Paleoindian Archaeology

UNIVERSITY PRESS OF FLORIDA

Florida A&M University, Tallahassee
Florida Atlantic University, Boca Raton
Florida Gulf Coast University, Ft. Myers
Florida International University, Miami
Florida State University, Tallahassee
New College of Florida, Sarasota
University of Central Florida, Orlando
University of Florida, Gainesville
University of North Florida, Jacksonville
University of South Florida, Tampa
University of West Florida, Pensacola

Paleoindian Archaeology

A Hemispheric Perspective

EDITED BY

Juliet E. Morrow and Cristóbal Gnecco

University Press of Florida
Gainesville/Tallahassee/Tampa/Boca Raton
Pensacola/Orlando/Miami/Jacksonville/Ft. Myers/Sarasota

13 12 11 10 09 08   6 5 4 3 2 1

First cloth printing, 2006
First paperback printing, 2008

Library of Congress Cataloging-in-Publication Data
Paleoindian archaeology: a hemispheric perspective/edited by Juliet E.
Morrow and Cristóbal Gnecco.
p. cm.
Includes bibliographical references and index.
ISBN 978-0-8130-3014-2 (cloth)
ISBN 978-0-8130-3389-1 (paperback)
1. Paleo-Indians. 2. Paleo-Indians—Implements. 3. Stone implements—
America. 4. Excavations (Archaeology)—America.
5. America—Antiquities.
I. Morrow, Juliet E. II. Gnecco, Cristóbal

The University Press of Florida is the scholarly publishing agency for the
State University System of Florida, comprising Florida A&M Univer-
sity, Florida Atlantic University, Florida Gulf Coast University, Florida
International University, Florida State University, New College of Florida,
University of Central Florida, University of Florida, University of North
Florida, University of South Florida, and University of West Florida.

University Press of Florida
15 Northwest 15th Street
Gainesville, FL 32611-2079
http://www.upf.com

For Chris and Jill
In gratitude for your love and patience

Contents

Figures

Tables

Preface and Acknowledgments

This volume is intended for archaeologists—professional and avocational alike. It would not have been possible without the help of many individuals and institutions. First and foremost we thank our families and our friends for their support and encouragement. Institutional support was provided by the Arkansas Archeological Survey (a department of the University of Arkansas system), the Universidad del Cauca in Colombia, and Arkansas State University in Jonesboro.

Subsequent to the 1997 Nashville symposium "Late Pleistocene Occupations of the Americas: A Hemispheric Perspective," we received valuable comments and suggestions from Robert Whallon, editor of *International Monographs in Prehistory*, and from Darrin Pratt at the University of Colorado Press that helped guide us in the right direction. David Anderson (University of Tennessee) and an anonymous reviewer took time from their busy schedules to carefully consider the papers and make suggestions that substantially improved the volume as a whole. Stella Phillips and Deborah Anderson provided editorial assistance during their tenure as undergraduate students at Arkansas State University. We are indebted to the staff of the University Press of Florida for their patience and their belief in this project.

Introduction

JULIET E. MORROW AND CRISTÓBAL GNECCO

Late Pleistocene occupations in the Americas have been researched from a variety of perspectives. Historically, first came the search for the clear proof of the coexistence of human beings and extinct fauna; once this coexistence was established, the search for early sites and assemblages became an important research endeavor. When a pancontinental culture (Clovis) linked to a specific technology (fluted bifaces) and an economic characterization (big-game hunting) emerged, models in the guise of culture history (that is, models dealing with the spatial and temporal structuring of archaeological materials) were offered to account for the apparent swift, compulsive, and directional occupation of the continent. The "oddities" that were noted in the intervening years, such as the possible existence of nonbifacial cultures predating Clovis, were eventually cast off as stochastic noise in an otherwise smooth and consensual disciplinary landscape dominated by empirical concerns.

The last years of culture history (which dominated archaeology for decades) witnessed a previously unknown interest in continent-wide perspectives in the research of early periods. The landmark work of Alex Krieger (1964) and Gordon Willey (1966, 1971) demonstrated that widening the scope of inquiry beyond the traditional borders of limited regions had much to offer: richer and informed comparative frameworks, holistic views, encompassing models reaching well beyond restricted (and mostly artificial) spatial segments. However, the interest on that wide perspective, which could have led to a more horizontal and balanced academic exchange between researchers from all the Americas, did not outlive culture history's heyday. Concentrated research on Clovis and other Paleoindian-era cultures in the western United States by key researchers, most notably George Frison (1982, 1987, 1991a, 1996) and C. Vance Haynes (1976, 1979, 1982), provided a wealth of data on the Paleoindian era of the region. However, the arrival of processualism (the focus on cultural process rather than time-space systematics) in archaeology did little to carry Paleoindian archaeologists past their preoccupation with time-space systematics. From our perspective, four factors contributed to this historical trajectory: (1) researchers were still preoccupied with accumulating sites and assemblages and avoided theoretical discussions that might have broadened the magnitude and scale of problems and questions; (2) North American academia dominated over those of Central and South America because of an academic colonialism that portrayed the South as a producer of data and the North as the builder of models and interpretations, and neglected the role that archaeologists from outside North America could have had in shaping research agendas; (3) the prevalence of English as the medium of scientific discourse, which made invisible the intellectual production published in Spanish and Portuguese; and (4) in the dominant processual paradigm, ecological-reductionist views attributed most cultural change to localized environmental conditions, thus fostering a research focus on local or regional ecology while discouraging inquiries of continental, subcontinental, or supraregional scope as theoretically unproductive.

There have been significant changes in archaeology during the past decade, which include a renewed interest in theoretical formulations; the construction of a more open and equal academic dialogue among researchers working in North, Central, and South America; and a greater propensity to consider human agency in archaeology, so that early settlers can be viewed as active transformers of their social and natural milieus. In addition to these changes within the discipline, three major recent events pushed the topic of the late Pleistocene settlement of the Americas onto the public stage: the 1996 discovery of one of the oldest, most complete skeletons yet found in North America, widely known as Kennewick Man; the 1997 publication of the final report on the Monte Verde site in Chile; and the 1999 "Clovis and Beyond" conference in Santa Fe, New Mexico. Since these pivotal events, increasing media attention has been focused on the early colonization of the New World.

Articles in weekly news magazines opened up for the public the issues surrounding the science and politics of Early Paleoindian archaeology, particularly with respect to Kennewick Man and the Native American Graves Protection and Repatriation Act. For archaeologists who concurred with the excavator's interpretations of the controversial Monte Verde archaeological site (Dillehay 1997a), there seemed to be a greater potential for discovering contemporary, and possibly even older, sites in North and South America. The broad acceptance of Monte Verde as an authentic circa-12,500-year-old human habitation spurred an intense search for pre-Clovis cultural remains in the New World and reassessment of numerous sites and interpretative models that had been previously dismissed from the standpoint of the dominant paradigm: Clovis First. The 1999 "Clovis and Beyond" conference brought together scholars and amateur archaeologists interested in Native American origins and Early Paleoindian archaeology. It provided a public venue for the strident defense of several controversial pre-Clovis sites, including Monte Verde, Meadowcroft Rockshelter, and Cactus Hill. The conference also served as a springboard for Dennis Stanford and Bruce Bradley's North Atlantic Corridor hypothesis (Stanford and Bradley 2002; Bradley and Stanford 2004), that is, that Clovis is descended from the western European Upper Paleolithic Solutrean culture.

This book as a whole reflects these recent changes and events; yet this collective work was not conceived as a new consensual synthesis, nor did it achieve such unanimity. Rather, we have attempted only to create a stimulating contemporary dialogue by juxtaposing different views of the early peopling and colonization of the continent; it could not be otherwise, given the diversity of strongly held opinions on many of the issues surrounding Paleoindian occupations during the late Pleistocene. This book does not pretend to solve such oppositions, nor do we offer a homogeneous approach; rather, we present informed contemporary interpretations, differing in many particulars but all sharing a wide hemispheric perspective. A horizontal and open communication between the North and the South is basic for telling the complete story. This volume represents an important step in this direction.

While we concede that the chapters do not achieve a new disciplinary consensus, this does not mean that they do not share important issues. In fact, the chapters in this volume are crosscut by recurrent themes: first, the development of new theoretical constructs that may help to explain the diversity of land-use strategies and territorial symbolization; second, recognition of the rapid transformation of ecosystems and the early appearance of a plethora of distinct stone tool styles; third, the need for a continental approach to the peopling of the Americas that will enable researchers to go beyond narrow interpretations; and fourth, the urgent need for substantive research comparing the late Pleistocene archaeological records in Central, South, and North America, which we hope will involve collaborative research between archaeologists from different corners of the continent that erases the traditional, colonial dominance of the North.

The majority of these chapters resulted from a symposium organized by the editors for the 62nd Annual Meeting of the Society for American Archaeology held in Nashville in 1997. The symposium, "Late Pleistocene Occupations in the Americas: A Hemispheric Perspective," brought together researchers from across the New World who were asked to consider archaeological data from geographic areas beyond their traditional scope. We think this shift toward a hemispheric perspective can facilitate intercontinental communication between archaeologists, enrich our current understanding of late Pleistocene archaeology in the various regions of the Americas, and provide productive avenues for future research. A hemispheric perspective allows us to go beyond traditional analytic perspectives, focused narrowly on specific regions or, if a greater scale is involved, at most considering phenomena of subcontinental scope. A narrowed focus has prevented a holistic approach to the topic of early colonization and settlement of the Americas and has produced fragmented views of a process that cannot be understood without acknowledging the interdependence of social units and the active role of culture. Since the symposium, the original papers have been substantially revised and updated, and some other contributions were requested.

The first section of the book, devoted to continental issues and comparisons, contains three chapters dealing with continent-wide issues. In chapter 1, "Paleoindians without Mammoths and Archaeologists without Projectile Points," Luis Alberto Borrero argues that models from North America should not be used to explain patterns in the South American archaeological record. From Borrero's perspective, North American archaeologists have focused on fluted points and mammoths to the exclusion of other Early Paleoindian evidence. He argues that North American archaeology has dominated the discipline as practiced in the rest of the western hemisphere and describes how this dominance has translated into research biases of several kinds. While these biases have also affected North American archaeology, in South and Central America the effect has been devastating because these regions have limited research regarding aspects as contentious as territoriality, ecosystemic transformation, and early stylistic diversity. Borrero views the role of megafauna hunting as marginal and the process of colonization in South America as slower, with new niches being occupied early on. Basing his interpretations on a thorough knowledge of the South American Paleoindian record, Borrero beckons us to open our minds to the potential for alternative economies, especially those oriented toward the exploitation of low-risk and scattered resources.

In chapter 2, "Points in Time," Stuart J. Fiedel addresses issues concerning the timing of the arrival and dispersal of the first colonists over the continent. He outlines the problems that historically have obfuscated the refinement of Early Paleoindian chronology and critically evaluates the available Early Paleoindian database pertinent to this topic. He uses new data generated from advances in radiocarbon dating and interdisciplinary paleoclimatic research to provide a balanced perspective of New World migration models. With increasing precision in dating techniques and additional Early Paleoindian sites with in situ, datable occupational debris, Fiedel thinks that decadal precision is achievable for the Clovis era and that we will eventually know specifics about the arrival time and routes taken by the earliest Americans.

In chapter 3, "Grassland Archaeology in the Americas," Eileen Johnson and her coauthors present a broad comparison of the floral and faunal resources, lithic assemblages, tool kits, artifact patterning, and land use of late Pleistocene grasslands-oriented hunter-gatherers in two regions of the western hemisphere: the pampas of Argentina and the U.S. southern plains. In their study, Johnson and her colleagues include the only glyptodont kill site in Argentina (La Moderna), a multicomponent stratified site (Arroyo Seco), and a series of new Fishtail-related sites along the Río Quequén Grande that indicate the killing and processing of large mammals, including guanaco. From the southern plains, they examine the stratified Lubbock Lake Landmark site and review evidence from other sites including Blackwater Draw, Aubrey, Jake Bluff, Bonfire Shelter, Cooper, Big Lake, San Jon, and Plainview. In both the pampas and the southern plains, they recognize a pattern of generalized foraging during the Clovis era followed by specialized collecting during the early Holocene.

Part II contains three chapters highlighting a South and Central American perspective about the late Pleistocene peopling of the continent. The first chapter adheres to the traditional perspective that some other chapters seek to challenge, yet it also shows the importance of extraregional comparisons to the archaeology of the early peopling of the Americas. In "The Clovis Colonization of Central America," Anthony Ranere compares fluted points and preforms from Clovis quarry workshop sites in the midcontinental United States and those from La Mula West in Panama and Turrialba in Costa Rica, arguing that the late Pleistocene colonization of Central America was a rapid expansion because populations often leapfrogged great distances in establishing new colonies and because the focus of subsistence was on hunting. Recent improvements in the application of evolutionary ecological theory to hunter-gatherer behavior, in the modeling of population movements in prehistory, and in comparative analyses of Paleoindian technology and typology are brought to bear on this question. In particular, his chapter presents a detailed description of the bifacial reduction sequence for a Clovis workshop in Panama that closely parallels what is seen in North American early Clovis workshops and, therefore, attests to the close cultural and chronological ties between Central American and North American Clovis sites.

In "Early Humanized Landscapes in Northern South America," Cristóbal Gnecco and Javier Aceituno take exception to the received, North American–produced view of the first colonists of the continent as highly nomadic and directional (a view that would seem to preclude territoriality of any kind as early as late Pleistocene times). They argue that there is evidence in northern South America of Early Paleoindian "agrilocalities." The early archaeological record in these areas shows regular spatiotemporal patterns reflecting the emergence and development of "agroecology." They propose that these occupations (premised upon territoriality, restricted mobility, and the focal use of resources) led to structural transformation of ecosystems.

In "Fluted and Fishtail Points from Southern Coastal Chile," Lawrence J. Jackson reflects on Junius Bird's early work at Fell's Cave that drew the world's attention to the presence of Early Paleoindian peoples in southernmost South America. Fell's Cave produced a convincing association of deep stratified deposits and distinctive Paleoindian projectile points/knives known as Fishtails—later radiocarbon-dated by Bird to the same period as Folsom. The fluting of South American Fishtail points is enigmatic, and the absence of North American fluted point styles (that is, Clovis, Folsom, Gainey, Barnes, Cumberland) has contributed to the perception of a divergent Paleoindian sequence in South America. Jackson's chapter highlights Clovis and Clovis-like points from coastal Chile and suggests that Fishtail points are a regional development on a common Clovis theme.

Chapters in Part III involve Clovis-era archaeology in North America. In "New Radiocarbon Dates for the Clovis Component of the Anzick Site, Park County, Montana," Juliet Morrow and Stuart Fiedel highlight the significance of the Anzick site, the only known burial associated with the Clovis culture. Analysis of osseous material used to manufacture the foreshafts verified that they were made of antler rather than bone or ivory. Two accelerator mass spectrometry (AMS) radiocarbon assays were obtained for two of the Anzick foreshafts, and one AMS radiocarbon assay was obtained on human bone associated with the foreshafts. The human bone date corroborates many earlier dates on collagen from this same skeleton. The authors discuss the chronological placement of the Anzick site and implications for Early Paleoindian occupations and migrations in light of these new data. "The Rancholabrean Termination" by C. Vance Haynes is a hypothetical scenario based on data generated from nearly half a century of geological and archaeological research in the San Pedro River valley of Arizona. Focused surveys revealed a large number of paleontological sites, with and without associated Clovis debris, and resulted in an unprecedented amount of detailed information on terminal Pleistocene ecology and Paleoindian behavior. From this unique and interdisciplinary perspective, Haynes offers catastrophic drought as a plausible explanation for the demise of megafauna and Clovis groups in the San Pedro Valley circa 11,000 uncalibrated years BP. The final chapter, "Paleoindian Archaeology in Florida and Panama," by Michael K. Faught, summarizes some of the evidence for early occupations in Panama and Florida in an attempt to understand the tantalizing similarities exhibited in hafted projectile points/knives from late Pleistocene sites in Florida and Panama. Faught underscores the lack of good dates and stratified sites in both of these regions and thus the need for continued research.

The word *radiocarbon* has, in appropriate cases, been replaced by the character symbol ^{14}C. Unless otherwise stated, radiocarbon dates in this volume are presented without applied correction factors, in uncalibrated radiocarbon years before present (BP). Calibrated dates are followed by "cal BP."

We hope the professional and the avocational archaeological communities will find these chapters useful and even inspiring. In this volume, we have tried—within the rules of science—to "return history to the human process of dispersal that eventually, but coincidentally, led to a global humanity" (Gamble 1993: 318).

I

Continental Issues and Comparisons

1

Paleoindians without Mammoths and Archaeologists without Projectile Points?

The Archaeology of the First Inhabitants of the Americas

LUIS ALBERTO BORRERO

For decades the results of North American archaeology were inspirational in the search for evidence of the initial settlement of South America (Borrero 1988; Ardila and Politis 1989; Dillehay et al. 1992; Whitley and Dorn 1993). Thus, fluted projectile points and megamammals were the selected indicators. This search model was helpful in many ways but distracted attention toward a limited body of evidence, such as the association of megamammals and humans (Montané 1968; Sanguinetti 1976; MacNeish 1979; Nuñez et al. 1994). This is expressed quite frankly by some South American archaeologists. Lautaro Nuñez and colleagues, for instance, in a comment on their results at Taguatagua 2[1] (one of the more convincing early sites in South America, where megamammals and associated projectile points dated to circa 10,000 BP[2] were found), wrote, "Fell [Cave] patterns seem to play a similar role to that of Clovis in relation to the extinction of mammoths in North America" (Nuñez et al. 1994: 517). But how representative of the early South American archaeological record is Taguatagua 2? I think not very, because the appropriation of megamammals and the use of projectile points do not characterize ancient sites in South America. At best they are a small part of the picture. Only with the use of a different search mode—one not centered on megamammals or projectile points—were significant results achieved. In this chapter I comment on these results and use this knowledge to assess the case for the early human occupations in North America.

Importance of Megamammals

The hypothesis that the early inhabitants of South America were big-mammal hunters is inconclusive at best. The process of extinction of Pleistocene faunas on this continent is not well known; what is known, with increasing certainty, is that circa 10,000 BP, *Mylodon* sp., *Hippidion* sp., *Equus* sp., and many other megamammals were already extinct (Borrero 1997). Most early sites display both modern and Pleistocene faunas, usually with the former being dominant (Borrero 1984). This is the case even in the northern regions of South America.

In Tequendama, Colombia, the remains of deer (*Odocoileus* sp. and *Mazama* sp.) as well as small mammals (*Dasypus* sp., *Cavia porcellus*, *Sylvilagus braziliensis*) were recovered in levels dated to circa 10,000–11,000 BP (Correal and Van der Hammen 1977). This tendency is also recorded at other sites dated at the Pleistocene-Holocene transition, including El Abra (Hurt et al. 1972). Moreover, sites such as San Isidro and Piedra Roja inform us that some of the earlier hunter-gatherer adaptations relied heavily on plants, particularly palms (Gnecco and Mora 1997: 689; Gnecco 2000; Mora and Gnecco 2003). There are also sites where megamammal bones are numerous, including Tibito, in Colombia, dated to between 10,000 and 11,700 BP, which is interpreted as a kill and butchering site of mastodon (*Cuvieronius hyodon* and *Haplomastodon* sp.) and horse (*Equus* sp.) (Correal 1986); El Vano, in Venezuela, where cut-marked bones of *Eremotherium rusconii* were found in association with artifacts dated around 10,700 BP (Jaimes 1999); and Taima Taima, in Venezuela, dated to between 12,600 and 13,400 BP (Ochsenius and Gruhn 1979), also considered a mastodon kill. But in these cases, the remains of modern fauna, such as deer, are also present.

Moving south there is the case of the Paiján Complex along the Peruvian coast, dated to between 8000 and 11,000 BP (Gálvez 1992; Briceño 1997; Dillehay, Rossen, Netherly et al. 2003). Excavated middens produced evidence of deer, snails, fish, reptiles, small mammals, and crustacea (Chauchat 1982; Gálvez 1992). Mastodon bones dated to between 10,500 and 12,300 BP were found at the La Cumbre site (Ossa and Moseley 1972), but their cultural significance is difficult to assess and may be unrelated to the Paiján people. One specialist interpreted Paiján as "the first adaptation to marine resources on the Peruvian coast during the Pleistocene-Holocene transition" (Chauchat 1988: 66). Similar indications of early Holocene utilization of coastal resources are also found in Ecuador (Stothert 1985), southern Peru (Sandweiss et al. 1998; Sandweiss 2003), and central Chile (Llagostera 1979; Jackson 1993, 1997; Jackson et al. 2003).

Although the subsistence patterns of the highlands are not very well known, owing to a lack of paleontological work, highland inhabitants do not appear to have focused on megamammals. The discovery of horse in the Ayacucho Valley (MacNeish et al. 1970) and the Puna of Junín (Matos 1992) indicate, however, that horse was available (Alberti and Prado 2004). Subsistence remains found in sites dated to before 10,000 BP in highland Peru, as well as northwestern

Argentina and northeastern Chile—all in puna habitats—consist of primarily modern species (Aschero 1979; Lynch 1980; Rick 1988; Santoro 1989; Yacobaccio 1995; Elkin 1996a; Rick and Moore 2001). A single fossil horse bone was found at Tuina 5, in the Chilean puna (Cartagena et al. 2002). In Argentina, rodents were important in sites such as Inca Cueva 4, while other sites, including Quebrada Seca and Huachichocana, point toward camelids as the mainstay since the early Holocene (Yacobaccio and Madero 1992; Elkin 1996b). In sum, a wide variety of resources—including medium-sized rodents, Cervidae, Camelidae, and invertebrates—occur in the highlands.

Evidence for a wide-spectrum diet circa 10,500–11,000 BP has been found in the Brazilian lowlands in Caverna da Pedra Pintada in Monte Alegre, near the Amazon River (Roosevelt et al. 1996), at the site of Boquete in Minas Gerais (Prous 1991), and at other sites attributed to the Paranaiba phase in Goias (Schmitz 1986, 1987). Despite the heated debate surrounding the Monte Alegre evidence, especially about the age of the site—with some researchers disputing the older dates of 11,000 BP but accepting dates around 10,500 BP (Fiedel 1996; C. V. Haynes 1997; Fiedel, this volume)—nobody doubts that the forest-oriented subsistence remains indicate use of a wide variety of resources. Remains of palm seeds, birds, fish, turtles, and mollusks comprise the majority of subsistence remains at this site. Incidentally, the chronological sequence of Monte Alegre—based on fifty-six ^{14}C dates and several thermoluminescence (TL) and optically stimulated luminescence (OSL) dates—appears to be reliable enough to accept that around 11,075 ± 106 BP, people were present in the central Amazon (Roosevelt et al. 2002).

In the pampas, the lower component of the Arroyo Seco 2 site, dated to between 7,320 and 12,240 BP, contains a wide array of faunal resources (Politis 1996a). These include guanaco (*Lama guanicoe*), a large flightless bird (*Rhea* sp.), the remains of nine genera of megamammals (*Megatherium americanum*, *Equus* sp., *Hippidion* sp., *Palaeolama* sp., *Toxodon* sp., *Glossotherium* sp., *Eutatus seguini*, *Glyptodon* sp., and *Macrauchenia* sp.), and smaller resources; however, the guanaco—a modern species—is the most abundant animal and appears to have been the main food source (Politis et al. 1995). The Paso Otero 5 site is characterized by the remains of megamammals, with guanaco comprising only 6 percent of the faunal assemblage (Martínez 2001; see Johnson et al., this volume). However, this abundance of megamammals may reflect the collecting of bones for use as fuel (Martínez 2001). At the site of La Moderna, there is an association between flakes and *Doedicurus clavicaudatus* bones with early Holocene ^{14}C dates (Politis and Gutierrez 1998).

Perhaps more surprising is the case of Monte Verde in south-central Chile, dated to circa 12,500 BP. This is one of the most frequently mentioned sites in discussing the early peopling of South America, but the remains of megamammals are not what characterize the site. Even when mastodon (*Cuvieronius* sp.) bones are present, soil remains found embedded in the bones suggest that they were scavenged (Dillehay 1997b; Karathanasis 1997). At least one fragment of mastodon tusk is probably a tool (Shipman 1997). The presence of more than sixty vegetal species suggests that plants were probably the mainstay for the inhabitants of Monte Verde (Dillehay and Rossen 1997; Ugent 1997).

Many late Pleistocene sites in Patagonia display human occupations associated with remains of extinct ground sloth (*Mylodon darwinii*) and horse (*Hippidion saldiasi*). While the evidence for the hunting of horse appears to be well substantiated at sites such as Cueva del Medio, Cueva del Lago Sofía 1, and Piedra Museo (Nami and Menegaz 1991; Prieto 1991; Miotti 1996; Alberti et al. 2001), whether ground sloth was ever hunted is not at all clear. The evidence is ambiguous at best and can be used to support either a hunting or a scavenging tactic (Borrero et al. 1991). I believe that this uncertainty also applies to most cases of ground sloth remains in South America. Again, horses may have been hunted in South America, but never in high numbers (Borrero 2001).

Fell's Cave is one of the most cited examples of an association between megamammals and humans, and it is used in almost every text as a "representative" site from southern South America (for example, Willey 1971). The remains of ground sloth, horse, canid, guanaco, birds, and small mammals were recovered (Saxon 1979; Bird 1988a; Clutton-Brock 1988; Humphrey et al. 1993). However, it is not clear that humans were responsible for the accumulation of all the faunal remains recovered from the lower levels of that cave, dated to between 10,000 and 11,000 BP. On some of the horse bones, carnivore marks were found that, by their size and location, were attributed to felids (Borrero and Martin 1996). In considering this evidence, postulating that those marks were produced after human use of the bones is difficult. Two possibilities remain open: that the horse bones represent a carnivore accumulation or that humans scavenged big-cat kills. This in no way diminishes the archaeological importance of the site, since other bones from the lower levels display cut marks. What is needed is clarification of the importance of modern versus extinct species in the human diet.

The association of ground sloth and humans presents an interesting case in northern Patagonia, where there is a ^{14}C-dated paleontological location indicating that sloths were available between 10,800 and 12,600 BP (see Nami 1996a). The oldest archaeological sites in the region are dated to circa 9000 BP (Ceballos 1982; Crivelli et al. 1993; Crivelli et al. 1996; Nami 1996a). In some of these sites, sloth bones were found, but never in a context suggesting human intervention. Only at the site of El Trébol, near the Nahuel Huapi Lake, is there a context in which remains of Mylodontinae and human artifacts are associated and cut marks were identified. Unfortunately, this site is not yet dated, and only some results have been published (Hajduk et al. 2004). One interpretation of this evidence is that humans arrived in the area immediately after the extinction of sloths. A similar case can be constructed for the Argentine puna in relation to the Pleistocene horse (Fernández et al. 1991; Yacobaccio 1995, 1996) or for the northern desert of Chile (Dillehay et al. 1992: 177). Agua de la Cueva, in the Andes of Mendoza, was also used by humans exploiting modern species between 10,200 and 10,900 BP (García 1995, 1997a, 2003).[3] There are thus regions in which megamammals were still available when humans arrived (such as northern Venezuela and the pampas) and regions in which megamammals apparently were already extinct. These data are important for evaluating the process of Pleistocene faunal extinctions.

Many differences appear when a comparison of Early Paleoindian faunal exploitation is made between North and South America, but understanding the importance of these differences is difficult. For example, horses constituted an important resource in South America, but they were never intensively exploited in North America (Frison 1987; G. Haynes 1995; Frison and Bonnichsen 1996). In reviewing the evidence, however, one can clearly see that most of the early stratified sites known in North America have the presence of mammoth bones in common (C. V. Haynes 1980, 1993; G. Haynes 2002; Grayson and Meltzer 2003). These remains are usually attributed to the hunting skills of the initial inhabitants of America, but alternative explanations—including sampling bias attributable to the high visibility of mammoth bones (Meltzer 1988)—are sometimes offered. Even when the exploitation of megamammals took place in several regions, the importance of alternative resources is clear (see Meltzer 1993: 303). Bison was clearly exploited in North America, but intensive exploitation of this large-mammal species is not in evidence in the earliest sites. Except at Mill Iron (Kreutzer 1996) and Jake Bluff (Bement and Carter 2003), the presence of bison is usually minimal. Later, during the early Holocene, bison was more central to subsistence (Frison 1987). A recent analysis of several Clovis assemblages indicated that "Clovis hunting behaviors appear more closely aligned with a specialized, rather than generalized strategy" (Waguespak and Surovell 2003: 348). However, other researchers reached a different conclusion and "seriously question the model of early Paleoindians as megafaunal specialists and suggest that foragers should have pursued a wide array of taxa" (Byers and Ugan 2005: 1624). Since this issue clearly is not settled, a critical consideration of some of the available data becomes necessary.

Evidence obtained in Alaska, California, Pennsylvania, and southeastern North America demonstrates that early inhabitants of the New World did not need to focus on mammoths or other large fauna. The utilization of megamammals is evident at some sites, but at others, a different economic orientation is indicated by the presence of a wide array of resources, including small mammals, fish, and birds (Meltzer and Smith 1986; Beaton 1991; Johnson 1991a; Stanford 1991; Hofman 1994; Erlandson and Moss 1996; Morse et al. 1996; Chilton 2004). In Alaska, at the Broken Mammoth site, whose early levels date to circa 11,000 to 11,800 BP, large-mammal remains include bison (probably *Bison priscus*), wapiti (*Cervus elaphus*), and caribou (*Rangifer tarandus*). In addition to these herbivores, a large variety of small mammals were recovered, as well as birds and fish, but bird remains dominate the assemblage. The only mammoth remains are fragments of tusk (Yesner 1996a). Moreover, at least some of the ^{14}C dates on the tusks, both at Broken Mammoth and at other sites nearby, are older than those produced on other materials, ranging between 15,800 and 17,000 BP. In this case, then, the likely explanation is that mammoth tusks were scavenged (Yesner 1995). Perhaps they were a source of raw material for artifacts. In any case, Broken Mammoth is an early site that clearly is not a kill or butchering location (Yesner 1996a: 267). Modern fauna also characterize the archaeological assemblage of Dry Creek, in the Alaska Range (Hoffecker et al. 1993). An important conclusion is that "there is no demonstrated evidence of humans killing mammoths in eastern Beringia" (Yesner 1996b: 248). As recent reviews show, central Alaska hosts the oldest well-dated multisite evidence for the presence of humans in the New World, and these humans clearly were not dependent on megamammals for their living (Hamilton and Goebel 1999; Roosevelt et al. 2002).

For years it was difficult to find early, stratified sites in eastern North America, but once they were found, associations with mammoth or mastodon were very rare (Meltzer 1988: 22; G. Haynes 1991: 445; Storck and Spiess 1994; Tankersley 1997; Walker et al. 2001).

The situation is also changing on the plains. Two mammoth rib fragments, at least one of which is a tool, were found at the Mill Iron site in Montana. The Mill Iron site is contemporaneous with or slightly younger than Clovis, according to two different sets of accelerator mass spectrometry (AMS) ^{14}C dates of about 11,250 and 10,900 BP, respectively (Frison et al. 1996). Bison remains dominate the faunal assemblage (Kreutzer 1996); whether the inhabitants of the Mill Iron site hunted mammoth or scavenged the bones is unclear. A burned mammoth radius recovered together with a Goshen projectile point in Kaufman Cave "is believed to have been partially fossilized at the time it was burned" (Frison et al. 1996: 207) and therefore was not necessarily the result of human killing (see Grey 1963). At the Sheaman site, an ivory foreshaft was found in a level dated to circa 10,600 BP, in a context lacking any other mammoth or mastodon remains (Frison and Zeimens 1980; Walker 1982). The Aubrey Clovis site in Texas, dated to circa 11,000–11,500 BP, contained mostly bison, deer, and turtle, within a context clearly suggesting a campsite. Four partial ribs of mammoth/mastodon were exposed by erosion near the excavations (Ferring 1995). Evidence for the consumption of plants, as measured by the presence of specialized tools or facilities, is minimal (G. Haynes 2002: 180, 227). Finally, the archaeological evidence for coastal human settlement near the end of the Pleistocene is increasing every year (Erlandson 2001; Faught 2004), not only indicating an early focus on maritime resources but also making attractive the coastal migration hypothesis (Dixon 1999).

All of these findings suggest a lesser role for megamammals in subsistence, yet most of the sites still used to characterize the initial peopling are dominated by mammoth remains (C. V. Haynes 1980, 1993; G. Haynes 2002). Even some sites that are not, such as Broken Mammoth, were studied under the initial impression of the potential importance of megamammals in the diet (Holmes and Yesner 1992). Today, together with the relevant evidence just reviewed, these sites inform us of the importance of alternative resources. This discussion is not intended to minimize the quality of the evidence for Clovis peoples as hunters of large game (G. Haynes 2002; Waguespak and Surovell 2003) but instead should underline the importance of exploring alternative resources, such as those found at both Clovis (Ferring 1995) and non-Clovis sites (Yesner 1996a). From a South American perspective, the fact that sites such as Broken Mammoth exist is not remarkable, since the absence of megamammals is not viewed as a problem. In summary, evidence from South America together with that provided by a few sites in North America suggests the need to develop alternative models for the colonization of America—models not necessarily centered on a big-mammal-hunting way of life (Dixon 1999; Dillehay and Rossen 2002; Meltzer 2002; Byers and Ugan 2005).

Importance of Collective Kill Sites and Prey Utilization

An important difference between North and South America concerns the role of collective kill sites. These became frequent in North America immediately after initial human settlement (Frison and Bonnichsen 1996; but see Hofman 1994), while in South America they were almost absent (Borrero 1990). One of the largest bone accumulations is in the locality of Taguatagua, in Chile, but this probably resulted from separated hunting or scavenging events. The bone remains were found in at least two different stratigraphic members (#5 and #6) and were distributed across a wide area. Detailed records from the more recent excavations at Taguatagua 2 suggest that the mastodon exploitation events took place during a short period (Nuñez et al. 1994: 512), perhaps a thousand years after the occupation of Taguatagua 1 (Montané 1968). Collective kills were not indicated at Taima-Taima (Casamiquela 1979), Tibitó (Correal 1986), or other early sites for which extensive faunal information is available.

Degree of utilization of prey is clearly related to food abundance. In South

America, most sites with early faunal assemblages display evidence of intensive processing (Silveira 1979; Rick 1980; Borrero 1990; Prieto 1991; Elkin 1996b; Miotti 1996). In Patagonia there is no evidence for underutilization of prey. Usually only a few (rarely in excess of five individuals) of a particular taxa are represented. Moreover, these animals may not have been complete when they arrived on the sites (Silveira 1979; Borrero 1990); this is probably the reason why the parts represented were intensively used.

In contrast, mammoth carcasses do not appear to have been extensively utilized in Clovis times (Kelly and Todd 1988; Hannus 1990; G. Haynes 1995: 26, 2002: 227). Some examples are the mammoth remains found at Colby, dated to circa 11,000 BP, which were cached but never used (Frison and Todd 1986), and the occupation of Murray Springs, dated to circa 10,900 BP (C. V. Haynes 1980, 1993). This general pattern is also valid for the early Holocene, as recorded at the Agate Basin site (Folsom level: 10,690 BP; pre-Folsom: 11,650 BP [Frison 1982; Frison and Stanford 1982]) and other sites.

To what degree collective appropriation resulted from the ethology of the main prey (mammoth and bison in North America and camelids in South America) is an open question. Mammoth hunting can create a surplus of food even with a single animal (Frison 1987: 189), and the same can be said of bison hunting. Moreover, bison live in large migratory groups that can produce large quantities of food. The few records of mastodon exploitation are in agreement with this view, since the carcasses appear to have been less intensively used. In contrast, the social organization of camelids is based on small family groups, which are widely distributed over steppes or prairies. Large all-male and all-female groups are also available, but family groups are the most abundant and stable formation. If family groups were targeted, then it follows that the collective appropriation of camelids was not a regularly used strategy.

The contrast between North and South America may be indicative of different hunting strategies, perhaps related to different human demographic patterns. Site size and site frequency suggest the existence of larger groups in North America, associated with the already mentioned emphasis on collective kills. Also, the earliest inhabitants of western North America seem to have avoided caves and rockshelters (Kelly and Todd 1988: 237). Use of caves and rockshelters becomes apparent only later, in the early Holocene, probably in relation to a "fundamental reorganization of hunter-gatherer mobility strategies" (Walthall 1998: 231). In contrast, caves and rockshelters are the most common geological context for late Pleistocene archaeological deposits in South America (Correal and Van der Hammen 1977; Flegenheimer 1986; Schmitz 1986; Bird 1988a; García 1995; Roosevelt et al. 1996; Borrero and Franco 1997; Mazzanti and Quintana 2001; Massone 2005). Whether this contrast results from our sampling biases or from different human land-use strategies is an issue in need of relevant research.

Projectile Points

An important question concerns the presence of fluting in South America, a trait classically used to suggest a Clovis origin (Lynch 1974), although other models of projectile points exhibiting wide distributions are also important (Bryan 1986; Mayer-Oakes 1986a; Dillehay 2000). But fluting in South America "appears almost exclusively on stemmed points, not lanceolate forms" (Dillehay et al. 1992: 146), which is an important technological difference between the two continents. Variation is evident in many regions, especially in northwestern South America (Dillehay et al. 1992: 182–83). In Colombia, where Carlos López has presented evidence about a variety of projectile points lacking fluting or basal thinning from the middle Magdalena River, some of them are dated to between 10,000 and 11,000 BP (López 1994). However, fluting is present in the Cauca region (Gnecco and Salgado 1989). Unifacial complexes are also important, especially in the Sabana de Bogotá (Hurt et al. 1972; Correal and Van der Hammen 1977; Ardila 1991). Other point morphologies are found in Venezuela, where several sites, including Taima Taima and Muaco (Cruxent 1970; Ochsenius and Gruhn 1979), exhibit willow-leaf projectile points.

A well-known shape is that of the so-called Fishtail, or Fell's Cave projectile point, initially found by Junius Bird in the Palli Aike region, in Chile. Fishtail points have since been recorded at several sites in Patagonia, including Piedra Museo and Cueva del Medio, and at localities around 38 degrees south latitude in Uruguay, Argentina, and Chile (Flegenheimer 1986; Nuñez et al. 1994; Martínez 2001). These points also exhibit wide variation in form, raw material, and size. They have usually been compared to Clovis, but important differences in their morphology (Politis 1991) and reduction sequences (Nami 1996b, 1997) suggest separate origins. Gustavo Politis (1991) suggested that fluting was not important in the Fell's Cave projectile points and concluded, "Technological characteristics suggest that beyond some general bifacial traits, there is no clear evidence to strongly support the hypothesis that FTPPs [Fishtail Projectile Points] derived from North American fluted points" (Politis 1991: 298). However, this issue is not settled, because on the basis of the technological analysis of Fell's Cave projectile points from the Guardiria site in Costa Rica, where they are associated with Clovis-like points, Georges A. Pearson found some similarities in the bifacial thinning and flute removals of both types of points (Pearson 2004). His findings are in accordance with observations made by previous researchers (Morrow and Morrow 1999).

The importance of projectile points in furthering research can be discussed in light of Monte Verde in central Chile and Tres Arroyos in southern Chile. Although leaf-shaped projectile points were found at the former (Collins 1997), they are quantitatively unimportant, no matter what role they played in the acceptance of Monte Verde by the archaeological community. At Tres Arroyos, in Tierra del Fuego, the remains of megamammals are stratigraphically associated with fragments of projectile points (Massone et al. 1993; Jackson 2002). The existence of projectile points is not necessary to accept the dating or the interpreted use of any of these sites, nor is it necessary to accept that bifacial reduction took place at those sites. Hugo Nami (1993) demonstrated through debitage analysis the presence of bifacial reduction at several early archaeological sites in southern South America (including Tres Arroyos), even when bifacial forms were not recovered. Even when sampling problems may be involved (Dillehay 2000; Pearson 2004), the unifacial complexes of the Sabana de Bogotá must also be mentioned. Finding a site that is functionally different—a site in which there was no reason for projectile points to be deposited—seems a much more promising way of acquiring new knowledge than adding another example to a long list of a well-known site type (for example, camp, kill, quarry, and so forth).

The panorama is not substantively different in North America. Several studies have demonstrated the variability that was hidden under the "Clovis" label (Bonnichsen 1991), a situation highlighted by the question of the Goshen Complex (Frison 1991c, 1996; Frison et al. 1996) that led George Frison and Robson Bonnichsen (1996: 314) to suggest the concept of cotraditions to explain diverse cultural configurations. On a continental scale, the lack of fluting on projectile points of the Nenana Complex in Alaska must be noted (Goebel 2004: 355).

However, a tendency toward the use of local (not necessarily the highest knapping quality) lithic sources in South America is evident in some of the older known archaeological assemblages (Borrero and Franco 1997). This tendency contrasts with the situation in North America during Clovis times, where good-quality exotic rocks were frequently used (Kelly and Todd 1988; Meltzer 1988, 1993). This means that archaeological landscapes generated synchronously in North and South America could be dramatically different, inviting consideration of the hypothesis that independent technological trajectories can be traced throughout both continents. Continental- or semicontinental-wide analyses of the distributions of Clovis and other related fluted projectile points also exhibit variety (Dincauze 1993a; Tankersley 1994; Morrow and Morrow 1999; Anderson and Faught 2000; Anderson and Gillam 2000) and may help bring the patterns to light. But it is probable that variation in associated artifacts, not only on projectile points, will play a decisive role in extending our knowledge. This is clear in the discussion about similarities between Clovis and Siberian assemblages (Goebel 2004: 355). The tendency toward the use of local and rarely the best lithic sources indicates that the model of hunter-gatherer expansion developed by Robert Kelly and Lawrence Todd (1988) is less applicable in South America than in North America. Moreover, and in full agreement with this concept, the proportion of bifaces and the abundance of artifact caches (Meltzer 2002; Redmond and Tankersley 2005) appear to be less important in South American assemblages.

Conclusions

In the first place we must acknowledge the recent improvements produced by the study of early human occupation of South America. Only a few years ago, it was still possible to maintain that "little is known about early human utilization of plants in forest and savanna environments" (Dillehay et al. 1992: 148). Today abundant data exist that attest to the importance of those resources and the human use of lands in which megamammals were not important. This and other changes in our perception of the earliest record increasingly complicate subsuming the first settlers under the label "Paleoindian" (Sanguinetti and Borrero 1977; Dillehay et al. 1992: 150; García 1997b; Roosevelt et al. 2002), since a wider spectrum of adaptations have been found than can be admitted by that term. Archaeological work from prior decades shows an excessive use of terms such as "Paleoindian" and "Archaic." For example, in northeastern Chile, the lack of megamammals was one reason to classify the earliest sites as Early Archaic (Santoro 1989). Are we going to change that label if a single megamammal bone is found? The important issue is the economic orientation and not the label.

A volume on the archaeology of the Pleistocene-Holocene transition (Straus et al. 1996) examined worldwide human responses to global environmental changes. In reviewing the evidence for America, David Yesner (1996b: 247) asked the relevant question "to what degree did populations shift to a broader spectrum of higher-cost, lower-return resources such as small game, birds, fish, or shellfish?"[4] The answer, it now appears safe to say, is "to no small degree." Indeed, some of the adaptations indicated by recent analyses of culturally associated remains from the earliest known sites in South America are very expensive, implying that energy was extracted from resources that were difficult to obtain or process, such as seeds (see O'Connell and Hawkes 1981), or very dispersed, such as plants and birds. The role of megamammals appears to have been marginal, and this certainly points toward a slower process of colonization in South America, since new niches had to be defined. This appears to contradict one of the implications of Kelly and Todd's model, that there was no need for the first inhabitants of any given region to occupy new niches (Kelly and Todd 1988: 235). Shifting of resources appears to be a selected strategy in South America. Thus, Kelly and Todd's model makes more sense in North America than in South America.

The extreme environmental gradients in South America are more pronounced than in North America. This situation means not only that probably more time was needed to successfully colonize a variety of habitats, but also that substantial differences in the material culture are to be expected from environmental circumstances alone. The search for early sites is "a geological problem first and an archaeological one second" (Meltzer 1995: 36), and a greater role for geoarchaeological studies can be called upon (for example, Holliday 1997). We should try to avoid focusing our research on archaeological landscapes based almost entirely on the distribution of projectile points or on the fortuitous finding of megamammal remains. The archaeological landscape constructed by many North American archaeologists is still centered on projectile points, and we see this reflected in the mammoth-killing model. Perhaps attention should focus on other kinds of artifacts.

South American archaeologists committed many sins in the past, and using Clovis as a reference was only one of them. Another was to accept long chronologies on very limited evidence (Schobinger 1969; Ibarra 1971; MacNeish 1979), a situation that blocked our understanding of the past. The South American experience suggests that a better approach would be to expend resources in trying to recognize alternative economies, especially those oriented toward the exploitation of low-risk and scattered resources; but for this to occur, archaeologists will need to resist the appeal of mammoths and projectile points.

Notes

1. The reader may note a lack of reference in this paper to sites or chronologies in excess of 15,000 years BP, even when some claims were recently published (Guidon and Delibrias 1986; de Lumley et al. 1988; Schobinger 1988). These claims have many problems, including the reliability of the artifacts (Parenti 1996), interpretation of cut marks (Beltrao et al. 1997), and the association of dates and artifacts (de Lumley et al. 1988).

2. All dates are presented in uncalibrated ^{14}C years.

3. See Gil et al. 1997 about the possibility of the presence of extinct camelid at Agua de la Cueva.

4. See Meltzer 2002: 29 for an alternative view, in which *small* means "more readily exploited."

Points in Time

Establishing a Precise Hemispheric Chronology for Paleoindian Migrations

STUART J. FIEDEL

A precise chronological framework is the sine qua non for modeling and explaining the process of initial human colonization of the Americas. Recent advances in ^{14}C calibration and paleoclimate research outlined in this chapter have radically altered our understanding of the terminal Pleistocene. However, three major difficulties impede further refinement of Paleoindian chronology: disagreement about the temporal baseline for human occupation, a paucity of reliable dates from stratified contexts, and complications arising from ^{14}C fluctuations during the terminal Pleistocene.

The Baseline Problem

The first and most intractable problem is the continuing, perhaps irresolvable, uncertainty about the temporal baseline for human arrival in the Americas. It is not impossible that we will someday find a site earlier than any yet discovered (Meltzer 1989); as the banal saying goes, "Absence of evidence is not evidence of absence." True believers in "Early Man" still anticipate that sites older than 13,500 years, perhaps even older than 30,000–40,000 years, will be found (for example, Bryan and Gruhn 2003). Indeed, Nième Guidon and her colleagues (Guidon and Delibrias 1986; Watanabe et al. 2003) contend that they already have evidence of 50,000-year-old human occupation of Pedra Furada and other sites in northeastern Brazil. Ironically, the stone "tools" from Pedra Furada were dismissed as geofacts by a team that included Tom Dillehay and James Adovasio, both vocal proponents of the pre-Clovis antiquity of their own sites, Monte Verde and Meadowcroft Rockshelter, respectively (Meltzer et al. 1994).

Several authors have noted a significant contrast between American and Australian research on initial colonization (Adams et al. 2001; Jelinek 1992;

Kelly 2003). Despite the much larger number of archaeologists and the rapid pace of landscape disturbance in North America, the evidence of early peopling is much better in Australia. Although early lithic industries in Australia lacked the finely crafted bifaces characteristic of American Paleoindian assemblages, there is little difficulty in distinguishing tools from geofacts. Arguments in Australia have thus focused not on ambiguous artifacts but on their age. The main problem in Australia has been that the first people arrived at a time just beyond the effective limits of ^{14}C dating. Thermoluminescence (TL) dates have suggested a human presence before 117,000 BP (Fullagar et al. 1996), but dates derived by optically stimulated luminescence (OSL) and by an experimental acid-base-wet-oxidation (ABOX) radiocarbon method now appear to fix the date of entry at about 46,000–50,000 cal BP (Gillespie 2002; Roberts et al. 1998; Turney et al. 2001). It is likely not a coincidence that the extinction of giant birds and marsupial megafauna appears to have been nearly contemporaneous with initial human settlement (Flannery 1999; Miller et al. 1999; Roberts et al. 2001).

The obvious inference to be drawn from the Australian case is that if there were any archaeological traces of a very early human occupation in the Americas, we should have found unambiguous sites by now. However, the true believers in American Early Man might be encouraged by recent developments in European prehistory. In the early twentieth century, the "eolith" controversy was resolved as European archaeologists realized that nature could mimic crude stone tools (Warren 1914). Claims of Pliocene human occupation based on these geofacts were thus discredited. Nevertheless, as the earliest hominins of Africa were dated earlier and earlier, some prehistorians claimed comparable antiquity of more than one million years for ostensible pebble tools and odd bone accumulations that were interpreted as evidence of hominin activity in Europe. By the mid-1990s, however, skeptical assessment of these ambiguous sites, along with refinement of biostratigraphy, underpinned a "short chronology" for the European Paleolithic (for example, Gamble 1999: 118–25; Roebroeks and Van Kolfschoten 1994, 1995). For adherents of the short chronology, the appearance of well-made Acheulean hand axes (for example, at Boxgrove, England) at about 500,000 BP marks the first human occupation of Europe. The significance of these bifaces is exactly analogous to that of fluted points in the Americas. But just as consensus was being achieved on the 500,000 BP date, startling discoveries of hominin remains and Oldowan-like tools in Spain (Gran Dolina) and Georgia (Dmanisi) pushed the date of first "peopling" by very primitive *Homo* back to about 800,000 BP in Iberia and 1.8 million BP on the southeastern periphery of Europe. In response to these confounding finds, Robin Dennell and Wil Roebroeks (1996) proposed a "revised short chronology," which allowed for intermittent hominin occupation of the Mediterranean rim starting around 1,000,000 BP but stable occupation only at 500,000–600,000 BP.

Will some American or northeastern Siberian equivalent of Dmanisi force a radical reassessment of New World prehistory? We are still coming to terms with the potential implications of the Diring Yuriakh site in Siberia. The ostensible pebble tools there are evidently not quite as ancient as Yuri Mochanov has contended, but the age of circa 300,000 years, indicated by OSL dating and stratigraphic analysis (Waters et al. 1997), is still unnerving for such a high-latitude location. If hominins, presumably of *H. erectus* grade, could sustain themselves in northern Siberia, is there any good reason to doubt their ability to migrate, along with other mammals, across Beringia and into North America? Other recent finds—the finely crafted and miraculously preserved wooden javelins from Schöningen, Germany, and evidence of hominin arrival (by a water crossing circa 840,000 BP) on the island of Flores in Indonesia (Morwood et al. 1999)—indicate an unforeseen behavioral complexity of early *Homo*. However, recent revelations of the extensive fraudulent activity by Shinichi Fujimura at Japanese "sites" (Normile 2001) have cast doubt on all evidence of a human occupation there before 30,000 years ago. In contrast to Siberia and Indonesia, such settlement would not have required coping with a water crossing or extreme climate.

Thus, although very ancient peopling of the Americas is improbable, we should not be shocked to discover a site in America that is 250,000 or 300,000 years old. Claims of such antiquity, however, that have already been advanced for a few sites—notably Valsequillo, Mexico (Steen-McIntyre et al. 1981; Szabo et al. 1969), and Toca da Esperança, Brazil (de Lumley et al. 1988), are not credible. Also, the *erectus*-like calvarium from Brazil reported by Alan Bryan (1978) has been conclusively demonstrated to be a fraudulent amalgam composed of disparate animal bones (S. Mendonça de Souza, cited by Dewar 2002).

If, against all odds, such an early arrival were documented, what would it mean? It would mean very little, really. If there ever was a successful, widely distributed, and long-lasting Lower or Middle Paleolithic occupation of the Americas, we would have found the evidence by now. Even Karl Butzer, who argued for the likelihood of an entry of humans circa 40,000 BP, saw no evidence of an evolutionary transition from these supposed early migrants to the post-15,000 BP biface markers. He wrote,

When the expansive Paleoindian populations and their descendants subsequently dispersed through the Americas, they settled some regions for the first time and, in others, they would have swamped any low-density,

older occupants. It would be naïve to expect tangible linguistic or biological traces of such mid-Wisconsin immigrants in the modern indigenous
population . . . any more than Neanderthal lexical or dental components
can be expected in the human mosaic of contemporary Europe. (Butzer
1991: 152)

If early hominins somehow got to America, they died out quickly. Unlike Europe, where Neanderthals slowly retreated into refugia and ultimately met with
extinction under pressure from anatomically modern humans after 40,000 BP,
there was no interaction between expanding Paleoindian ancestors and pre-
sapiens natives in the Americas.

By inference from the Eurasian record of Upper Paleolithic expansion, one
would anticipate a migration of anatomically modern humans across Beringia about 20,000 to 35,000 years ago. People bearing an Upper Paleolithic
industry had reached southern Siberia by 40,000 BP (Goebel and Aksenov
1995; Vasil'ev et al. 2002). The recent spectacular discovery of stone and bone
tools at the Yana RHS site (Pitulko et al. 2004) demonstrates that people were
living (at least for short visits) above the Arctic Circle in northeastern Siberia at 27,000 BP (about 30,000 cal BP). Why would they have waited 15,000
years before pushing on across Beringia? Indeed, a hypothesized human entry into the Americas about 25,000 BP was the focus of a recent Society for
American Archaeology symposium and a volume arising from that session
(Madsen 2004). Nevertheless, the archaeological record of both Beringia and
the Americas indicates that there was, in fact, an inexplicably long delay in human expansion until about 12,000 BP (14,000 cal BP), when Beringia was first
inhabited (Vasil'ev et al. 2002). Apart from the ambiguous (probably naturally
fractured) broken bones of the Old Crow Basin and Bluefish Caves (Cinq-Mars
and Morlan 1999), the earliest human occupation sites in eastern Beringia are
located in the Nenana and Tenana valleys of Alaska. These sites (Broken Mammoth, Swan Point, Walker Road, and Mead) date from about 11,200 to 11,800
BP (Hamilton and Goebel 1999), or about 13,200 cal BP to 13,800 cal BP (a
cluster of three dates around 12,000 BP from the deepest component at Swan
Point, which includes microblades, and one of 12,360 ± 60 BP suggest that the
first settlement may have occurred there about 14,000 cal BP [Largent 2004]).
The earliest Alaskan dates are thus marginally earlier than Clovis-associated
dates.

Several authors (for example, Turner [1992]) have speculated that competition from the indigenous carnivore guild may have prevented colonization of
Europe by early humans. Similar suggestions have been advanced to explain
the long delay in Northeast Asia. Valerius Geist (1999) identifies the short-

faced bear of North America and eastern Beringia as the fearsome predator that was too tough for humans to handle. Christy Turner (2002), instead, posits the giant hyena of Northeast Asia as the most dangerous competitor threatening colonizers. Recent genetic evidence implying that American dogs, along with their Old World relatives, descend from a single domestication event in eastern Asia around 15,000 BP (Leonard et al. 2002; Savolainen et al. 2002) lends credibility to Turner's suggestion that dogs may have played a critical role in overcoming the challenge of these formidable predators (Fiedel 2005).

Even if predators were not an insuperable problem, it may simply have been too cold in the far north, even before the Last Glacial Maximum at 18,000 BP (22,000 cal BP), for humans to successfully cope with arctic winters, particularly in the absence of trees for firewood. If any people did successfully traverse Beringia between about 12,000 BP and 20,000 BP (14,000–24,000 cal BP), they would have encountered an impassable ice barrier at the eastern edge, where the Laurentide and Cordilleran ice sheets coalesced (Dyke, Moore, and Robertson 2002). Even the hypothesized Pacific coastal route (Fladmark 1979; Josenhans et al. 1997), currently the focus of research and speculation by archaeologists (for example, Dixon 1999; Mandryk 1998) desperately seeking to explain the anomalous Monte Verde site, would have been sealed off by ice until about 13,000 BP (15,500 cal BP) (Clague et al. 2004). The ice sheets began to retreat about 12,000 BP (14,000 cal BP) (Dyke, Andrews, et al. 2002), probably in response to dramatic northern hemisphere warming at 14,700 cal BP. People were living in eastern Beringia at 11,800 BP, and a passage between the retreating ice sheets opened by about 11,500 BP (13,400 cal BP). I do not think it is coincidental that the first sure signs of human occupation south of the ice sheets date between 10,900 BP and 11,500 BP.

I will not belabor, in tiresome detail, the weaknesses of each of the remaining sites (Meadowcroft, Monte Verde, Cactus Hill, Chesrow Complex) for which pre-Clovis claims continue to be advanced. Suffice it to say that I do not find any of the evidence compelling (Fiedel 1999a, 1999b, 2000, 2002). The main issues yet to be resolved, in my opinion, are as follows:

1. Did the Clovis culture develop along the northern edge of Alaska and, once formed, move south? Or
2. Did Clovis develop within North America after migration southward from Alaska, from an offshoot of the Nenana Complex? And
3. Did the Paleoindian Fell I, or Fishtail point complex of Central and South America, derive from an actual continued Clovis migration or (much less plausibly in my opinion) by independent convergent stylistic development from an already ubiquitous Nenana-like ur-culture (as recently hypothesized by Roosevelt et al. in 2002)?

The Need for More Reliable Dates from Stratified Contexts

A second major obstacle to a refined chronology is the paucity of early sites that have been, or can be, securely dated using ^{14}C samples and/or stratigraphic superposition. Remarkably, the best Paleoindian sites in both North and South America (with respect to clarity of stratigraphic sequences, datable contexts, and unambiguous associations of typologically distinctive artifacts with well-preserved Pleistocene fauna) were discovered in the 1930s, not long after the initial recognition of a Pleistocene human presence at Folsom in 1927. In 1932, at Blackwater Draw near Clovis, New Mexico, fluted points were found embedded amid mammoth bones (Cotter 1937). Subsequent excavations revealed a stratified sequence in which Folsom points overlaid the Clovis artifacts. Until recently, Blackwater Draw was the only site with clear stratigraphic superposition of Clovis and Folsom components. However, preliminary reports indicate a Clovis-to-Folsom sequence at the Gault site in Texas (Collins 2002). In southernmost Patagonia, Junius Bird excavated from 1934 to 1936 at Palli Aike Cave and Fell's Cave. He discovered fluted Fishtail stemmed points in close association with bones of horse, giant sloth, and guanaco (Bird 1938a). Bird guessed that the earliest material might be about 5,400 years old.

Radiocarbon dates obtained three decades later put the first occupation of Fell's Cave at 11,000 ± 170 BP (Bird 1970). Carbonized plant remains from Blackwater Draw also were ^{14}C-dated in the 1960s, yielding dates of 11,630 ± 400 BP (A-491), 11,170 ± 360 BP (A-481), and 11,040 ± 500 BP (A-490) (C. V. Haynes 1964, 1993). These dates are not very precise, and as Anna Roosevelt and colleagues (2002) have observed, the dated material was not closely associated with the human activities documented at Blackwater Draw—it was neither hearth fuel nor food refuse. More precise dates have been obtained for other southwestern Clovis sites, such as Lehner, where twelve charcoal-based dates ranging from 10,620 ± 300 BP to 11,470 ± 110 BP provide an average date of 10,950 ± 40 BP, and Murray Springs, where eight charcoal- based dates ranging from 10,710 ± 160 BP to 11,190 ± 180 BP provide an average of 10,900 ± 50 BP (C. V. Haynes 1993). Thus there is no statistical difference between the Clovis dates and the Fell's Cave date. Their ostensible contemporaneity must be explained somehow if Clovis and Fishtail point makers are considered related as ancestors and descendants. I return to this issue below.

Unfortunately, the great majority of the more than thirteen thousand North American fluted points found over the past eight decades were collected from the surfaces of plowed fields or from shallow soils on upland sites. In these settings, there is no meaningful association with any organic materials that might be ^{14}C-dated (or might, for that matter, provide any useful information about Paleoindian subsistence). The lack of deep stratified sites is a particularly frustrating problem in northern Alaska and the Mid-South. These two regions seem the most likely to be Clovis homelands—the first because of its proximity to the assumed trans-Beringian migration path, the second because of the sheer abundance and variety of fluted points (Anderson and Faught 1998, 2000; Mason 1962).

In Alaska, some of the fluted points (for example, from Batza Tena) were made of obsidian. Some of the surface-collected fluted points from the Great Basin and most of the Fell I–type points from the highlands of Ecuador were also made of obsidian. Attempts to directly date these artifacts by measurement of microscopic obsidian hydration rinds have produced dates that are sometimes credible but often clearly erratic (for example, Basgall 1995; Bell 1977; Clark 1984). The limitations of this technique are now better appreciated, as specialists have identified the variables that affect hydration rates (Anovitz et al. 1999; Jones et al. 1997; Ridings 1996). Surface finds now appear to be unsuitable samples, which unfortunately excludes reliable dating of most Paleoindian-age artifacts.

Various other putative techniques for direct dating of artifacts or sediment matrices have been applied to Paleoindian materials. Some methods have proved useless, while others show promise. Both radiocarbon and cation dating of rock varnish on tools and petroglyphs, once touted as proof of pre-Clovis occupation of western North America (Whitley and Dorn 1993), have proved completely unreliable (Dorn 1996). As already noted, improved OSL dating of sediments has resulted in greater chronological precision in Australia. TL can be used to obtain dates from chert artifacts if they were ever heated to a sufficient temperature. This method has produced apparently reliable dates for Old World Paleolithic sites, such as circa 95,000-year ages for early *Homo sapiens* in Israel (Mercier et al. 1995). However, the precision of TL is currently limited to about 5 percent at best, so Paleoindian-era dates would have irreducible error margins of at least 650 years. Furthermore, TL can be affected by matrix moisture and other factors.

Archaeologists generally resort to luminescence only in desperation—when ^{14}C dating is impossible. However, in one recent application of this technique to a Paleoindian site (Pedra Pintada, Brazil), the results can be compared to an unusually large suite of ^{14}C dates (forty-nine AMS and seven conventional dates) (Roosevelt et al. 1996). All of the accelerator mass spectrometry (AMS) dates clustered around 10,000–10,500 BP (circa 11,300–12,500 cal BP). The TL dates ranged from 9530 ± 780 to 16,190 ± 930 BP; the OSL dates were 12,491 ± 1409, 12,536 ± 4125, and 13,106 ± 1628 BP. At Cactus Hill, OSL dates for an Early Archaic level (with Fort Nottoway points) are 9189 ± 1101 BP and 12,391 ± 1864 BP; the expected calibrated age was about 10,000 cal BP (Mc-Avoy et al. 2000). The Clovis component of the Gault site in Texas was recently

OSL-dated by Steve Forman. The dates reported are 12,820 ± 880, 12,940 ± 880, 12,960 ± 880, and 13,120 ± 1220 BP (Collins 2003). A date obtained for the Clovis-Folsom contact is 12,010 ± 830 BP. These dates are in remarkably close agreement with the anticipated calendar age of Clovis, although the Folsom date appears too recent (but becomes accurate when the large error factor is added). Apparently, when enough OSL dates are obtained, the average may correspond pretty closely to the age established by ^{14}C dating. However, researchers have not yet determined just how many dates are enough for confidence or how the large sigmas and frequently erratic dates should be explained or interpreted (Feathers 1997; Hilgers et al. 2001; Rich and Stokes 2001).

Even in the exceptional circumstances where datable organic materials are closely associated with artifacts, ^{14}C dating is not a simple procedure. Adequate sample size is no longer the problem it once was. Since the 1980s, ^{14}C dating using the AMS technique has yielded much more precise dates, even from small samples, than could be obtained previously by the conventional method. The Shawnee-Minisink site in Pennsylvania provides an illustration of the advantages of the AMS technique. Conventional dates obtained in the 1970s, with sigmas ranging from 300 to 1,000 years, suggested an age of about 10,600 BP for the Clovis occupation. Fortunately, some carbonized hawthorn plum seeds from a hearth had been saved, and two recently run AMS assays—10,900 ± 40 BP (Beta-127162) and 10,940 ± 90 BP (Beta-101935) (Dent 1999)—show that this eastern Clovis site is coeval with classic southwestern Clovis sites such as Lehner and Murray Springs.

AMS redating of several Paleoindian sites in the Southern Cone that had previously yielded pre–12,000 BP conventional ages has resulted in similar clarification, but in this case the AMS ages are all appreciably younger (Steele et al. 2001). With the exception of two dates on bone (12,070 ± 140 and 12,240 ± 100 BP) from Arroyo Seco 2 (not unequivocally associated with human activities), all of the new dates fall between circa 10,300 and 11,000 BP. These dates agree with the established range for Fell I components. They not only remove an obstacle to temporal seriation of North and South American fluted points but also underline the isolation and anomalous character of the circa 11,900 to 12,700 BP dates reported at the controversial Monte Verde "settlement" in southern Chile—a "site" where debitage is absent, the lithic assemblage consists mainly of naturally fractured and rounded stones supposedly used expediently by humans, and the proveniences of the half-dozen indubitable artifacts cannot be ascertained (Dillehay 1989, 1997a, 2002).

Recent research at the Brook Run jasper quarry in Virginia presents a cautionary case (Voigt 2002). One of the first dates obtained on associated charcoal was a conventional date of 11,670 ± 330 BP (Beta-145346). Coupled with ostensible evidence of prismatic blade production (subsequently reinterpreted), this date seemed to indicate early Clovis, perhaps even pre-Clovis, occupation. However, numerous additional AMS dates for the site clustered around 9900 BP (11,300 cal BP), and a charcoal sample from the same stratigraphic context as the Beta-145346 sample was AMS-dated at 9990 ± 50 BP (Beta-157322).

Despite its evident precision, AMS cannot guarantee accuracy. Take the perplexing case of the Mesa site in Alaska; twelve AMS dates on charcoal associated with Agate Basin–like unfluted lanceolate points clustered around 10,000 BP. Among these was a date of 10,060 ± 75 BP (Beta-52606) on a split sample; part of this charcoal piece had previously yielded a conventional date of 7620 ± 95 BP (Kunz and Reanier 1994). Two dates, however, came out much earlier than the rest: 11,660 ± 80 BP (Beta-55286) and 11,190 ± 70 BP (Beta-57430). Rather than greatly extending the antiquity of the lanceolate points on this basis (Kunz and Reanier 1996: 503), a more prudent approach might be to attribute these anomalous dates to a previous Paleoarctic occupation (Bever 1998). The puzzle does not stop there: the two early dates were derived from a single split sample! Even taking into account the widest 95 percent (two-sigma) confidence ranges and calibrating the dates, they do not overlap. At least one of them must be off the mark. This is particularly worrisome because, as we will soon see, determining whether the earliest North American Paleoindian sites date to 11,600 BP or 11,200 BP is crucial.

The Mesa ^{14}C dates illustrate a problem that is even more evident in the case of Roosevelt's Pedra Pintada site. As Michael Shott (1992) has cautioned, fully a third of ^{14}C dates may be inaccurate, just based on statistical probabilities. We are rightly suspicious of any single date, but our confidence grows as multiple assays converge on a targeted age. However, the more assays that are run, the greater the likelihood that a few dates will fall at the far ends of the probability curve. Roosevelt submitted fifty-six samples, fifty-two of which yielded remarkably consistent and precise AMS dates, falling within the range of 10,000 to 10,600 BP (which, unfortunately, places them on the Younger Dryas–era ^{14}C plateau). However, four dates are earlier: 11,145 ± 135, 11,110 ± 310, 10,905 ± 295, and 10,875 ± 295 BP. In view of the large sigmas, it should come as no surprise that these older dates are conventional ^{14}C dates. In assessing their validity, one could simply note their relative imprecision and large error factors and set them aside as problematic. Instead, Roosevelt, after being challenged on the site's reputed Clovis-equivalent antiquity, chose to defend the accuracy of the early dates. She had initially reported them as derived from separate contexts (proveniences 8231 and 8314), each with additional AMS dates of circa 10,400–10,550 BP for the Initial phase of the Monte Alegre culture. Later, however, Roosevelt and colleagues (1997, 2002) published a revised stratigraphic profile indicating that the seemingly older material had actually been excavated from a slightly lower and distinguishable level (Stratum 17c). The greater depth would explain the older age. This chronological evidence is too tenuous to support the far-reaching culture-historical revisions that Roosevelt and her colleagues (1996, 2002) have proposed.

Unfortunately, in South America there is a tendency to accept, at face value, dates that would be regarded very skeptically in North America (a commendable exception is Nami's [1994, 1996a] cautious assessment of the anomalous early date [12,390 ± 180 BP] from Cueva del Medio; the same hearth produced several dates of circa 10,500 BP). A good illustration of the North American attitude toward anomalously old ^{14}C dates is David Brose's (1994) interpretation of dates from the Paleo Crossing site in Ohio. These dates also show how AMS dating, dealing with small particles instead of pooled samples, can create new interpretive problems. Charcoal derived from a single feature, possibly a post mold, yielded dates ranging from circa 9230 BP to 13,100 BP. The excavator (Brose 1994) discounted the oldest and youngest dates to arrive at an acceptable Clovis date of 10,990 BP. We must ask, however, how did much older carbonized material intrude into a Clovis-era feature? Would this apparent contamination have been noticeable if conventional dating had been used?

The most famous Paleoindian sites are not encampments but kill and butchery sites where no cooking was done. At these sites, charcoal is lacking but bone is available. Even where artifacts are not associated, the bones of terminal Pleistocene megafauna offer a potential source of precise dates for the extinction of these large mammals, which may have been a consequence of human activity. Unfortunately, ^{14}C dating of bone has long been problematic, but Tom Stafford's recent development of protocols for AMS dating of purified amino acids from bone allows direct dating of late Pleistocene faunal and human remains (Stafford 1994) with a precision of ± 60 years.

The apparent precision of the new bone dates is not always definitive, however. Consider, for example, the range of reported dates for the Anzick infant burial, which was associated with a spectacular Clovis artifact cache. Should we put greatest reliance on a date of 10,240 ± 120 BP (AA-2978), 10,710 ± 100 BP (AA-2980), 10,820 ± 100 BP (AA-2979), 10,940 ± 90 BP (AA-2981), or 11,550 ± 60 BP (CAMS-35912)? Stafford regards the oldest age, despite its ostensible precision, as inexplicably erratic and unacceptable; he takes the average of circa 10,700 BP as the best estimate. A new collagen-derived AMS date run by Beta-Analytic Laboratories on a rib from the infant skeleton puts it at 10,780 ± 40 BP (Beta-163833), but two new dates on associated antler foreshafts are 11,040 ± 40 BP (Beta-168967) and 11,040 ± 60 BP (Beta-163832) (Morrow and Fiedel, this volume).

Stafford obtained a series of ^{14}C dates on mammoth bones from the Dent kill site. The average of five dates on separate amino acids is 10,690 ± 50 BP.

An older date of 10,980 ± 90 BP (AA-2941) was obtained for an XAD purified fraction. Several other dates in the same range have been reported, but their large sigmas render them useless in solving this problem. It is possible that some conservative band was searching the plains for the very last mammoths to kill with their antique Clovis points, while their progressive contemporaries used Folsom points to hunt bison. In fact, a bison kill site at Jake Bluff in Oklahoma, where two Clovis points were found in association, was recently dated to about 10,750 BP, apparently coeval with Folsom (Bement and Carter 2003). However, a more likely explanation of the Dent dates is that the bone-derived dates are simply too young. In view of many such cases, C. Vance Haynes (personal communication, 1999) generally takes the oldest of any series of bone dates as the most credible. However, this stance also poses logical and practical difficulties. For example, does the 11,550 BP ^{14}C date from Anzick negate all of the younger ages? Will it stand as valid until one of a potentially infinite series of replicate dates comes out even older?

Preliminary reports of the faunal dating project undertaken by Thomas Stafford, Russell Graham, and Holmes Semken (for example, Graham 1998; Graham et al. 2002) indicate that terminal Pleistocene extinction was very rapid. Final dates for seventeen megafauna species cluster between 10,800 and 11,400 BP. Although Graham has suggested, based on dates of circa 10,800 BP, that the proboscideans were the last to go, we should recall that dates of 10,800 BP have also been obtained for Clovis sites that appear to be of late Allerød age. I explore the reasons for this phenomenon in greater detail below. Furthermore, because of the rapid increase in ^{14}C at the Younger Dryas onset, dates drop from about 11,200 BP to 10,800 BP in about a century of real time around 12,900 cal BP (Hughen et al. 2000).

Also, we cannot preclude the nagging possibility that the youngest dates may be inaccurate because of intrinsic and insuperable uncertainties in dating collagen. The Oxford Radiocarbon Accelerator Unit recently installed a new ultrapurification protocol for bone collagen dates, with the consequence that late Pleistocene ages are generally becoming older when samples are rerun. For example, a human skull from Tlapacoya, Mexico, was originally dated to 9730 ± 65 BP using standard gel techniques; the date for the ultrapurified collagen is 10,200 ± 65 BP. Redating of European *Megaloceros* ("Irish elk") bones, previously dated to about 9400 and 9200 BP, produced significantly older ages of about 10,400 and 11,300 BP, respectively (Higham 2004).

The recent technical innovations in AMS ^{14}C dating clearly do not offer a panacea for problems of degraded, dislocated, or contaminated samples. These problems are particularly troublesome in the Northeast, where, all too often, dates from Paleoindian sites come out too young to be credible. Is the seemingly more recent charcoal derived from trees that grew and burned on these sites millennia after human occupation (Bonnichsen and Will 1999)? Conversely, fortuitous stratigraphic association of old charcoal with artifacts may account for a few other cases (Meadowcroft, Cactus Hill) where the dates seem too old to be accepted without hesitation.

The fact remains that the great majority of the Paleoindian archaeological material available to us is, and will surely remain, surface-collected projectile points. Can this material be useful for the construction of a precise chronology? Distinctive types are readily recognized, and western fluted points were quickly divided into Clovis and Folsom types. But as late as the 1970s, it was considered a real possibility (for example, Wilmsen 1984) that these were coeval functional variants. Even now, a naïve analysis of overlapping ^{14}C date ranges would support that interpretation. We must be explicit about the assumptions underlying stylistic seriation: that stylistic differences arise (1) through cultural drift caused by increasing geographic and social isolation, and (2) by innovation and inexact transmission of norms and techniques over time. The similarity of stylistic seriation to processes of biological speciation should be obvious; indeed, Michael O'Brien and colleagues (2001) recently used a cladistic approach to sort southeastern fluted points into a series of ancestor-descendant forms, as though they were trilobites. To pin down the beginning of a seriation sequence, one must designate one extreme form as the ancestral type. Ideally, this form would be absolutely dated early and would likely be more widely distributed geographically than later derived types. In the particular case of fluted points, the widely assumed directions of stylistic evolution run from larger to smaller points, short to long flutes, single to multiple flutes, flat to concave bases, straight to flaring basal ears, wide bases to contracting or fishtailed stems, percussion to pressure flaking, and finer-grained (often exotic) to coarser-grained (often local) lithic materials.

On a hemispheric scale, overriding all of these dimensions of variation is a basic north-to-south assumption; that is, the first people, originally from Northeast Asia, arrived from the north and moved south. If they invented fluted points early in their migration, North American points should be earlier and ancestral, and Central and South American Fishtail points should be later and derived (for example, Morrow and Morrow 1999; Pearson 2002). It must be strongly emphasized that basal fluting is a very unusual technique that has not arisen repeatedly in stone-flaking traditions around the world. It was not, for example, developed by the Solutrean biface-makers of Iberia—a fact that, aside from other temporal and geographic issues, fatally vitiates Dennis Stanford and Bruce Bradley's (2002) hypothesis of Solutrean ancestry for Clovis. In fact, unlike notching, fluting had a rather brief (perhaps 1,500-year) ubiquitous florescence at the beginning of American prehistory, and it never came back into style thereafter. Therefore, that fluting was independently and coevally invented by mutually isolated terminal Pleistocene populations in North America and South America is unlikely (but for an alternative view see Bryan and Gruhn 2003; Mayer-Oakes 1984; Miotti 2003b; Roosevelt et al. 2002).

Nevertheless, for now, the place of origin of fluted points is unknown. Could archaeologists even recognize "proto-Clovis" points, constrained as they are by the above assumptions about stylistic evolution? At 11,700 BP, the earliest known inhabitants of eastern Beringia were making small, unfluted, triangular and teardrop-shaped (Chindadn) points. If these people were the ancestors of North American Paleoindians, upon their arrival south of the ice sheets did they one day start making giant, flawless, fluted bifaces like the points from the East Wenatchee cache? Or should we be looking for a transitional series of smallish, paratriangular, basally thinned points as precursors to the classic Clovis type? Ironically, such points exist in several areas (Holcombe points in the Upper Midwest, late Paleo forms in the Southeast, small fluted points in the Great Basin, "stubbies" in Alberta, and small fluted points in northern Alaska [Clark 1991]), but they are all normally considered to be very late variants. The Meadowcroft Rockshelter (Adovasio et al. 1999) and Cactus Hill (McAvoy and McAvoy 1997) sites clearly raise this issue, since the supposedly early forms in each case are smallish, unfluted, paratriangular lanceolate points. In both cases, however, the points appear to have been reworked from originally longer lanceolate forms. They are equally plausible as Clovis prototypes or, alternatively, as late variants in reversed or misdated stratigraphic contexts. Roosevelt and colleagues (2002) have now advanced the hypothesis that an initial migration of Nenana descendants spread unfluted triangular points through North and South America. Clovis is viewed as a secondary, regionally limited, and adaptively specialized derivative from this wetland-focused ur-culture. This model underestimates the pan–North American and Central American range of Clovis and must deny, or explain away, the obvious technological and stylistic relationship of Clovis and Fell I points. Roosevelt's argument—that Fell I–type points in Central America are not ^{14}C-dated as pre-Holocene—may be technically correct for the moment, but it is logically untenable and will surely be undermined as more dates are obtained (for example, recently reported bracketing dates of circa 9,000–11,500 BP from the lowest stratum with Fishtail points at Cueva de los Vampiros in Panama [Pearson 2002]).

The Clovis lithic industry, with its end scrapers, gravers, and other artifacts, is ultimately derived from the Eurasian Upper Paleolithic. Old World Upper Paleolithic tool kits, while they may contain bifaces, are always dominated by blades struck from prismatic cores. The lithic industry of the Nenana culture, a credible Clovis ancestor in Alaska, is also macroblade-based (Goebel et al. 1991). Until recently, however, the blade element in Clovis assemblages had not been fully appreciated (Collins 1999; Morrow 1996, 1998, 2001b; Witthoft 1952). Now, we realize that big prismatic blades and cores are characteristic of Clovis industries from Texas (for example, Gault), the Midwest (Martens et al. 2004; Morrow 1996), and the Mid-South (that is, Kentucky [Freeman et al. 1996], Tennessee [Broster and Norton 1996], and Alabama [Futato 1996]). Years ago, John Witthoft (1952) argued that the assemblage from the Shoop site in central Pennsylvania was blade based and therefore represented a very early fluted point culture, not far removed from its Upper Paleolithic roots. Witthoft's analysis of the Shoop industry has since been questioned (Cox 1986), and very few true blades seem to have existed in northeastern Paleo-indian assemblages. Nevertheless, Witthoft's more general argument may be correct; the earliest Clovis sites probably should have the highest percentage of prismatic blades, which should fall off over time and distance from the point of first entry. Prismatic blades are very rare in Central American Paleoindian assemblages (Pearson 2002), but they seem to recur, along with burins, at El Inga in Ecuador (Mayer-Oakes 1984).

Plateaus and Jumps: Radiocarbon and Climate Events

The recent realization that ^{14}C dates for the terminal Pleistocene grossly under-estimate real age is another complicating factor in chronological refinement. Since the 1970s, archaeologists have known that fluctuating ratios of ^{14}C and ^{12}C in the past affected ^{14}C dates significantly; thus, ^{14}C ages were about 1,000 years too young around 8000 BP. Preliminary indications suggested that this difference narrowed in the early Holocene, and Paleoindian specialists were not too concerned about the possible effects of calibration on their chronol-ogy. However, it is now evident that late Pleistocene ^{14}C dates are about 2,000 years younger than calendrical ages (Stuiver et al. 1998; for a detailed discus-sion, see Fiedel 1999a). Clovis-associated dates ranging from 10,700 to 11,100 BP correspond to a short period from about 12,800 to 13,200 cal BP (Taylor et al. 1996). Thus, Ernst Antevs' (1935, 1953, 1959) estimate of 13,000 years old for Clovis turns out to have been correct, after all.

Most of the dates earlier than 11,100 BP for Clovis have large sigmas or are derived from samples without secure behavioral association (Roosevelt et al. 2002). An exception is the date of 11,470 ± 110 BP from Lehner—although that date looks like an outlier, as numerous other dates for this site cluster around 10,900 BP. The problematic early date for the Anzick burial has already been mentioned; the new assays indicate a date of about 11,040 BP. Charcoal-derived dates of 11,540 ± 110 BP (AA-5271) and 11,590 ± 90 BP (AA-5274) are reported from the Aubrey site, in northern Texas (Ferring 1995, 2001). The samples came from a Clovis occupation surface but not, apparently, from a defined hearth. Although C. Reid Ferring (2001) discounts any possibility of contamination, old wood could have skewed the results (Roosevelt et al. 2002). Apart from Aubrey, numerous ^{14}C dates repeatedly place Clovis occupations in the East and West about 10,950 BP. The most precisely dated Clovis sites are Lehner and Murray Springs, both in Arizona. The ^{14}C date for Lehner, averaged from twelve charcoal assays, is 10,930 ± 40 BP. The date for Murray Springs, averaged from eight assays, is 10,900 ± 50 BP (C. V. Haynes 1993: 221). The most precise of the Lehner dates are 10,950 ± 90 (SMU-290), 10,940 ± 100 (A-378), 10,950 ± 110 (SMU-194), and 10,710 ± 90 BP (SMU-340). The most precise date from Murray Springs is 10,840 ± 70 BP (SMU-41). Most of the Murray Springs samples were pieces of charcoal found in eroded deposits. The only dates from definite Clovis cultural contexts are 10,760 ± 100 and 11,150 ± 450 BP.

As of now, the limit of precise calibration, based on the oldest German tree rings (12,450 cal BP) (Friedrich et al. 1999, 2001 ; Schaub et al. 2003), falls just short of the era of Paleoindian migrations. Older "floating" tree-ring sequences of Bølling-Allerød age from Switzerland and Germany may soon be tied securely to the later continuous sequence (Friedrich et al. 2001, 2004; Kromer et al. 2004). Until then, there are several ways to translate ^{14}C dates of 12,000–10,000 BP into "real" calendrical or sidereal years. Combined high-precision Thermal Infrared Multispectral Scanner (TIMS) U-Th and AMS ^{14}C dates on corals (for example, Burr et al. 1998) have some utility, but uncertainty about late glacial fluctuations of localized marine reservoir effects limits their reliability. Radiocarbon dating of terrestrial macrofossils (for example, twigs) incorporated within varved lakebed deposits avoids this problem, but uncertainties in this method arise from the possibilities of missing or duplicated varves, vertical displacement of dated samples, and the peculiar carbon contents of some plant materials (Turney et al. 2000). Furthermore, the varve sequences need to be anchored to some fixed event to be more reliable. The ^{14}C-dated varves from Lake Suigetsu in Japan (Kitigawa and van der Plicht 1998, 2000) and the varved marine sediments in the Cariaco basin off Venezuela (Hughen et al. 1998, 2000) overlap the German dendrochronological record at the recent end and can be tied to the latter by wiggle-matching the ^{14}C dates. There is, nevertheless, approximately a 100-calendar-year difference between Cariaco and Suigetsu dates. The Cariaco ^{14}C dates are derived from marine foraminifera embedded in the sediments. A correction for reservoir effect must, therefore, be applied. Although the assumption of an invariant local reservoir effect of 420 years throughout the late glacial is defensible (Hughen et al. 1998, 2000), the possibility of intermittent spikes cannot be precluded.

Temporal variations in thickness of the Cariaco varves (the "grey scale") are correlated with the synchronous fluctuations of oxygen isotope ratios in

Greenland ice sheet cores. The rapid onset (cooling) and termination (warming) of the Younger Dryas (YD) climatic episode are crucial marker events for correlation of these records. Both events are clearly recorded as dramatic changes in snow accumulation, temperature, chemical composition, and dust content in both the Greenland Ice Core Project (GRIP) and Greenland Ice Sheet Project 2 (GISP2) cores from the Greenland ice sheet. Based on counts of annual accumulation layers, the dates for YD termination (the start of the Holocene) are approximately 11,550 ± 90 cal BP (GRIP) and 11,645 ± 200 cal BP (GISP2). European tree rings indicate a similar date of 11,590 cal BP for this event (Friedrich et al. 2004), and the Cariaco date is 11,580 ± 16 (Hughen et al. 2004). Unfortunately, there is an unresolved 200-year discrepancy between the two ice cores, centered on the 12,500–12,800 cal BP span at the start of the Younger Dryas (Southon 2002): the GISP2 date for YD onset is 12,940 ± 260 cal BP, but the GRIP date is about 12,700 ± 100 cal BP. The Cariaco date of circa 12,950 cal BP supports the GISP2 date, but several varved lakebeds in central Europe indicate a YD duration of only 1,100 years and seem to verify the GRIP date.

The cause of the Younger Dryas stadial remains to be determined. The prevailing theory attributes the sudden temperature decline (about 15°C in Greenland and 6°C in northern Europe) to a breakdown of the ocean's thermohaline circulation system, perhaps caused by Laurentian ice sheet meltwater pouring into the North Atlantic (Broecker et al. 1988). If the ocean surface suddenly became colder, thus absorbing less atmospheric carbon, the same process could account for the peculiar ^{14}C increase that accompanies the YD onset. This increase of about 70 per mil is manifested as a jump in dates from about 11,100 to 10,700 BP within a century from 12,900 to 12,800 cal BP (Hughen et al. 2000; Reimer et al. 2004). After this steep decline, ^{14}C dates within the Younger Dryas form a long plateau with several descending steps: samples dating from circa 12,650–12,750 cal BP yield dates of circa 10,600 BP; samples dating between circa 12,150 cal BP and 12,650 cal BP produce ^{14}C dates of about 10,400–10,500 BP; and ^{14}C dates from the 11,800 to 12,150 cal BP span are circa 10,200–10,300 BP. The last section of the plateau extends beyond the YD termination (circa 11,590 cal BP); ^{14}C dates for samples in the interval from 11,250 cal BP to 11,800 cal BP are around 10,150–10,000 BP (Hughen et al. 2000).

The steep decline in ^{14}C age attributable to abruptly increased atmospheric ^{14}C is evident not only in the Cariaco and Suigetsu sequences but also in the ^{14}C date series from the YD onset in Swedish varves (Wohlfarth et al. 1998) and pond sediments from Kodiak Island, Alaska (Hajdas et al. 1998) (see figure 2.1). The falloff is not as sharp in two Polish varved lakebed series reported by Tomasz Goslar and colleagues (2000), but numerous dates from these loca-

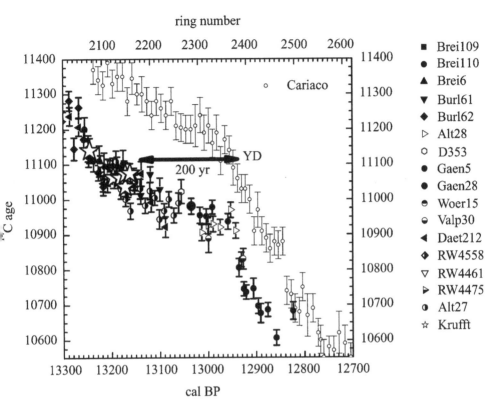

Figure 2.1. Calendar-year calibration of ^{14}C dates of Late Glacial German tree rings compared with equivalent Cariaco basin varve dates (from Kromer et al. 2004: fig. 2, reprinted with permission from the University of Arizona Press). Stars indicate dates for outer rings of trees killed by Laacher See eruption, dated to circa 200 years before onset of Younger Dryas. Note the radiocarbon "cliff" at the onset of the Younger Dryas, which was used to anchor the German sequence to the Cariaco curve; ^{14}C dates drop from circa 10,600 to 11,000 BP between 12,860 and 12,950 cal BP. Also note the approximately 200-year disparity between tree-ring and Cariaco dates, as well as the Clovis-era plateau (12,950–13,200 cal BP) with calendrical dates of circa 10,900–11,000 BP.

tions appear anomalous and may be from dislocated or contaminated samples. Two lakebeds in the Southern Cone (Huelmo in southern Chile and Lake Mascardi, 120 kilometers to the east in Argentina) show what appears to be the same event (Hajdas et al. 2003). However, these records show a cold event starting at about 11,400 BP, well before the ^{14}C falloff and perhaps 500 calendar years prior to the beginning of the YD in the northern hemisphere. This offset underscores the difficulty of correlating late glacial climate events on a global scale.

The climatic effects of the Younger Dryas are most evident along the rim of the North Atlantic. Moving away from that area, the effects on indicators such as vegetation, microfauna, and lake chemistry become subtler and may be obscured by lack of resolution and problems in dating pollen cores (Yu 2000; Yu and Wright 2001). Regional effects are also likely to have been out of phase because of changes in air circulation patterns. The black mats recognized by C. Vance Haynes (1991, and this volume) in the Southwest and southern plains probably mark the onset of the regional equivalent of the YD (Fiedel 1999a). However, we cannot be sure that they are exactly synchronous with YD onset in the North Atlantic. Calibration using the new Cariaco data (Hughen et al. 2000; Reimer et al. 2004) implies that the black mats may date to about 100–200 years after the isotope signature of YD onset in the Greenland ice cores. Clovis artifacts and mammoth skeletons occur just beneath the black mats but never above them; Folsom points are always within or above the mats. These features are attributable to increased spring discharge (Quade et al. 1998) and thus imply a higher water table, increased precipitation, and reduced evaporation, resulting in relatively wet and cold conditions. Globally, however, the YD is generally characterized as a dry period.

Only in the Northeast is there the potential to establish an unambiguous stratigraphic correlation of the YD as a North Atlantic rim phenomenon (Mayle et al. 1993; Williams et al. 2002) and Paleoindian occupation. The ^{14}C dates of circa 10,600 BP (circa 12,700 cal BP) from the Debert site (MacDonald 1968) suggest that it was occupied just after the YD onset. Recognition of permafrost effects at the site supports this interpretation. However, Robson Bonnichsen and Richard Will (1999) have raised doubts about dates from Debert and other Paleoindian sites in the Northeast. They speculate that presumed cultural features may actually be tree burns unrelated to human activities; trees may have become more susceptible to fire during the Younger Dryas because of climatic stress and regional aridity. Although there does indeed appear to be a global pattern of increased burning during this period (Haberle and Ledru 2001), this argument seems dubious in the case of Debert, where the clustering of artifacts and charcoal features in "hot spots" (MacDonald 1968) is not easily dismissed as fortuitous. In any case, the strongly concave bases and long ears of Gainey-like northeastern fluted points from Debert, Vail, and Lamb appear to be derived elaborations of the basic Clovis prototype and should, therefore, be expected to yield relatively late dates.

Abrupt Younger Dryas climate changes left clear signatures in numerous European lakebeds, where there are synchronous sharp transitions in oxygen isotopes and microfauna such as midges, pollen, and sediments. Vegetation responded rapidly to the changes in temperature and precipitation, with lag times that rarely exceeded 100 years (Williams et al. 2002). In northern South America, the vegetation responded about 25–50 years after the Younger Dryas onset (Hughen et al. 2004).

In 1999, on the basis of examination of the available ^{14}C series derived from sediments stratified below YD-onset markers, I suggested that there had been a date reversal or short plateau about 150–200 years before the onset of the Younger Dryas. I posited that this hypothesized event was causally related to the brief, perhaps 200-year, cold snap in the Allerød called the Gerzensee oscillation or Intra-Allerød Cold Period (IACP). A reversal of this kind, I thought, might account for the anomalous circa 10,700–10,800 BP ages obtained from Clovis sites that, on stylistic and stratigraphic grounds, ought to be older (Folsom dates, which should be later than Clovis, average about 10,600 BP, with some as early as 10,900 BP). The initially reported Cariaco basin date series (Hughen et al. 1998) seemed to show the same ^{14}C event at 13,150 cal BP, but the later, more detailed, decadal sequence revealed no significant break in the ^{14}C dates of circa 11,300 BP for this time (Hughen et al. 2000).

However, the matter does not end there; the reversal/plateau has been recognized in additional lakebed records (Andresen et al. 2000; Goslar et al. 1999: 33). A date reversal at circa 13,200 cal BP (based on GISP2 correlation) also appears in ^{14}C dates from preserved tree stumps of the Bølling-Allerød period at Dättnau, Switzerland (see figure 2.1). K. F. Kaiser (1989) constructed a floating tree-ring chronology for these stumps. He suggests that an 8-year period of thin rings represents the trees' stunted growth in response to the eruption of the Laacher See volcano in Germany. The Laacher See tephra from this eruption (LST) serves as another critical stratigraphic marker within varved lakebed sediments in central Europe. Varve counts, as well as the Dättnau tree rings, show that the LST dates from roughly 200 years before the YD onset (13,140 cal BP using the GISP2 date for YD of 12,940; 12,836 cal BP [Schwander et al. 2000] using a GRIP and varve-based date of 12,693 for YD onset; or 12,916 cal BP [Baales et al. 2002]). Although a ^{14}C age of 11,230 ± 40 BP has been reported for the LST (Hajdas et al. 1995b), the thin rings at Dättnau provide a later date for the eruption (11,070 ± 60 BP), and German poplars buried by the tephra have been dated to 10,986 ± 46 (Baales and Street 1996) and 11,063 ± 12 BP (Friedrich et al. 1999). In fact, Michael Baales and colleagues (2002) show that forty-four dates for wood or charcoal samples from below or within the LST fall into distinct old, middle, and young clusters. They interpret the weighted mean value of 11,062 ± 11 BP for the middle cluster as the best date for the eruption. The young cluster, with a weighted mean of 10,911 ± 49 BP, "represents an inversion in the ^{14}C timescale not included in the INTCAL98 record" (Baales et al. 2002: 283). Thomas Litt and colleagues (2003: 9) present additional high-precision dates from late Allerød tree rings in which "a clear, two-step ^{14}C age plateau at 10,950 BP and 11,060 BP is evident, each extending for at least 100 rings (calendar years)." The astute reader will note the correspondence of these dates to those most often reported from Clovis contexts.

For the moment, we are faced with an unexplained discrepancy of about 250 ^{14}C years between the Cariaco varves (where 13,140 cal BP is equivalent to 11,280–11,300 ± 50 BP) and the German trees. One plausible explanation is that the oceanic reservoir effect in the Cariaco basin changed significantly between 11,000 BP and 12,000 BP, so the standard 420-year correction is not applicable to this period (also suggested in Litt et al. 2003: 10 and Kromer et al. 2004). A marked disparity between floating dendrochronological dates and their probable Cariaco equivalents is now also apparent in the period from about 13,400 cal BP to 13,700 cal BP; tree-ring dates are about 150–200 years younger (Litt et al. 2003: 11; Kromer et al. 2004). A new calibration based on Pacific corals (Fairbanks et al. 2005) agrees with the German trees for this period and differs from Cariaco and INTCAL04. If the Aubrey dates of circa 11,550 BP are accurate, this is where they would fit on the correction curve.

Some additional factors will be noted that might exaggerate the apparent ^{14}C age of South American sites (see Kelly 2003 for additional speculations along the same lines). In arid environments, old wood can last quite a long time on the surface and may be used as fuel. As recently suggested by Douglas Kennett and colleagues (2002), on the coast of Peru, shell dates from Archaic sites may actually be more reliable than wood or charcoal dates. This effect could also account for the earliest dates (11,088 ± 220 BP [BGS-2024] and 11,105 ± 260 BP [BGS-1942]) from Quebrada Jaguay (Sandweiss et al. 1998). The next oldest date there is 10,770 ± 130 BP (BGS-1702), and several other dates of circa 10,700 BP were obtained from sequential overlying strata. This pattern begins to suggest a Younger Dryas–era ^{14}C plateau, although the anticipated dates for this period would be about 10,400 BP in the northern hemisphere. A similar stacking of circa 10,750 BP dates, ostensibly marking a radiocarbon plateau, was reported recently from a core at Lake Doubtful in New Zealand (Turney et al. 2003).

Unpublished ^{14}C dates for tree rings sampled from a Tasmanian Huon pine log (Barbetti n.d.) show a generally close agreement with Cariaco (and

Table 2.1. Radiocarbon Dates Equivalent to Calendar Years BP (Northern Hemisphere) from Cariaco Basin Varves, Southern Cone Lake Sediments, and Huon Pine-Tree Rings from Tasmania

INTCAL04 (cal BP)	Cariaco	Lake Huelmo	Lake Mascardi	Tasmania
12,800	10,715±30	10,740±75		~10,650
12,600	10,510±30	10,800±85	10,480±80	~10,600
12,500	10,480±30	10,700±85		~10,350
		10,585±70		
12,400	10,490±25	10,530±85		
12,100	10,325±25	10,400±90	10,620±80	

INTCAL04) dates during the first 500 years of the Younger Dryas, but there are two evident discrepancies. At 12,700 cal BP, the Tasmanian date is 100 years older than Cariaco (10,650 versus 10,550 BP in Cariaco), but at 12,500 cal BP, the Tasmanian date is 150 years younger (10,350 versus 10,500 BP). Also, some of the dates from Lake Huelmo and Lake Mascardi in the Southern Cone, when fitted to the Cariaco calibration curve, are as much as 200–300 years older than the age-equivalent Venezuelan dates (Hajdas et al. 2003: fig. 5).

Bernd Kromer and colleagues (2001) showed that even the small latitudinal difference between Germany and Turkey created, via seasonal variation in $^{14}CO_2$ uptake by trees, age differences of 22 years around 3600 BP. This latitude effect might, they suggested, be exaggerated during cold periods. Gerry McCormac and colleagues (2004) have determined that between AD 950 and 1850, the ^{14}C offset between the northern and southern hemispheres varied periodically, with values ranging from 8 to 80 years; there was a particularly large offset between AD 1245 and 1355. Table 2.1 indicates that there were episodes during the Younger Dryas when the offset between hemispheres may have been on the order of 100 to 200 years. However, the Huelmo and Mascardi dates, derived from bulk samples of *gyttja*, are not as reliable as dates on terrestrial plant macrofossils; thus they must be regarded as merely suggestive, not probative.

Invoking speculative interhemispheric ^{14}C offsets to account for the extant data is unnecessary. Let us take the earliest of the most precise (one-sigma <100), internally consistent ^{14}C dates from good stratigraphic contexts for Fell I assemblages in southernmost South America (Miotti and Salemme 2003): Piedra Museo, 11,000 ± 65 BP (AA-27950) and 10,925 ± 65 BP (OxA 8528); Tres Arroyos, 11,085 ± 70 BP (OxA 9248); Cerro Tres Tetas, 10,915 ± 65 BP (AA-22233); and Cueva Casa del Minero 10,999 ± 55 BP (AA-37207) and 10,967 ± 55 BP (AA-37208). I have arbitrarily excluded from this analysis dates that have large sigmas and are probably outliers, as well as dates on presumed

Table 2.2. Allerød-era Radiocarbon Inversion in Lake Mascardi Sediment Record

Depth (cm)	^{14}C date	Cariaco calendar year equivalent
783.4	10,480±180	12,600
789.4	10,900±110	ca. 12,800
791.5	10,810±85	ca. 12,900
796.5	10,960±85	ca. 12,950 (YD onset)
801.5	11,240±85	13,000
811.1	[10,440±95] (rejected)	
812.1	11,050±90	ca. 13,100
813.5	10,930±80	ca. 13,100
816	11,170±110	ca. 13,150

old wood or shell. Among the excluded dates are 12,390 ± 230 BP from Cueva del Medio; 11,560 ± 140 BP and 11,100 ± 150 BP from Cerro Tres Tetas; and 11,880 ± 250 BP from Tres Arroyos (for a graphic representation of ^{14}C dates from selected Southern Cone sites see Jackson, figure 6.1, this volume).

Clearly the makers of Fell I Fishtail points had reached the southern tip of South America by 11,000 BP (Flegenheimer and Zarate 1997). At first glance, this would be as early as, or even earlier than, most well-dated Clovis sites in North America (circa 10,950 BP). The geographic and stylistic logic of north-to-south migration makes this most obvious inference unlikely, as it leaves no time for the population movement or cultural drift implied by the Clovis-to-Fishtail transformation. Based on the available knowledge of late glacial radiocarbon fluctuations, the simplest solution is that some Clovis sites date to about 200 or 250 years before the YD onset (that is, circa 13,100 cal BP), and the first Fell I sites date to the cusp of the YD onset event at about 12,900 cal BP. This solution fits the dates to the now-demonstrated late Allerød ^{14}C inversion (which also seems to be present in the Lake Mascardi sequence (Hajdas et al. 2003) (see table 2.2). It also accommodates the most parsimonious model of the Clovis–Fell I relationship (Jackson, Ranere, and Faught chapters, this volume; also see Pearson 2002 for a consideration of alternatives based on Central American data). This solution allows some eight to twelve human generations for the migration from a Clovis staging area in Texas (for example, Gault) to the tip of South America. If the Aubrey dates of circa 11,550 BP (circa 13,300–13,600 cal BP; see Litt et al. 2003: 11, figure 4) turn out to be accurate, the time available for migration and population growth could be as much as 700 years.

To demonstrate that the calendar age of the Clovis culture is pre-YD, we need somehow to fix its position relative to the ice cores or other annually laminated records that can be securely linked to global climate events. This may be possible in the northwestern United States.

A spectacular cache of giant Clovis points at the East Wenatchee site in Washington state lies directly on sediments that contained particles of Glacier Peak tephra (Mehringer and Foit 1990). C. Vance Haynes (n.d.) speculates that the cache might have been a ritual offering to appease the spirits responsible for the eruption that the Paleoindians had just witnessed. This tephra is widespread in the Northwest and northern plains. In several lakebeds, dates for Glacier Peak tephra layers, actually representing three sequential eruptions—G, M, and B—that are chemically indistinguishable, cluster around 11,200 BP (Foit et al. 1993; Mehringer et al. 1984). At Indian Creek, Montana, the tephra date is reported as 11,125 ± 130 BP, and a Clovis occupation stratified above it (with intervening sediments) was dated to 10,980 ± 150 BP (Davis 2001). Minute particles of volcanic glass from the Glacier Peak eruptions could have been aerially transported to Greenland and deposited in the ice. Particles traceable to the eruption of Mount Mazama, another volcano in the Cascade Range, have recently been detected in the annually layered GISP2 core and allow a precise dating of that event (7627 ± 150 cal BP) (Zdanowicz et al. 1999). Diagnostic particles from the Laacher See volcano, virtually contemporaneous with Glacier Peak, might also be identified. Barring that, chemical signatures of these events (sulfate peaks) may be identifiable in the ice. Curiously, there are no reported signatures of eruptions so far in the GISP2 core dating between 13,553 cal BP and 13,084 cal BP (Zielinski et al. 1996). Recent examination of the NGRIP core has detected no signature of the Laacher See eruption (Mortensen et al. 2005). Finding ice-core records of the Laacher See and Glacier Peak eruptions in this interval would establish a neat correlation of Old World and New World chronologies. Even without such a discovery, a larger corpus of AMS dates on macrofossils from northwestern lakebeds could fix the age of the Glacier Peak eruptions more precisely. For now, the stratigraphic location of the tephra, relative to vegetation records in a few pollen cores, suggests that it occurred within the unnamed relatively warm interval (GI-1a) between the IACP and the Younger Dryas onset (circa 12,950–13,100 cal BP). This is a credible age for the first Paleoindians in the Northwest. I expect that we may soon know, perhaps with decadal precision, exactly when Paleoindians arrived in America, which routes they traversed, how long it took them to people the continent, and how they affected the native fauna. Establishment of a precise chronology is critical for modeling and understanding the colonization process. Once a precise chronology has been established, there will be profound theoretical repercussions for ethnology, genetics, historical linguistics, demography, and ecology.

3

Grassland Archaeology in the Americas

From the U.S. Southern Plains to the Argentinean Pampas

EILEEN JOHNSON, GUSTAVO POLITIS, MARÍA GUTIERREZ,
GUSTAVO MARTÍNEZ, AND LAURA MIOTTI

The vast grassland ecosystems of the Americas contain long, extensive records of early peoples in the late Pleistocene and the transition to the early Holocene. A seemingly analogous cultural development between the North American southern Great Plains and the South American Argentinean pampas appears to be emerging: hunter-gatherers exploiting the grassland herd herbivores during the late Wisconsinan (18,000–11,000 BP).

The southern plains and the pampas are extensive grassland ecosystems analogous to each other in temporal, climatic, environmental, and geomorphic development (figure 3.1). The core of the pampas—much like the North American southern plains—has remained a grassland since at least the late Pleistocene (Prieto 1996; Quattrocchio et al. 1993; Tonni et al. 1999, 2003; Salemme and Miotti 1987; Miotti and Salemme 1999; Tecchi 1983), although the character of these grasslands and the faunal communities of both regions changed throughout this period (Ferring 1995, 2001; Holliday 1995a, 1995b; Johnson 1986, 1987; Johnson and Holliday 1986, 1989; Lundelius et al. 1983; Martínez and Gutierrez, 2004; Miotti and Salemme 1999; Salemme and Miotti 1987). For both the Great Plains and the pampas, the regional primary depositional units are aeolian and lacustrine. Loess units are a regional phenomenon for the pampas, laid down in extensive blanket sheets (Fidalgo et al. 1973; Fidalgo and Tonni 1981; Tonni 1992; Zárate 1989; Zárate and Blasi 1993; Zárate and Flegenheimer 1990) similar to the extensive loess deposits of the northern Great Plains of North America (Feng et al. 1994; Maat and Johnson 1996; Martin 1993).

For the southern plains, thousands of internally drained lake basins, known as playas, dot the landscape (Sabin and Holliday 1995), while on the pampas, similar abundant lake basins are known as lagoons. On the pampas, different geological and faunistic evidence recognized at several localities indicates a

Figure 3.1. Major grassland ecosystems of North and South America (adapted from Coupland 1992a: frontispiece).

middle Holocene regional climatic change known as the Hypsithermal, lasting from about 8,000 to 5,000 years ago, with warm and humid conditions (Aguirre and Wathley 1995; Bonadonna et al. 1995; Fidalgo et al. 1986; Fidalgo and Tonni 1981; Isla 1989; Zárate and Blasi 1993). The Great Plains also experienced a regional climatic change during this period (circa 7,000 to 4,500 years ago), known as the Altithermal, but conditions there were hot and dry (Holliday 1989, 1995b).

The hunter-gatherers who occupied both regions as early as 12,100 years ago (uncalibrated radiocarbon years before present) used a similar lithic tool kit consisting of a stylized weapon and a variety of percussion-flake tools. In general, these earlier peoples had a broad-spectrum, meat-related subsistence base that, by early Holocene times, focused on a particular herd herbivore—bison on the Great Plains and the guanaco on the pampas. Smaller game animals supplemented the subsistence base in the southern plains (Ferring 1995; Johnson 1987, 1995a) and the pampas (Fidalgo et al. 1986; Mazzanti and Quintana 2001; Miotti and Salemme 1999; Martínez and Gutierrez 2004; Politis 1984; Salemme 1987). Fluted and unfluted Fishtail projectile points seem to be synchronous with fluted styles on the Great Plains but may have independent origins (Borrero 1983; Flegenheimer 1980, 1987; Miotti 1996; Politis 1991: Politis et al. 2003).

Setting

The major uninterrupted North American grassland stretches from Canada through the central United States and into Mexico (Coupland 1992a). Much, but not all, of this grassland biome occupies the Great Plains physiographic province (Fenneman 1931; Hunt 1967). Although the two labels are frequently regarded as synonymous, the boundaries of the grassland biome and the Great Plains are not the same (figure 3.2). In characterizing grasslands in general, the concept of binding species is used to denote the dominant forms (Clements and Shelford 1939; Coupland 1992a). Major physiographic features and indicator plants and animals bind the grassland together over the vast Great Plains (Coupland 1992a), but regional variations occur. At least six major regions have been identified (Coupland 1992a: 148)—each with its own subset of climatic conditions, soil types, water regime, binding species, grass species associations, and faunal communities—creating a mosaic grasslands.

Today, two of these regions—the mixed-grass prairie and the short-grass steppe—are wholly within the Great Plains, and the mixed-grass prairie forms the core of the Great Plains grassland. This lineal extent is divided into a northern and southern mixed-grass prairie and short-grass steppe. Informally, this same area is divided into northern, central, and southern plains (Fenneman 1931). The southern plains includes the Mescalero (Querecho) Plains, a portion of the High Plains, the Llano Estacado (southern High Plains), the southern Central Lowlands (Osage Plains), and the Edwards and Stockton plateaus (Fenneman 1931; Holliday et al. 2001). Much of the southern short-grass steppe is coincident with the southern High Plains (figure 3.3).

This region is dry-subhumid (mixed-grass prairie) to semiarid (short-grass steppe) with periods of severe drought. Winds, particularly during the spring, are frequent and strong. Across the southern plains, average winter temperatures vary but are generally mild, whereas summer mean temperatures are high. Two hundred or more frost-free days provide a warmer and longer growing season than on the northern plains. Evaporation rates increase from north

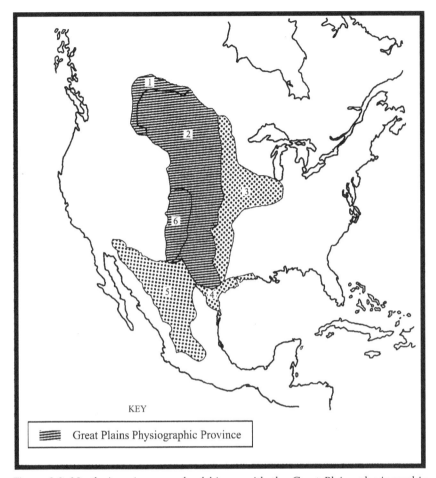

Figure 3.2. North American grassland biome with the Great Plains physiographic province superimposed and the major regions numbered: (1) fescue prairie; (2) mixed prairie; (3) tallgrass prairie; (4) coastal prairie; (5) desert grassland; (6) short-grass steppe (adapted from Coupland 1992a: 148).

to south and from the mixed-grass prairie to the short-grass steppe (Coupland 1992b). Summer is the major rainy season, with rains coming primarily from convective thunderstorms. Stream courses are broad, and valleys are separated by gently undulating (mixed-grass prairie) or flat (short-grass steppe) upland plains. Grama grasses (*Bouteloua* spp.), bison (*Bison bison*), and pronghorn (*Antilocapra americana*) are the binding species that tie the southern plains together as a grassland region. The dominant grass association in the mixed-grass prairie is of grama and needle (*Stipa* spp.) grasses, while the short-grass steppe association is blue grama (*Bouteloua gracilis*) and buffalo (*Buchlöe*

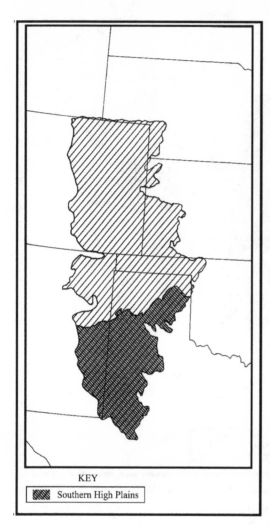

Figure 3.3. The short-grass steppe with the southern High Plains physiographic province superimposed (adapted from Lauenroth and Milchunas 1992: 186).

dactyloides) grasses (Coupland 1992a; Lauenroth and Milchunas 1992). Overall for the southern plains, the most important grass tribes are Paniceae and Agrosteae, as they contribute almost twice the global average to the grass flora (Coupland 1992a: 149; Hartley 1950).

When the binding species of bison is used as an indicator, the Great Plains grassland biome extended southward to the Valley of Mexico during the late Pleistocene and into the early Holocene. Historically, much of this area was discontinuous desert grassland characterized by various grama grass associations and pronghorn (Schmutz et al. 1992: 352). While modern bison are missing from the desert grassland archeological record, ancient bison occurred during the late Pleistocene and into the early Holocene in the grassland of this region (Bement 1986; Dibble and Lorrain 1968), indicating a change in grass association (as a reflection of the different climatic conditions at the time). By 9,000 years ago, bison were absent from the Pecos region of western Texas, and the Chihuahuan Desert vegetation returned (Bryant and Holloway 1985).

The major uninterrupted South American grassland stretches from southern Brazil through Uruguay and Argentina (Soriano et al. 1992). Located on a vast and continuous plain, this grassland biome is known as the Río de la Plata grassland (figures 3.1 and 3.4). Major physiographic features and indicator plants and animals bind the grassland together over this vast geographical area (Soriano et al. 1992), but regional variations occur. Two major subregions and seven units have been recognized (Prieto 1996; Soriano et al. 1992: 373)— each with its own subset of environmental conditions, soil types, hydrology, geomorphology, grass species associations, and faunal communities—creating a mosaic grasslands (figure 3.4) similar to the situation on the North American plains.

The major subregions are the campos of southern Brazil and Uruguay (northeast of the Río de la Plata) and the pampas of Argentina (southwest of the Río de la Plata). The pampas are located in the southern part of the Pampasia, an extensive geographic region of flat to gently undulating landscape (Frenguelli 1946), having a deep mantle of loess and loessic silts. Two mountain systems, Sierra de Tandil and de la Ventana, rise above the pampas along the southern and southwestern borders of the grassland. The pampas are divided into four units based on relief and fluvial characteristics (Soriano et al. 1992). The climate and grassland of the pampas are similar to those of the southern plains mixed-grass prairie (Walter 1967).

The Río de la Plata grassland is temperate subhumid (mixed-grass prairie) with periods of severe summer drought. Winds occur primarily in the summer. Mean winter temperatures are variable, and mean summer temperatures are moderate. For the pampas, the mean annual temperature difference between winter (7°C) and summer (22°C) is less drastic and cooler than that of the southern plains (10°C and 28°C) (Coupland 1992b: 153; Soriano et al. 1992: 376). Around 240 frost-free days on the pampas provide a long growing season. Evaporation rates decrease from east to west and from the campos (humid) to the pampas (dry subhumid). Across the pampas, rates decrease from east (humid pampas) to west (dry pampas) (Soriano et al. 1992). Spring and fall are the rainy seasons; rains primarily are generated from frontal storms. Stream courses are broad, and valleys are separated by flat to gently undulating upland plains.

Needle grasses (*Stipa* spp.), guanaco (*Lama guanicoe*), pampas deer (*Ozotoceros bezoarticus*), and greater rhea (*Rhea americana*) are the binding species that tie the pampas together as a grassland region (Perrins 1996; Redford and

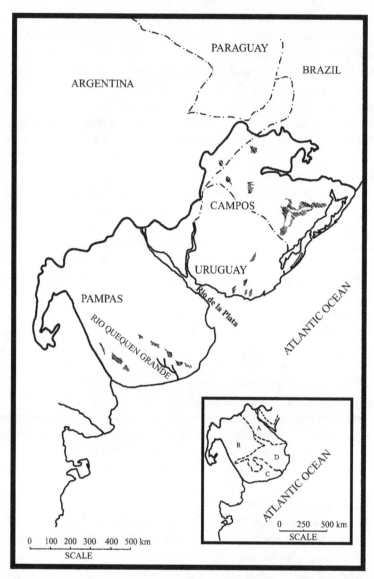

Figure 3.4. The Río de la Plata grassland biome in South America with the major pampas subdivisions lettered: *A*, rolling pampa; *B*, inland pampa; *C*, southern pampa; *D*, flooding pampa (adapted from Soriano et al. 1992: 368).

Eisenberg 1992; Soriano et al. 1992). Overall, for the pampas, the most important grass family is that of Poaceae; its tribe Paniceae contributes almost twice the global average to the grass flora (Coupland 1992c: 363; Hartley 1950; Soriano et al. 1992: 380).

During the late Pleistocene and into the Holocene, Patagonian faunal elements (such as Patagonian cavy [*Dolichotis patagonum*], Patagonian fox [*Pseudalopex culpaeus*], and Patagonian opossum [*Lestodelphis halli*]) moved up into the pampas (Tonni 1985; Tonni et al. 1988). These faunal elements indicate that environmental conditions in the pampas during this time probably were similar to those of northern Patagonia (Miotti and Salemme 1999).

Selected Sites

A long-term comparative study of grassland hunter-gatherers on the Argentine pampas and the North American southern plains has focused on select stratified dated sites (that is, those being investigated by the authors) to note the similarities and differences. Peoples across time and within the same geologic time period were hunter-gatherers living in a grassland ecosystem exploiting a grassland biota under similar climatic regimes. This apparent commonality provides a mechanism for exploring differences in decision making and adaptation strategies, as well as cultural development and change. The emphasis for this chapter is on commonalities such as location, particular game animals, technology, and human behavioral patterns. The discussion and comparisons are in general terms rather than detailed site specifics.

SOUTHERN PLAINS

While a fair number of late Quaternary sites are known for the southern plains of the United States, the emphasis in this joint comparative study has centered on the Lubbock Lake Landmark (Johnson 1987), a 315-acre archaeological and natural history preserve within a meander of Yellowhouse Draw (an ephemeral tributary of the Brazos River drainage system) within the southern High Plains (figure 3.5). Over a hundred archaeological occurrences have been excavated from five major stratigraphic units, spanning the past 11,100 years. The earlier part of the Paleoindian record is found within fluvial deposits on a gravel bar. While flaked lithics were not found with the bone bed at the point of contact with the gravel, a Clovis point came from dredged deposits adjacent to the excavation area. Bucket-teeth rows are preserved in the bone bed from the 1930s dredging operation that led to the discovery of the site (Johnson 1987).

Although in a fluvial environment, these elements are not waterworn; detailed orientation analysis demonstrates that water has not played a role in site

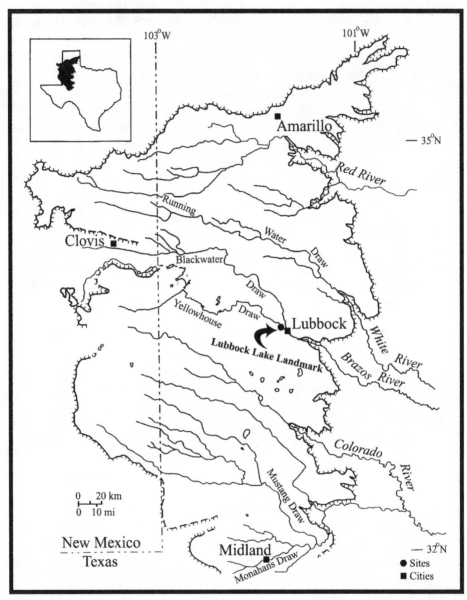

Figure 3.5. Southern High Plains of western Texas and eastern New Mexico, locating the Lubbock Lake Landmark.

formation but was a factor in site disturbance through realignment (Johnson 1995a; Kruetzer 1988). Carnivore activity also has played a role in site disturbance (Johnson 1995a). The late Pleistocene megafaunal processing station (11,100 BP) documents a broad-spectrum, meat-related subsistence base, with site activities focused on secondary butchering and deliberate bone breakage for marrow and tool use. Among the game animals present are giant short-face bear (*Arctodus simus*) and giant pampathere (*Holmesina septentrionalis*), both South American forms that were part of the great American faunal exchange during the Pleistocene (Webb 1985). This pampathere, with its homeland in Argentina and Brazil, is a relative of the South American glyptodont (Edmund 1985). Neither of these animals has been found at other southern plains late Pleistocene sites.

Evidence of use is based on cultural modification to the bones. Limb elements of the bear and pampathere have been dynamically impacted mid-diaphysis to produce helical fracture surfaces and leaving a remnant impact zone (Johnson 1985, 1989). Pry marks occur on the articular surface of the bear radius. The cut marks (confirmed through scanning electron microscopy [SEM] analysis) along the diaphysis are deep, wide, multiple-stroke marks (Johnson 2005). Multiple strokes within the same mark indicate repeated motion at the same spot to accomplish the action. Having to take more than one stroke to free an area indicates some resistance to tissue removal or joint separation. The bear remains most likely represent a scavenged carcass.

Subsequent early Holocene occupations (8600 to 10,800 BP) found in lake and marsh sediments document a focused, meat-related subsistence base related to bison, with site activities concentrated on primary kills and deliberate bone breakage for tool use. Archaic occupations (2000–8600 BP) within eolian and marsh deposits document the continuation of bison kills, but with the addition of plant-processing activities by the middle of the period. The tool kit is expedient in each of these periods, composed of a multipurpose projectile point style, amorphous lithic flake tools, and fracture-based bone butchering tools (Johnson and Holliday 1986, 1989). Bone piling is typical of the bison kill and butchering locales.

While the Lubbock Lake Landmark record is used to exemplify the southern plains, not all activities or site types are represented for all periods. Among the activities not represented in the landmark's late Pleistocene and early Holocene records are caching, residential settlement, and lithic procurement. Caching is a type of risk management strategy—or insurance—to buffer against the lack, or limited supply, of adequate lithic resources in the area. Late Pleistocene caches occur across the southern plains (Collins 1999) and are focused on sequestering blades (for example, Collins 1999; Green 1963; Montgomery and Dickenson 1992) or blade cores (Goode and Mallouf 1991). Dated early Holocene caches and those with diagnostic points are rare. The Ryan site (Hartwell 1995) is a cache of points, large bifaces, and large flakes found within stratified lacustrine deposits of a small extinct playa that overlooked Yellowhouse Draw (within the southern High Plains). A few quarries and lithic workshops are known (Collins 1999), although most are not in stratified or dated context.

The majority of late Pleistocene sites within the southern plains are focused on subsistence procurement, with mammoth being the main commodity. These sites are found along ancient waterways (river or creek valleys, ponds, or playa basins), and procurement was through either hunting or scavenging. Sites such as Aubrey (Ferring 1995, 2001), Jake Bluff (Bement 2002), and Gault (Collins 1999, 2001), located in the mixed-grass prairie of the Osage Plains and Edwards Plateau, provide an expanded perspective. Aubrey, found along the Elm Fork tributary of the Trinity River, also documents a broad-spectrum, meat-related, late Pleistocene subsistence base, with site activities focused on secondary butchering. However, those activities are in a residential setting where tool refurbishing occurred (Ferring 2001). Jake Bluff, in a buried arroyo along the North Canadian (Beaver) River, is a subsistence procurement site focused on ancient bison. It represents a kill site at which bison were run into the arroyo (Bement 2002). Gault, located at springs along a tributary of the Lampasas River (Edwards Plateau), is a residential site with lithic procurement and tool production activities (Collins 1999, 2001). Camps, bison kills, and lithic procurement sites are rare in the general late Pleistocene grasslands record.

Bison kill sites are the most common early Holocene type of stratified, dated site. The size of kill varies both seasonally and through time, with later kills exhibiting an increase in numbers of animals. Both small-scale and large-scale bison kills occur with associated carcass treatment differences. For the large-scale kills, bone distribution ranges from articulated skeletons to disarticulated carcasses and disassociated elements (for example, at Cooper [Bement 1997] and Bonfire Shelter [Dibble and Lorraine 1968]). At Blackwater Draw Locality #1 (Hester 1972), in a basin tributary of Blackwater Draw (an ancient river valley within the southern High Plains), small-scale bison kills occur around the edge of the pond in the early Holocene, with larger-scale episodic kills in the same location by 9000 BP (Johnson and Holliday 1997). On the Osage Plains, Lipscomb (Hofman et al. 1991) is the largest single-event, early Holocene, southern plains bison kill, with at least fifty-four animals present. Several of these large kills are repeat events in which thirty to fifty bison were killed in a single episode (for example, at Cooper [Bement 1997], Bonfire Shelter [Dibble and Lorraine 1968], and Plainview [Johnson 1989]). The basic tool kit is the same at these localities, composed of a stylized weapon reused as a butchering tool and expedient, amorphous flake tools. Fracture-based bone butchering tools sometimes occur (for example, at Bonfire Shelter [Johnson 1982]).

Although small-scale bison kills occur, stratified, dated, late-early and middle Holocene sites are rare on the southern plains. At Big Lake, an internally drained saline lake basin on the Osage Plains, a bison kill is located in the mud flats of the drying lake (Turpin et al. 1992, 1997). Articulated units and disarticulated elements occur along with some concentrations of the same elements. A short-term camp is located at the edge of a now-extinct playa at San Jon (on the southern High Plains), where tool refurbishing was conducted.

PAMPAS

Most of the late Pleistocene sites in the pampas are located in the Tandilia hills and in the plains between these hills and the Ventania range (the Interserrana area). It is not yet clear whether this concentration of early sites is related to the demography of the region during the late Pleistocene or a result of sample bias. Almost all the early sites are in small caves in Tandilia; the only exception is Cerro El Sombrero (Flegenheimer 1987). On the plains, they are more expansive, open-air sites that include Arroyo Seco 2, Paso Otero 5, La Moderna, and Campo Laborde (figure 3.6).

Arroyo Seco (Fidalgo et al. 1986; Politis 1984, 1989; Politis et al. 1992) is a large, geologically stratified, multicomponent site from the late Pleistocene through late Holocene period situated on a rise between a stream and a lagoon (figure 3.6). Habitation and burial activities appear to represent the two major occupation types at the site through time. Numerous occupation events representing camping activities have been uncovered. The recovered materials consist primarily of lithics and bone. The lithics are produced from regionally available quartzite and chalcedony in the Tandilia range, flake tools (including end and side scrapers and marginally retouched flakes) being the most common tool type (Fidalgo et al. 1986). Faunal composition changes through time, with extinct pampean megamammals in the lowest level and the Holocene pampean faunal community in the upper levels. Guanaco is the main prey species throughout the late Quaternary sequence (exhibiting both cut marks and helical fractures), but other animals also formed part of the subsistence base at different times. Although cut marks have been difficult to confirm on the megamammal remains (primarily giant ground sloth [*Megatherium americanum*] and American horse [*Equus* (*Amerhippus*) *neogeus* and *Hippidion* spp.]) from the earliest levels, numerous long-bone segments are helically fractured—presumably for marrow processing.

Technological features such as intersecting fracture fronts, large bending flake scars, and hackle marks have been identified on megamammals bones

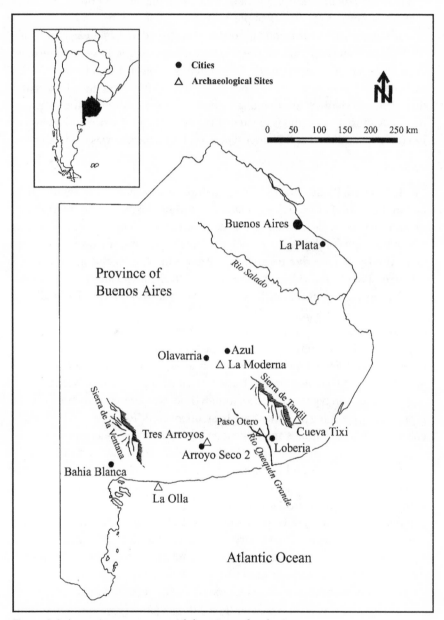

Figure 3.6. Argentinean pampas with locations of early sites.

(Gutierrez et al. 2000). Characteristics of the archaeological record such as the associated lithic artifacts, presence of selective skeletal parts (appendicular skeleton), great diversity of species, and location of the site (top of a paleodune, not a location for the natural death of several different mammals) indicate the cultural origin of the lower levels of the site. The fracture pattern indicates the bones were very fresh when broken through dynamic impact. That pattern provides further evidence of a cultural origin for the lower levels. The processes involved in site formation included a variety of natural factors that disturbed the deposit (Gutierrez 2004). This disturbance, however, does not invalidate either the antiquity of the site nor the human origin of the modifications on the megamammal bones.

Radiocarbon ages secured on bone collagen and charcoal date the lowest component (Fidalgo et al. 1986; Politis 1984; Politis et al. 1995). Earlier attempts at dating collagen from megamammal bones yielded ages between 7300 and 9000 BP (Fidalgo et al. 1986: 262; Politis and Beukens 1991: 6). However, recent AMS dating (n=12 dates) of megamammal bones recovered from a different area of the site has yielded ages between 11,200 BP and 12,100 BP (Steele et al. 2001).

To date, forty-four human burials have been uncovered from different levels dating from circa 4,500 to 7,800 years ago (Barrientos 1997; Barrientos et al. 2003; Politis 1989; Politis et al. 1992; Scabuzzo and Politis 2006). The burials occur as single-individual and multi-individual burials of both adults and children—sometimes with grave goods of marine shell beads and necklaces of carnivore canines and powdered red ochre around the head (Barrientos 1997; Fidalgo et al. 1986; Politis et al. 1992). A secondary burial has been dated to 7,600 BP (Scabuzzo and Politis 2006).

Geologically, the Paso Otero cluster spans the late Quaternary period (figures 3.6 and 3.7). Archaeologically, they are terminal Pleistocene to middle Holocene floodplain sites along the Río Quequén Grande, involved with megamammal processing (terminal Pleistocene, Paso Otero 5) or guanaco kills (Holocene, Paso Otero 3). Paso Otero 5, on the bank of the Río Quequén Grande (figure 3.7), is the first recorded site in the Interserrana area of the Pampean region that shows a clear association between Fishtail projectile points and megamammals (Martínez 2001; Martínez et al. 2005).

The Río Salado Member profile at this site exposed numerous buried soils, indicating previous stable landscape surfaces (Holliday et al. 2003). The megamammal bones and flakes came from the lowest A horizon that separates the Río Salado Member from the Guerrero Member of the Luján Formation. Radiocarbon dating of burned megamammal bones yielded ages between 10,200 and 10,450 BP (Martínez 1999, 2001; Martínez et al. 2004).

The flaked stone assemblage of Paso Otero 5 primarily is composed of arti-

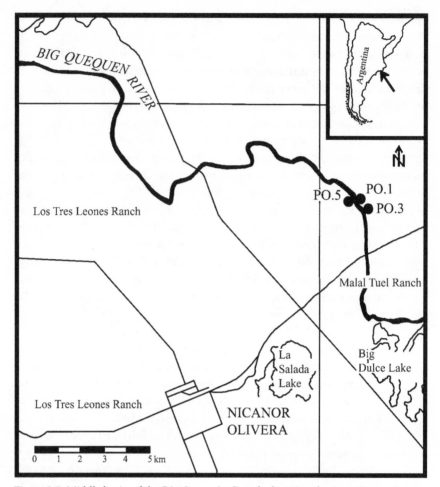

Figure 3.7. Middle basin of the Río Quequén Grande, locating the Paso Otero sites.

facts made on quartzite. Tools include Fishtail projectile points with fractured stems (one of which appears manufactured on silicified dolostone, an exotic raw material), a small bifacial tool fragment, and informal unifacially retouched tools. Both extinct megamammals (ground sloths [*Megatherium americanum, Glossotherium* sp.], horse [*Equus neogeus*], and llama [*Hemiauchenia* sp.]), and modern species (guanaco) are represented. The bone assemblage has a high degree of fragmentation and an extremely high proportion of burned bone (about 91%).

The site reveals a great faunal diversity for the Pleistocene-Holocene transition. The presence of at least 10 species of megamammals is explained by: a) the reoccupation of the same place for specific activities (hunting and processing); and b) by the use of megamammal bone as fuel. Paso Otero 5 represents a special purpose site of short-term occupations related to secondary processing of megafauna hunted or scavenged nearby (Martínez and Gutierrez 2006).

Two sites indicate the Holocene survival of Pleistocene megamammals: La Moderna and Campo Laborde. Both sites are on the banks of Holocene marshes, at the dual heads of the Arroyo Tapalque (figure 3.6). La Moderna (Politis 1984; Politis and Gutierrez 1998; Politis et al. 2003) is a glyptodont (*Doedicurus clavicaudatus*) procurement site located on the banks of a late Pleistocene to early Holocene marsh (figure 3.6); it is the only known glypotodont procurement site in Argentina. The locality is geologically stratified, with the occupational materials just above the Pleistocene sediments (Guerrero Member of the Luján Formation).

Part of the axial skeleton and carapace of a glyptodont was recovered in close association with nearly 2,000 quartz flakes and debris. Although the glyptodont remains did not exhibit cut marks or other evidence of cultural modification, microwear and polish studies of the associated lithics indicated their use in meat-cutting (primary) and wood-scraping (secondary) activities (Politis and Olmo 1986). Three bone collagen dates assayed from glypotodont elements provided an age of circa 7,000 to 7,500 BP (Politis and Gutierrez 1998). Two additional dates from soil humates supported these Early Holocene dates, giving ages of 8,356 and 7,448 BP (Politis et al. 2003).

Campo Laborde (figure 3.6) is a single-component site in the same stratigraphic position as La Moderna, where the hunting and primary butchering of a giant ground sloth (*Megatherium americanum*) took place (Messineo and Politis 2006; Politis et al. 2004). A few quartzite flakes and a fractured piece of a bifacial tool (possibly the stem of a lanceolate point) have been recovered in association with the well-preserved bones. Three radiocarbon dates from bone place the occupation between 7,800 and 8,800 BP.

The faunal assemblage recovered in Paso Otero 1 (Johnson et al. 1998; Politis et al. 1991; Gutierrez 1998) was composed of a large number of guanaco bones in discrete piles of mixed adult to fetal remains (figure 3.7). The bones came from highly organic marsh sediments within a geologic context of the Río Salado Member of the Luján Formation. These stratified deposits recorded three major periods of stable landscape environments in the river valley (Johnson et al. 1998) represented by buried A horizons. The bone piles came from the middle stable landscape period at around 4,900 BP. Small flakes and a bipolar artifact made on a coastal pebble were recovered in close spatial association. Cut marks and helical fracturing were identified on the guanaco bones (less than 2%) (Gutierrez et al. 1997; Gutierrez 1998; Johnson et al. 1998).

The site originally was interpreted as a primary processing guanaco kill site (Politis et al. 1991; Johnson et al. 1998). However, further geoarchaeological, taphonomic, and site formation studies now indicate that water was the main responsible agent for the guanaco bone accumulation. Bones were in contact with a sedimentary erosional unconformity with a channel structure that yielded evidence of a turbulent flow (Favier Dubois 2006). Bone accumulations would have originated during this time. Some of the skeletal parts that belonged to guanaco carcasses processed and exploited by hunter-gatherers in areas close to the site augmented those from the rest of the animals that died naturally. This addition resulted in a mixture of material of both natural and cultural origin (Favier Dubois 2006; Gutierrez and Kaufmann 2006; Kaufmann and Gutierrez 2004).

At Paso Otero 3 (Martínez 1999; Martínez 2002–2004), approximately 0.5 km downstream on the same side of the river from Paso Otero 1 (figure 3.7), excavation exposed a 1.6 m profile that contained numerous buried soils, indicating previous stable landscape surfaces. The archaeological record came from the lowest A horizon dated circa 4800 BP. A guanaco bone pile also was uncovered. Guanaco, pampean deer, vizcacha (*Lagostomus maximus*), and rhea eggs showed evidence of consumption, with some bones exhibiting helical fractures and cut marks. Fragments of marine gastropods and red ochre were found on the top of the bone pile.

The large lithic assemblage primarily was composed of informal unifacial flakes and flake tools manufactured on quartzite. Fracture-based bone butchering tools also were recovered (Martínez 1999; Martínez et al. 2001). Paso Otero 3 initially was interpreted as a kill-processing site, but now is considered a short-term base camp (Martínez 2002–2004, 2006).

Comparisons

The North American southern plains Paleoindian period generally is characterized by a major climatic change at the end of the Pleistocene and widespread extinctions. Another climatic shift around 9000 BP to 8500 BP heralded the end of pluvial conditions, increased warming and drying conditions, and the transformation to a different ecosystem and cultural lifestyle. Mosaic open grasslands dominated the drainage systems, but the mixed-grass prairie and bison retracted their ranges from the Pecos region of western Texas. The middle Holocene drought is characterized by considerable eolian deposition. By the beginning of the late Holocene (circa 4500 BP), the modern continental climate was established (Holliday 1995b; Johnson and Holliday 1995).

The Argentinean pampas also are characterized by a major climatic change and widespread extinctions. The faunistic shift occurred by the end of the early Holocene and heralded the transition to a different ecosystem and cultural lifestyle. A mosaic open grassland likewise dominated the pampas, which experienced a regional warm and humid period during the middle Holocene. Cooler and more arid conditions prevailed, from about 1000 BP to 5000 BP, when a modern pampean ecosystem was established (Politis and Tonni 1997; Tonni and Cione 1997).

The Lubbock Lake Landmark, exemplifying the North American southern plains sites, is in an ancient river valley and contains activity areas at the water's edge, along the valley margins, and on the adjacent uplands overlooking the draw. Megafaunal secondary processing activities and bison kill sites are represented in the numerous activity areas related to differential use of the topography and changing hydrology. Repeated use of the landscape is typical, and the numerous buried soils attest to stable landscapes, as well as changing topography across time along the waterway.

Butchering and processing tool kits discovered at the Lubbock Lake Landmark consist of fracture-based utilitarian bone butchering tools and amorphous flake tools—both expedient technologies (Johnson 1985, 1987). The main difference is the changing projectile point style. Amorphous flake tools are the standard for plains Paleoindian butchering tools in general (for example, Frison 1991a, 1996; Wheat 1972, 1979), and bone piling is typical at bison kill sites (Frison 1991a; Johnson 1987; Wheat 1972). A variety of large-game animals, including extinct pampathere and ancient bison, were hunted in the late Pleistocene. After megafaunal extinctions, bison emerged and continued into the ethnographic present as the major game resource (Johnson 1987, 1995b, 1997).

During the late Pleistocene and into the early Holocene, the Argentinean pampas were a vast, temperate, subhumid-dry grassland (Prieto 1996; Quattrocchio et al. 1993) with a variety of herbivores, such as glyptodont and guanaco, that were hunted by early peoples. Most of these sites are along waterways and on uplands near lagoons. After the extinction of the megamammals, guanaco became the prime game-animal resource. Bone beds are a result of an ungulate processing pattern (Bonomo 2005; Martínez and Gutierrez 2004; Mazzanti and Quintana 2001). The pattern of prey acquisition and processing of middle Holocene guanaco-oriented exploitation resembles some of the early Holocene bison kill sites (for example, Bement 1993, 1994; Dibble and Lorrain 1968; Johnson 1987; Wheat 1972, 1979) of the U.S. southern plains. Thus in both regions similar subsistence patterns were recorded but at different time periods. An expedient tool kit based on unifacial flake technology is the hallmark of the pampas (Crivelli et al. 1997; Fidalgo et al. 1986; Martínez 1999; Oliva et al. 1991; Politis 1984), with informal flake tools as the common element. Completing this kit are the occasional stylized projectile point and bola stones. The record at the Paso Otero sites of numerous buried soils attests to stable landscapes, as well as changing topography through time along the waterway.

With these changing climatic and ecosystemic conditions, hunter-gatherers underwent adaptive change brought about by climatic stress and alterations in density and distribution of food resources. On the southern plains, the late Pleistocene hunter-gatherers were organized as foragers in their approach to subsistence, utilizing opportunistic (primary) and targeted (secondary) behavior patterns that allowed the hunting and scavenging of animals. They followed the practice of exploitation of bone resources with the use of a minimal lithic tool kit and general conservancy of lithic materials (Johnson 1991a). Early Holocene hunter-gatherers were organized as collectors in their approach to subsistence, utilizing targeted (primary) and opportunistic (secondary) behavior patterns that allowed both focused hunting of bison and the taking of small game. Exploitation of bones as tool resources, a minimal lithic tool kit, and general conservancy of lithic materials continued (Johnson 1991b). Middle Holocene hunter-gatherers may have been organized as foragers, utilizing behavior patterns that incorporated both hunting and systematic plant harvesting (Johnson and Holliday 1986).

Evidence from Paso Otero 5 (Grill et al. 2005), along with regional trends for the southern pampas, indicates that paleoclimatic conditions during the end of the late Pleistocene were semiarid or arid (Prieto 1996; Quattrocchio et al. 1995; Tonni and Cione 1995; Tonni et al. 1999; Tonni et al. 2003). Absence of a vegetation cover, environmental disturbance, and strong aeolian activity are suggested for the period 12,000 to 10,000 BP. Stable conditions associated with soil development and the presence of temporary ponds occur at the Pleistocene-Holocene transition (Grill et al. 2005; Prieto 1996; Quattrocchio et al. 1995; Tonni and Cione 1995; Zárate et al. 2000). The climatic trends for the middle Holocene indicate humid and warmer conditions and the presence of a humid grassland prairie associated with lacustrine settings. Expansion of the grass and sedge steppe during the middle Holocene occurs as does a marine transgression (Aguirre and Whatley 1995; Isla 1989; Isla et al. 1990).

The faunal evidence for the late Pleistocene–early Holocene pampean sites suggest a high taxonomic diversity and richness and a subsistence pattern composed of a broad diet. This economic strategy is characterized as a generalized regional economy (Martínez and Gutierrez 2004). A broad spectrum of resources (including extinct mammals) are exploited by hunter-gatherers. Among 38 species found in the archaeological record, at least 16 are food sources.

Based on lithic raw material, site function diversity, home ranges and place, and technology-oriented strategies (Flegenheimer et al. 2003; Martínez 2001;

Mazzanti 2003; Politis et al. 2004; Kelly and Todd 1988), these earlier hunter-gatherers (between 10,000 to 12,000 BP) appear to have had a differentiated settlement system. A well-planned schedule for lithic procurement and artifact production is indicated by several lines of evidence: 1) an uneven distribution of high quality lithic raw material throughout the landscape; 2) great variability of artifacts (for example, Fishtail projectile points, preforms, recycled tools, burins, knives); 3) evidence of retooling, resharpening, and primary and secondary trimming; and 4) good knowledge and management of specific places with the presence of lithic resources. This evidence suggests that technological organization mainly was based on a curated strategy and that mobility would have included a logistical component. This early settlement system basically is characterized by a collector strategy (Binford 1980) although the presence of forager components may be present.

For the end of the early Holocene (6500–8800 BP), the archaeological sites (La Moderna, Campo Laborde, La Olla) record monospecies faunal assemblages associated with informal flake tools and occasional bola stones (Johnson et al. 2000; Politis and Gutierrez 1998; Messineo and Politis 2006; Politis et al. 2003]). The taking of ground-birds, particularly their eggs, and the occasional seasonal exploitation of sea mammals (La Olla, circa 7000 to 8000 BP [Politis and Lozano 1988, Bayón and Politis 1997]) may be viewed as an opportunistic behavior pattern. This situation proceeds a subsistence pattern characterized as a specialized regional economy with emphasis on guanaco during the middle Holocene (3500–6500 BP) (Martínez and Gutierrez 2004).

The prevalence of specific task sites, occupations in different areas of the region (coast, hills, pampas), and lithic assemblages composed primarily of informal tools during the early and middle Holocene indicate a broader geographic occupation with a less redundant use of sites and a greater residential mobility (Martínez 1999, 2006). Arroyo Seco 2 is the exception.

On a global basis, the transition from the Pleistocene to the Holocene is characterized by widespread extinctions (particularly of megamammals). By convention, the boundary is placed at 10,000 BP (Hageman 1972) on the basis of data available at the time and in an attempt to make sense of what appeared to be conflicting and confusing information. This boundary date is still used today (for example, Graham and Lundelius 1994; Straus et al. 1996) even though the larger, more refined, modern database underscores its static and arbitrary nature (for example, Grayson 1991). Species react differently to changing climates and ecosystems, and the timing and regional extinction of species varies (for example, Graham and Lundelius 1984; Guthrie 2003). The dynamic nature of this transition is exemplified by the data from the U.S. southern plains and the Argentinean pampas.

On the southern plains of North America, 11,000 BP marks the biotic and ecosystemic end of Wisconsinan conditions (Baker 1983; Johnson 1986, 1987; Lundelius et al. 1983). Although the small, now-extinct antelope *Capromeryx* survived into Folsom times (10,300 BP to 10,800 BP) (Johnson 1987), megamammal extinctions occurred quite distinctly around the 11,000-year mark (Ferring 1995; Holliday et al. 1994; Johnson 1986, 1987; Johnson and Holliday 1997). The only large herd herbivore to survive the extinction filter was ancient bison.

On the pampas, the time of extinction is controversial; scholars debate whether it occurred at the end of the Pleistocene or during the early Holocene. This region has been proposed as one of the few continental places where certain Pleistocene megamammals survived into the early Holocene (Politis et al. 1995). La Moderna and Campo Laborde provide evidence to address this controversy.

If megamammals did not become extinct until well into the early Holocene, then the retention of a rich diversity of game animals could be one of the reasons for explaining the differences between early Holocene general subsistence patterns and social organization of the hunter-gatherers on the southern plains (specialists with a targeted game animal, that is, bison hunters) versus the Argentinean pampas (retention of a broad-based subsistence). Furthermore, this chronological difference could underscore the fact that the process (that is, patterns and sequence of patterns) is the same. What is being examined is the response to a grassland setting with abundant resources that later are reduced. It is the timing of that response that is different (early Holocene for the southern plains versus middle Holocene for the pampas) in dealing with similar subsistence patterns and general social organization. What also must be taken into account in explaining these patterns is the influence that the fluctuating climate and grassland ecosystem conditions may have had on hunter-gatherer populations (early Holocene, increasing warming trend and decreasing humidity; Hypsithermal, warm and humid).

The major differences between the two grasslands regions are the timing of megamammal extinctions, the effect that timing had on hunter-gatherer organization and hunting patterns, an element of the tool kit, and different behavioral patterns of bison and guanaco. Apparently minimal in the pampean tool kit, in comparison with southern plains tool kits, are fracture-based bone butchering tools. This type of tool is rare in pampean sites, known only from La Olla (1 tool: Johnson et al. 2000) and Paso Otero 3 (2 tools: Martínez 1999; Martínez et al. 2001), and a few examples are known for later Tierra del Fuego sites (Scheinsohn and Ferretti 1995). This kind of tool may not have been as frequent a component of the tool kit as on the Great Plains or its minimal presence in the tool kits of the pampas may be attributable to a lack of recognition or to the small number of excavated kill and butchering and processing sites. Although bison and guanaco are both herd herbivores and share some general behavioral characteristics, specific differences would affect hunting strategies and should temper archaeological expectations.

Acknowledgments

Support for this research was provided by the National Science Foundation International Programs (INT-9218457 and INT-9603078) and the Museum of Texas Tech University (EJ) and represents part of the ongoing Lubbock Lake Landmark regional research into grasslands hunter-gatherers and adaptations to ecological changes. The ongoing work in the eastern pampas (GP, MAG, and GM) is supported by Consejo de Investigaciones Científicas y Technicas Nacional (CONICET) (National Agency of Scientific and Technical Researchers), Agencia Nacional de Promoción Científica y Técnica, the Universidad Nacional del Centro de la Pcia. de Buenos Aires, and the National Geographic Society. Tara Backhouse (documentation specialist, Museum of Texas Tech University) finalized the illustrations. Interpretations herein along with any errors are those of the authors.

II

Perspectives from the South

4

The Clovis Colonization of Central America

ANTHONY J. RANERE

The expansion of Clovis and later fluted point traditions throughout the Americas is an important chapter in human history. One of the fundamental questions concerns the linkage between the cultural tradition called Clovis and the human populations that bore this tradition. The circumstances that would have permitted such a rapid expansion from temperate environments of North America through multiple environmental zones of tropical America and back into temperate environments of South America have taken on additional significance in light of the now widely appreciated fact that this expansion did not take place through vacant terrain.

In this chapter, I argue that the rapid Clovis expansion was demic rather than an adoption of a particular technology by already-resident populations, and that the speed of this expansion was possible only because the focus of the subsistence effort was on hunting. Recent improvements in the application of evolutionary ecological theory to hunter-gatherer behavior, in the modeling of population movements in prehistory, and in comparative analyses of Paleoindian technology and typology are brought to bear on this question. In particular, this chapter presents a detailed description of the bifacial reduction sequence for a Clovis workshop in Panama that closely parallels North American early Clovis workshops and, therefore, attests to the close cultural and chronological ties between Central American and North American Clovis sites.

Reconsidering Paleoindians in Central America

Recently there have been some major shifts in our understanding of ancient human settlement in the Americas: for example, the publication of the second volume of the Monte Verde site investigations (Dillehay 1997a), increasing evidence for coastal occupations in Peru during the eleventh millennium (Keefer et al. 1998; Sandweiss et al. 1998), and support for similarly early occupations in the Amazon basin (Roosevelt et al. 1996). All of this has served to reinforce an already-growing feeling that Clovis was a Johnny-come-lately phenomenon in the peopling of South America. In the enthusiasm of the moment, there are new claims that Clovis may represent a reinvasion of North America from a South American base (Nichols 1998), a suggestion made considerably earlier (for example, Mayer-Oakes 1986a).

The fact that Clovis artifacts do not, in all likelihood, represent the earliest penetration of humans in Central America and South America demands a re-assessment of what exactly Clovis represents. Because human groups may well have been established throughout the Americas before the appearance of the Clovis tradition, the question arises whether the Clovis expansion was carried out by Clovis people or whether it is attributable to the adoption of the Clovis technology and lifestyle by already-resident folks. Given the rapidity of the spread, the distances involved, and the multiple environments traversed, the latter may seem the most likely answer. However, I argue here that the spread was demic, and I attempt to support this position by comparing the well-defined early Clovis technology for North America with that known for lower Central America. In the absence of skeletal remains or other traces of human physical remains, careful comparisons of technology may be the best evidence for or against demic expansion.

Evidence for the Late Glacial Occupation of Central America

The evidence for the human occupation of Central America during the Late Glacial is limited to remains that are all linked to Clovis and related techno-logical traditions. Most of this evidence comes in the form of fluted points found as isolates or in eroded and/or disturbed sites. There are only two sites where fluted points have been found in stratigraphic contexts with ^{14}C dates: Los Tapiales in highland Guatemala (Gruhn et al. 1977) and Cueva de los Vam-piros in the Pacific coastal plain of Panama (Pearson 2002; Pearson and Cooke 2003). At Los Tapiales (3,150 meters above sea level), ^{14}C dates of 8810 ± 110 BP and 11,170 ± 200 BP bracket deposits that yielded an assemblage that includes a fluted point base, a channel flake, bifaces, unifacial points, burins, gravers, spurred end scrapers, blades, and nearly 1,500 flakes. The excavators view the occupation as short term and consider the ^{14}C date of 10,710 ± 170 BP as most closely approximating the age of the site (Gruhn et al. 1977). At Los Vampiros, ^{14}C dates of 8970 ± 40 BP and 11,550 ± 140 BP bracket deposits that contain a distal fragment of a fluted Fishtail point (the base is missing), overshot flakes characteristic of Clovis reduction techniques, a spurred end scraper, a thumb-nail scraper, and bifacial thinning flakes with ground platforms (Pearson and Cooke 2003). Two other central-Pacific Panama sites have eleventh-millennium ^{14}C dates associated with sparse habitation debris that includes bifacial thin-ning flakes with ground platforms but no diagnostic points. The Aguadulce Shelter, located on the coastal plain, has yielded ^{14}C dates of 10,725 ± 80 BP,

10,675 ± 95 BP, and 10,529 ± 284 BP for the earliest occupation of the site (Piperno et al. 2000). Farther inland in the foothills, the Corona Shelter (240 meters above sea level) yielded a single date of 10,440 ± 650 BP (Ranere and Cooke 2003). Finally, a 14,000-year-old lake core sequence from La Yeguada (650 meters above sea level) in central-Pacific Panama registered the initial firing of lakeside vegetation in its phytolith and particulate carbon record 11,000 BP (Piperno et al. 1991). While the timing of the Paleoindian occupation of Central America is not well controlled, two aspects of that record are relatively secure and deserve close examination: (1) the geographical and environmental contexts from which Paleoindian remains have been recovered, and (2) the nature of the lithic artifacts (Ranere 1980; Ranere and Cooke 1991).

The Central American Landscape during the Late Glacial

There have now been a sufficient number of paleoecological studies in Central America and neighboring regions to permit us to describe the climate and vegetation for the area during the late Pleistocene, or circa 10,500–20,000 BP (for example, Bartlett and Barghoorn 1973; Bush and Colinvaux 1990; Leyden 1984, 1985; Piperno et al. 1991; Piperno and Jones 2003). The data have been summarized by Dolores Piperno and Deborah Pearsall (1998), who note that temperatures for the late Pleistocene were on the order of five to seven degrees Celsius cooler than at present and annual rainfall was 25–50 percent lower than at present.

If the vegetation map of Central America is adjusted to account for these differences in rainfall and temperature, where do Paleoindian sites and isolated Paleoindian points fall? The Belize localities (Hester et al. 1981; MacNeish and Nelken-Terner 1983) are all found in what would have been some sort of thorn woodland, low scrub, or wooded savanna vegetation. A similar landscape would have been present in the lowlands of central-Pacific Panama (for example, at La Mula West [Ranere 2000], Vampire Cave [Pearson and Cooke 2003], and the Nieto quarry [Pearson 2003]) and northwestern Costa Rica (an isolated fluted point findspot [Swauger and Mayer-Oakes 1952]). The late Pleistocene phytolith record from the coastal plain Monte Oscuro sediment core documents the open nature of the vegetation in central-Pacific Panama (Piperno and Jones 2003). Closed-canopy lowland forests (albeit drier than those found today) would have blanketed the Chagres River watershed near the present-day Panama Canal (for example, at the Madden Lake/Lago Alajuela localities [Bird and Cooke 1978]) and the foothills of central-Pacific Panama (for example, at Cerro Corona and La Yeguada [Ranere and Cooke 1991, 1996]). An 11,300-year-old pollen/phytolith sequence from the Chagres basin (Bartlett and Barghoorn 1973; Piperno 1985) and a 14,000-year-old pollen/phytolith sequence from La Laguna de la Yeguada (Piperno et al. 1991) confirm this characterization of the vegetation in these two regions of Panama. Closed-canopy montane forests are reconstructed for the lower montane Costa Rican localities of Turrialba (Snarskis 1979) and Arenal (Sheets 1994), as well as San Rafael (Coe 1960) and the Quiche basin (Brown 1980) in the Guatemalan highlands. Alpine meadows are reconstructed for the landscape higher than 3,000 meters above sea level in Guatemala, where Los Tapiales is situated (Gruhn et al. 1977).

Although few Paleoindian localities have been identified, they are found in a diversity of environments and geographic regions: in both Caribbean and Pacific coastal lowlands, in highlands on both sides of the continental divide, in relatively open thornscrub/savanna vegetation, in both lowland and montane closed-canopy forests, and in alpine meadows. This includes most of the range of environmental and geographic settings present in Central America during the late Pleistocene. In the following paragraphs, I consider how populations using Clovis technology could have expanded into all of these different regions.

Modeling the Clovis Expansion throughout Central America

How could migrating populations from North America have reached the southernmost limit of Central America by 11,000 BP? Such a rapid expansion would have required both high mobility and high reproductive rates. While these two characteristics may seem incompatible at first glance, Todd Surovell's (2000) analysis of the relationship between mobility and fertility indicates that they are not. But how could this rapidly expanding population have adapted to the resources of the range of Central American environments—from alpine meadows to lowland tropical forests—within such a short time frame? I argue here that the rapid expansion of Clovis populations into new environments was possible only because they were focused on hunting and the eating of meat as their primary subsistence strategy. While Clovis populations undoubtedly ate some plant foods, they were probably limited to eating plant parts that are designed to attract animal consumers (for example, fruit) and generally pose little threat to humans. Those plant parts that are best retained by the plant (for example, leaves, branches, underground storage organs) or left uneaten by consumers (for example, seeds) are often chemically or mechanically defended from herbivores and oftentimes either cannot be eaten by humans or need special methods of processing to render their consumption harmless (Ranere 2000). In either case, the time it would take to identify plants that could be safely consumed or to devise ways to neutralize plant toxins to render them harmless seems incompatible with the rapid expansion of Clovis populations into the entire range of tropical habitats found in Central America.

Theoretical considerations and empirical evidence support a focus on animal procurement for Clovis populations in North America, although the extent to which Clovis hunters concentrated on megafauna remains actively debated (for example, Byers and Ugan 2005; Waguespak and Surovell 2003). More contentious is the claim that hunting would remain the subsistence pursuit of choice by Paleoindians as they moved from open habitats into the tropical forests of Central America. One can argue that Clovis populations were able to move rapidly through the range of environments found in the Americas precisely because of the nature of hunting/meat eating (Kelly and Todd 1988; Morrow and Morrow 1999; Ranere and Cooke 1991). Clovis colonizers were not so much adapted to particular environments as they were to a particular mode of food procurement—that is, hunting. Hunting techniques can be transferred, with minor modifications, from environment to environment; preparation and consumption of animals can certainly be transferred without difficulty. I am arguing that the initial Clovis colonists of Central American tropical forests were hunters, as were the initial Clovis colonists throughout North America, including the woodlands of eastern North America. Here it is particularly important to distinguish between initial colonizing populations and the subsequent descendant populations in a region (Dincauze 1993b; Kelly and Todd 1988). The subsistence strategies of the initial colonizers should be very similar to the strategies pursued in their previous homeland. Subsequent strategies will reflect changes in those initial strategies that more efficiently exploit/utilize the resources of the new zone.

Characterizations of Paleoindians in eastern deciduous forests as general foragers who consume more plant foods than animals (for example, Meltzer 1988; Meltzer and Smith 1986) may perhaps apply to the Late Paleoindian populations (or, more likely, Early Archaic populations), but not to the initial Clovis colonizers.

Migration models that envision populations moving long distances to set up colonies in unoccupied or sparsely occupied territories with later "filling in" of the spaces between mother and daughter populations (for example, Anderson 1990; Anthony 1990; Dincauze 1993b) appear to better account for the rapid dispersal of Clovis populations than does the "wave of advance" model (Martin 1973; Mosimann and Martin 1975). Dena Dincauze (1993b: 51) describes a two-step process in which an initial marshaling area—"a focus for the gathering, arranging, and allocating of resources and information"—may be occupied for only a brief period of time while the colonizing population scouts for an area with resources more suitable for a longer-term occupation. In eastern North America, David Anderson (1990, 1991) has identified a number of these high-resource zones, which he calls staging areas. While the availability of high-quality lithic materials seems likely to have played a part in the settlement choices of Clovis populations, as William Gardner (1974, 1983) has long maintained, the density of prey species would, I suspect, be the most important determinant.

Hunting as the primary subsistence strategy appears to have persisted longer in environments where game was plentiful and other resources scarce (the North American plains) than in environments where game was scarce (tropical forests). It follows that colonizing populations would have moved more quickly through areas with low game densities than through areas where game densities were high. Given the small land mass and the somewhat limited potential of terminal Pleistocene environments in Central America to support large numbers of game animals, movement through the isthmus by the initial Clovis populations may well have been extremely rapid. If colonizing populations "leapfrogged" (Anthony 1990) through Central America, then we should expect that the populations left behind would have quickly expanded their search areas to incorporate all of the territory in the gap left by the advancing hunters. Furthermore, these populations would have been under selective pressure to redirect their subsistence efforts toward activities that had previously been of minor importance. We might reasonably expect fish and other aquatic animals to enter the dietary mix relatively early in contexts where terrestrial game was sparse. We might also expect to see an early focus on plant exploitation, particularly in those areas away from the coastlines where aquatic faunal resources were not available.

It might be argued that hunting is not now nor was it ever a viable subsistence option in forested areas, particularly in the tropics. However, recent inventories of animal biomass in the neotropics suggest that they seem sufficient for supporting widely dispersed and highly mobile hunting bands. Piperno and Pearsall (1998) calculated that seasonal forests can sustain human population densities of nearly two persons per square kilometer with animals supplying most of the calories. This is not entirely unexpected, since terrestrial game provides the Ache foragers of Paraguay with over half of their dietary calories (Hawkes et al. 1982; Piperno and Pearsall 1998). It should also be noted that large forest fauna were not immune to the mass extinctions that occurred at the end of the Pleistocene (Martin and Guilday 1967). Moreover, if one takes into account the capacity of large herbivores (such as elephants) to affect the openness of the environment (Owen-Smith 1987), the terminal Pleistocene forests in Central America are likely to have been much more attractive to hunters than is currently the case (Ranere and Cooke 1991). Hunting, then, would have been a viable subsistence option in the forested tropics, particularly for highly mobile, widely dispersed bands (see Waguespack and Surovell 2003 for an extended discussion on the relationship between population densities and reliance on hunting among hunter-gatherers). In addition, the cooler, drier terminal Pleistocene climate in tropical America would have resulted in a more open landscape than occurred under Holocene conditions (see Piperno and Pearsall 1998 for a summary of the evidence).

Clovis Technology in North and Central America

In a recent study of Clovis technology in North America, Juliet Morrow (1995, 1996) identified a bifacial reduction strategy that is characteristic of the early Clovis assemblages of western North America and some (but not all) eastern fluted point sites—for example, Ready/Lincoln Hills (Illinois), Adams (Kentucky), Ledford/Roeder (Kentucky), Welling–Nelly Heights (Ohio), Carson-Conn-Short (Tennessee), Thunderbird (Virginia), and Williamson (Virginia). She argues that the appearance of this early Clovis technology at eastern sites indicates that they are closely related both culturally and chronologically with the western Clovis sites. A comparison of metric attributes of finished fluted points from North America indicates close affinities between western Clovis and some eastern fluted points (Morrow 1996).

Does the distribution of this early Clovis technology extend into Central America? A recent comparison of fluted points from North, Central, and South America seems to suggest that it does not (Morrow and Morrow 1999). However, only fourteen points from Central America (excluding Mexico) were included in the sample. If suitable measurements and illustrations of what appear to be early Clovis lanceolate points from both Turrialba, Costa Rica, and La Mula West, Panama, had been available for the 1999 Morrow and Morrow study, the resulting analysis would almost certainly have identified early Clovis technology as far south as Panama.

We are not limited to a small sample of isolated fluted points to assess relatedness between Central American and North American Clovis technology, however. Fortunately, Clovis lithic workshops have been identified at both Turrialba and La Mula West (figure 4.1). The lithic reduction represented at La Mula West was almost entirely devoted to the production of bifacial points. Bifacial points and a variety of other tools were manufactured at the much larger site at Turrialba, Costa Rica. The bifacial reduction sequence at both these sites closely parallels that identified by Morrow (1996) for the Ready site in Illinois, a sequence apparently shared with western Clovis and other eastern Clovis sites but not with later fluted point traditions.

The Turrialba (Finca Guardiria) site is located on terraces (700 meters in elevation) of the Reventazon River in the Atlantic watershed of central Costa

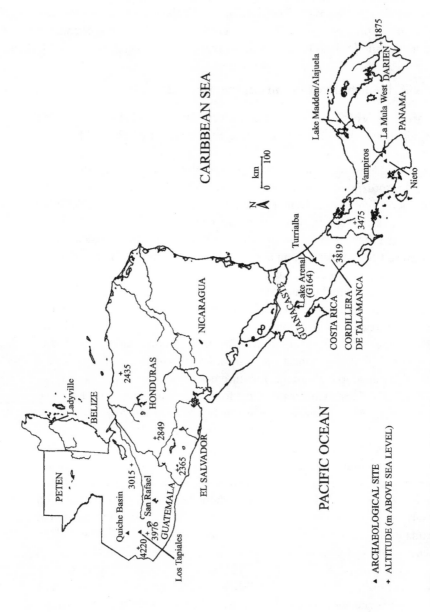

Figure 4.1. Paleoindian localities in Central America.

Table 4.1. Point Bases from La Mula West

Dimensions (mm)	5-1	5-194	7-27	8-S	21S/24S	27S	4-99-0/ Y4-30/W4-1	4-99-1	4-99-2
Length	>30	>28	>34	>23	?64	>76	>96	>24	>24
Maximum width	?29.7	?32	>17	?37.7	26.2	42.5	35	24	33
Maximum base width	27	?26	>15	29	?21	—	31	20	27
Maximum thickness	7.9	7.7	7	7	6.9	13.7	9.9	6	7
Basal concavity depth	1.5	0	?2.5	0	0	—	2	0	0
Flute 1, length	18	25	8	13	21	43	29	>24	>24
Flute 1, width	16	17	8	13	10	13	17.5	19	23
Flute 2, length	—	24	14	16	—	34	28	—	12
Flute 2, width	—	11	>10	14	—	>15	13	—	12

Note: A ? before a dimension indicates that the measurement likely applies to the entire point; a > before a dimension indicates that the measurement is not valid for a whole point but only for the fragment recovered.

Rica (Castillo et al. 1987; Snarskis 1979). The area today receives 4,000 millimeters of rainfall annually and at the time of its occupation would have been covered by a montane wet forest. However, the entire area has been cultivated, and all archaeological materials from the site have been recovered from surface contexts or the plow zone. At 10 hectares, Turrialba is by far the largest Paleoindian site yet reported in Central America. Paleoindians used the fine-grained siliceous rocks, which are still abundant as cobbles and boulders in the adjacent streambeds, to manufacture a wide variety of tools. Michael Snarskis (1979) has reported recovering in systematic surface collections and shallow excavations twenty-eight thousand lithic specimens, including eighteen fluted points, large numbers of bifacial preforms, and a series of tool types often found with North American fluted point assemblages: snub-nosed keeled end scrapers, end scrapers with lateral spurs, burins, bifacial and unifacial knives, and well-made side scrapers. The enormous amount of workshop debris, including broken preforms and bifacial thinning flakes, identifies a major activity at the site. The variety of finished tools, many of which have been reworked and/or show edge damage and polish, identify Turrialba as a habitation site as well. Pearson's (2002, 2004) reassessment of the Turrialba Clovis assemblage confirms the close parallels with early North American Clovis assemblages and lithic reduction strategies.

La Mula West is located on the margins of an intertidal salt flat along the central Pacific coast of Panama. Recent deforestation and overgrazing have led to erosion of the land adjacent to the salt flat. Dunes of salt-laden silt blown onto the land during the six-month dry season (December to May) impede plant growth and promote more erosion. Archaeological materials are left behind on the eroded surfaces as a lag deposit as the fines (silts, sands, and clays) are removed by wind and sheet erosion. Although extensive testing at La Mula

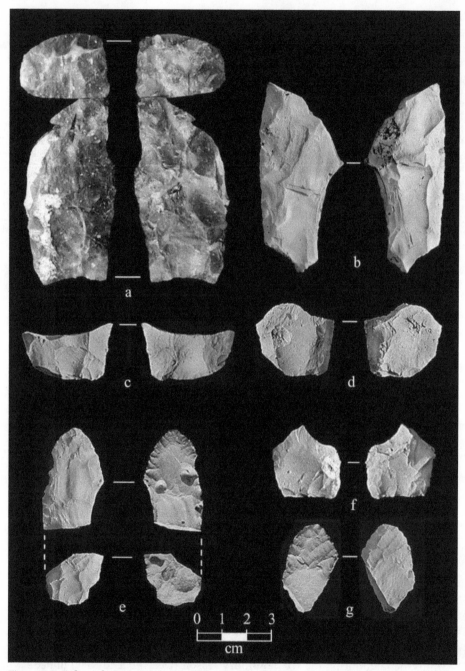

Figure 4.2. Bifaces from La Mula West, Panama: *a–d, f,* late-stage (4.3 or 5) fluted preforms; *e,* two fragments of the same finished point with pressure retouch at the tip (pot-lid fractures from heat damage are visible); *g,* tip of late-stage preform or finished point.

West failed to reveal any undisturbed deposits, charcoal collected during the 1960s from a hearth exposed in the tidal flat in the same general vicinity as the site yielded a date of 11,300 ± 300 BP (Crusoe and Felton 1974). Biface fragments, spurred end scrapers, burins, gravers, and blades with platforms prepared by grinding characterize the site assemblage. Translucent milky-white to brown agate (or chalcedony) was used almost exclusively by Clovis knappers. The site activity best documented is the manufacture of bifacial points. We recovered eighty-four biface fragments in total, most having been broken in the manufacturing process. Twelve of the fifteen basal fragments are either fluted or extensively basally thinned (table 4.1, figure 4.2a–f). The reduction sequence represented at La Mula West is compared in the following section with the sequence from the Ready site (Morrow 1996: 201–15).

STAGE 1: SELECTION OF NODULE OR FLAKE BLANK

Raw material availability apparently plays a major role in this stage. At the Ready site, both naturally occurring tabular spalls and flake blanks were used.

La Mula West contained a number of nodule fragments with cortex; none is large, and I estimate that the raw material here was cobble sized, probably not much larger than 15–20 centimeters in maximum dimension. The appearance of stage 2 fragments suggests that whole nodules were used for blanks. However, some stage 3 preforms are plano-convex to triangular in cross section; these suggest that the blanks might have been blades or bladelike flakes.

STAGE 2: INITIAL EDGING AND TRIMMING

During this stage, a bifacial edge is established around all or most of the specimen's perimeter, and prominent ridges and humps are removed from the faces.

The eight stage 2 bifaces from La Mula West are all small fragments that do not retain more than a portion of one margin (two are overshot flakes). I suspect that when chunks like these broke off the preform, the larger preform remnant was simply reshaped. Occasional edge remnants with grinding appear on stage 2 bifaces, but this is rare. The reduction techniques and flaking patterns are consistent with early-stage Clovis reduction at Ready and elsewhere but are not restricted to Clovis reduction sequences.

STAGE 3: PRIMARY THINNING AND SHAPING

Because this is the stage at which the biface first begins to be distinctively Clovis, I quote Morrow (1996: 207–9) at length about the diagnostic characteristics of stage 3 bifaces:

Following the initial edging and trimming, stage 2 bifaces were further reduced by the removal of deep, transverse percussion, thinning flakes.

This primary thinning produced large, fully flaked stage 3 bifacial blanks with regularized cross sections and roughly ovate outlines. In some cases, the flake removals were on opposing faces from opposite edges, as seen on many western Clovis bifaces (Bradley 1982, Frison 1991b, Gramly 1993), and in others, they appear to have been more random. This type of intensive biface thinning produces broad bifaces with flattened cross sections and a flaking pattern consisting of several very large, relative widely spaced, long, deep, flake scars. I propose that this biface thinning strategy is a hallmark of Clovis technology and is perhaps no less diagnostic of Clovis lithic assemblages than the Clovis point itself. . . . Clovis striking platforms are well isolated lobes that are positioned in the center plane of the biface and typically project at least 2 to 3 mm from the biface margin. . . . These isolated lobes occur around the entire circumference of the biface at fairly widely spaced intervals, and usually are aligned with prominent ridge crests located between previous flake removals. . . . Soft hammer percussion flakes detached using this type of striking platform have deep, narrow initiations and often span a large portion of the width of the biface, sometimes terminating in an outre passé, wherein a portion of the opposite edge of the biface is also removed. Using this flaking technique, one can greatly reduce the thickness of a biface with a minimum of flake removals.

Twelve stage 3 biface fragments were recovered from La Mula West (figures 4.3a and g). Unlike those of the Ready site, at La Mula West (LMW), stage 3 bifaces have subparallel sides rather than being ovate. This pattern conforms to Morrow's model of lithic reduction if the blanks being used are predominantly blades or blade-like flakes rather than cobbles. LMW stage 3 bifaces do have the characteristic large, widely spaced, long, deep flake scars and flat cross sections. Striking platforms are typically positioned in the center plane of the biface, but they are not isolated to the degree suggested by Morrow (2- to 3-millimeter projections); 1 millimeter is the maximum isolation witnessed in the La Mula West specimens. Nonetheless, LMW flakes initiated from these minimally isolated, sometimes ground platforms do expand from deep, narrow initiations to terminations near the opposite side of the biface (figure 4.3a). Occasionally overshot or outre passé flakes are produced, in which the opposite edge of the biface is removed (figure 4.3g). A pattern of flake removal on opposing faces from opposing edges is present but not dominant.

To sum up, stage 3 biface reduction at LMW looks very much like that from the Ready site and other North American Clovis sites. The only major difference is the absence at LMW of lobed, isolated striking platforms.

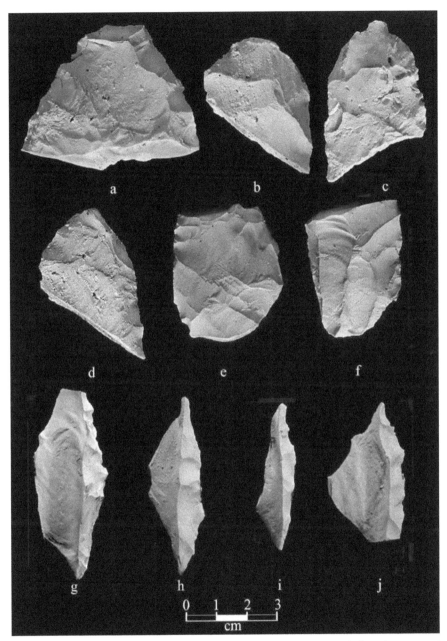

Figure 4.3. Biface fragments from La Mula West, Panama: *a*, stage 3 biface; *b–e*, stage 4 bifaces showing deep, narrow flake initiations and terminations near the opposite edge of the biface (the opposite edge of *e* has been removed by an overshot flake); *f*, stage 4 biface with two parallel flute scars on one face; *g–j*, outre passé or overshot flakes from stage 3 (*g*) and stage 4 (*h–j*) bifaces.

STAGE 4: SECONDARY SHAPING AND FLUTING

Morrow states that during this stage, the bifaces are thinned and shaped by "marginal lateral percussion trimming," leaving a distinctive boat-shaped outline. At this point in the reduction process, while the biface is still rather large, the fluting is done. The striking platforms that are produced (stage 4.1) are typically isolated, lightly to moderately ground projections at or near the center of a convex base and near the biface center plane. Flutes appear to be removed by soft hammer percussion and are often quite large and bold. Basal and lateral trimming follows (stage 4.2), often removing the step or hinge fracture at the flute termination. Preparation of the platform for the second flute (stage 4.3) parallels that for the first. The base is less convex than earlier and may be straight or even slightly concave.

At LMW, thirteen fragments consisting of tips, midsections, and overshot or outre passé flakes (figures 4.3b–e, h–j) are considered stage 4 examples. Without basal portions to examine, any further subdivision is impossible. Three bases are from very early stage 4 reduction, since no platform preparation for fluting is visible. Two base fragments have what appear to be remnants of isolated platforms prepared for fluting (Morrow's stage 4.1a), which collapsed in the flute removal attempts. One midsection and three base fragments appear to have fluting on one face (stage 4.1b); a fourth convex base fragment (figure 4.3f) has two narrow flutes that extend across the convex surface of a plano-convex biface. One base (figure 4.2f) has a flute on one side, a flat-facet "pseudo-flute" on the other, and evidence for some lateral trimming (stage 4.2). Four bases are fluted on both sides and could be either stage 4.3 or 5 (figures 4.2a, c, d, and f); the small size of most fragments prevents determination of whether final thinning and shaping was carried out. Finally, four midsections show evidence of two flutes and are therefore classified as stage 4.3 bifaces.

STAGE 5: FINAL THINNING AND SHAPING

After successful removal of the second flute, "light soft hammer *percussion*" around the entire perimeter of the point thins the point but leaves the fluting scars largely intact (Morrow 1996: 217; emphasis in the original). One or both sides are occasionally refluted, apparently by indirect percussion, to thin the haft element of the point.

At LMW this stage is best represented by the basal two-thirds of a point recovered in three pieces (figure 4.2a). The point appears to have been broken during the attempt to thin the upper portion of the blade. Two flake scars 25–28 millimeters from the base, and opposite each other, have removed part of the fluting flake. Only one other specimen from LMW, a midsection, shows evidence of two flutes and percussion trimming flakes that invade the edges of the fluting scar. This may be an artifact of the extremely fragmented nature of the bifaces left at the site or may reflect that stage 5 light trimming did not result in many broken preforms.

STAGE 5.9: EDGE RETOUCH AND HAFT GRINDING

Pressure flaking is used to straighten lateral and basal edges and to reduce the height of ridge crests between percussion flake removals. The lower lateral edges and base are moderately to heavily ground.

STAGE 6.0: FINISHED POINT

Pressure flakes quite evident on one point tip (figure 4.2g) from LMW identify it as stage 5.9/6.0. Two additional fragments, which appear to belong to a single point (figure 4.2e), are from a finished point that has been subjected to severe heat damage.

The manufacturing sequence for fluted point production at LMW is almost identical with the sequence described by Morrow for the early Clovis technology in North America. In particular, the stage 3 thinning process that Morrow considers a hallmark of early Clovis technology—producing broad, flat bifaces with large, widely spaced deep flake scars extending well beyond the midsection—is clearly present at LMW. These characteristic bifaces were, however, produced at LMW without the extreme isolation of striking platforms (2 to 3 millimeters from the biface margin) for bifaces found at Ready and some other North American Clovis localities. Flute removal in the LMW sequence occurs well before the final reduction stage, as is the case for North American Clovis. For both North American Clovis and LMW Clovis reduction sequences, pressure flaking is found only on stage 5.9 and 6.0 (or finished) bifaces.

The reduction sequence present at Turrialba parallels that just described for La Mula West. Turrialba biface fragments exhibit the widely spaced scars from deep transverse percussion flaking that are characteristic of stage 3 reduction. Fluting at Turrialba occurred well before the final thinning stage (figure 4.4b–d), and pressure flaking is found only on finished bifaces. The remarkably similar bifacial reduction strategies seen in these two Central American sites and early Clovis sites of North America, as well as the typology of the end product, imply close cultural and chronological connections between the two areas. This early Clovis pattern may even extend to the north coast of Venezuela, where a collection of fluted points and preforms has been reported from the Paraguaná peninsula (Jaimes 1997). The evidence suggests that Clovis populations were at the gateway to South America, if not already in South America, by approximately 11,000 BP.

Figure 4.4. Bifaces from Turrialba, Costa Rica (photo by Michael Snarskis): (*a*) base of completed point; (*b–c*) late-stage fluted preforms; (*d*) large fluted preform.

What Happened to Clovis Populations in Central America?

The distribution of Clovis points and that of fluted Fishtail points overlap throughout the territory between southern Mexico (Garcia-Barcena) and Panama and perhaps beyond, into Venezuela (Jaimes 1997). The most likely and often suggested explanation for the disappearance of the former and appearance of the latter is that Paleoindian populations in Central America adopted a somewhat different point form either for stylistic reasons or for some unrecognized functional advantage of stemmed points (for example, Pearson 2004; Ranere and Cooke 1991; Snarskis 1979; but see Mayer-Oakes 1986a). Population continuity appears to have continued in Central America, a pattern most clearly seen in central-Pacific Panama ("Gran Coclé"), where the same locations occupied by Paleoindians continued to be occupied by Early Archaic populations (Ranere and Cooke 1996). Unfluted bifacial stemmed and notched points continued to be manufactured in central Panama until 7000 BP (Cooke and Sanchez 2004a; Pearson 2004; Ranere 2000; Ranere and Cooke 1996). These same populations began cultivating domesticated squash (*Cucurbita* sp.), arrowroot (*Maranta arundinacea*), leren (*Calathea allouia*), and bottle-gourd (*Lagenaria siceraria*) early in the ninth millennium BP (Piperno et al. 1991; Piperno and Pearsall 1998) and may well have been ancestral to the large populations encountered by the Spanish in Gran Coclé early in the sixteenth century (Cooke and Sanchez 2004b).

It seems likely that Paleoindian populations, with their fluted point technology, entered South America around the time when the lanceolate Clovis form was being replaced by stemmed Fishtail forms. Whereas no evidence of occupation prior to the Clovis expansion in Central America has yet been recovered, a growing body of evidence suggests that populations were well established throughout South America by the time the Clovis/Fishtail populations entered the continent (Correal 1981; Dillehay et al. 2003; Hurt et al. 1972; López 1991; Roosevelt et al. 1996). Nonetheless, the similarity of the Fishtail points from the Southern Cone of South America to those from Central America suggests to me that the same focus on hunting that led to the rapid expansion of Clovis populations throughout North and Central America was also responsible for the rapid expansion of descendant populations down the length of the Andes into Tierra del Fuego. An alternative hypothesis is that there were already resident populations in South America that adopted the technology of manufacturing hunting weapons, including fluted Fishtail points. However, a number of populations living throughout South America at least as early as the eleventh millennium BP did not adopt fluted Fishtail point technology (for example, Dillehay et al. 2003; López 1991; Roosevelt et al. 1996) or even bifacial reduction technology (for example, Correal 1981; Keefer et al. 1998; Sandweiss et al. 1998; Stothert et al. 2003). I would argue that these already-established populations, rather than any environmental barriers, were what confined the expansion of Fishtail point populations primarily to inter-Andean regions before they reached the Southern Cone. After all, Clovis populations in Central America had already crossed the range of tropical environments that characterized the eastern two-thirds of South America.

Acknowledgments

This is a revised version of the paper entitled "Paleoindian Expansion into Tropical America: The View from Central Panama," which was presented at the 62nd Annual Meeting of the Society for American Archaeology held in Nashville in 1997. I thank my colleagues Richard Cooke and Patricia Hansell for comments on earlier drafts of this chapter.

5

Early Humanized Landscapes in Northern South America

CRISTÓBAL GNECCO AND JAVIER ACEITUNO

The early colonization of the Americas has been thought of largely from the standpoint of ecofunctional theory, that is, a process whereby humans adapted to a basically unknown environment using a limited cultural repertoire, salient among which were bifacial hunting weapons and tools. This perspective conceives of the environment as a powerful backdrop that limited and directed human behavior. However, the passivity that ecological reductionism accords to an ontologized culture (*sensu* Fabian 1983: 157) is giving way to a dynamic consideration, by virtue of which culture is no longer the submissive subject of nature and human beings no longer the submissive subjects of culture. Culture is seen as the active medium by which societies built their world around. In this perspective, the environment becomes landscape, that is, a semanticized space, utterly transformed (appropriated and contested) by human symbolization. The culture/nature dichotomy dissolves, casting off its modern clothes. How do we proceed, then, to understand the early peopling of the Americas, leaving aside ecological reductionism? The first step is to interpret how humans appropriated and gave meaning to the environment, that is, how they humanized the space from the very beginning of their American adventure. In this chapter we discuss the information from northern South America about early hunter-gatherers from such a perspective. First we discuss the temporal dimension in which these processes occurred; then we consider how the space was colonized and given meaning.

Time and Tools

The scant available information (table 5.1) indicates that humans were impacting and appropriating various ecosystems by late Pleistocene times. In arid coastal and inland northwestern Venezuela, Taima-Taima and El Vano (figure 5.1) have provided evidence of the association of El Jobo points (figure 5.2A) with extinct fauna as far back as 13,000 BP (Bryan et al. 1978; Ochsenius and Gruhn 1979; Jaimes 1999). At Santa Elena, in Ecuador, Karen Stothert (1988)

Table 5.1. Sites from Northern South America with Late Pleistocene/Early Holocene ^{14}C Dates

Site	Country	Sample	Date (BP)	Material
Rancho Peludo	Venezuela	Y-1108-IV	13.915±200	Charcoal
Taima-Taima	Venezuela	IVIC-655	11.860±130	Wood
		SI-3316	12.980±85	Wood
		Birm-802	13.000±200	Wood
		IVIC-191-1	13.010±280	Wood
		USGS-247	13.880±120	Wood
		UCLA-2133	14.200±300	Wood
		IVIC-191-2	14.440±435	Bone
Muaco	Venezuela	M-1068	14.300±500	Bone
		O-999	16.375±400	Bone
El Vano	Venezuela	B-95602	10.710±60	Bone
Provincial	Venezuela	B-22638	9.020±100	Charcoal
El Abra	Colombia	B-2134	10.720±400	Charcoal
		GrN-5556	12.400±160	Charcoal
Tibitó	Colombia	GrN-9375	11.740±110	Bone
Tequendama	Colombia	GrN-7115	9.740±135	Charcoal
		GrN-6730	9.990±100	Charcoal
		GrN-6210	10.025±95	Charcoal
		GrN-6732	10.130±150	Charcoal
		GrN-7113	10.140±100	Charcoal
		GrN-7114	10.150±150	Charcoal
		GrN-6731	10.460±130	Charcoal
		GrN-6505	10.590±90	Charcoal
		GrN-6270	10.730±105	Charcoal
		GrN-6539	10.920±260	Charcoal
Bedout	Colombia	B-40852	10.350±90	Charcoal
Palestina	Colombia	B-123565	10.230±90	Charcoal
		B-123565	10.260±70	Charcoal
		B-123566	10.300±70	Charcoal
		B-123566	10.400±90	Charcoal
Sueva	Colombia	GrN-8111	10.090±90	Charcoal
Sauzalito	Colombia	B-18, 441	9.300±100	Charcoal
		B-23, 475	9.600±110	Charcoal
		B-23, 476	9.670±150	Charcoal
San Isidro	Colombia	B-65877	9.530±100	Charcoal
		B-65878	10.050±100	Charcoal
		B-93275	10.030±60	Charcoal
Peña Roja	Colombia	GX-17395	9.125±250	Charcoal
		B-52963	9.160±90	Charcoal
		B-52964	9.250±140	Charcoal
Porce 045	Colombia	B-72375	9.120±90 AP	Charcoal
El Jazmín	Colombia	B-95061	9.020±60	Charcoal
OGSE-80	Ecuador	TX-3316	9.550±120	Shell
		TX-3772	9.800±100	Shell
		TX-4461	10.100±130	Shell
		TX-4706	10.300±240	Charcoal
		TX-3770	10.840±410	Charcoal
OGSE-201	Ecuador	TX-3774	9.460±100	Shell
El Inga	Ecuador	R-1070/2	9.030±144	Soil
Chobshi	Ecuador	Tx-1133	10.010±430	Charcoal
Cubilán	Ecuador	Ki-1642	10.300±170	Charcoal
		Ki-1640	10.500±1,300	Charcoal

Figure 5.1. Northern South American regions mentioned in the text: (1) northwestern Venezuela; (2) Gulf of Urabá; (3) middle Orinoco; (4) middle Porce; (5) middle Magdalena; (6) Middle Cauca; (7) Sabana de Bogotá; (8) upper Calima; (9) upper Cauca; (10) middle Caquetá; (11) Santa Elena.

excavated occupations that date to circa 11,000 years ago. Evidence indicates that hunter-gatherers exploited diverse and rich ecotones located between the coast and the water sources of the alluvial plain. The Ecuadorian highlands have also very likely been populated since the late Pleistocene,[1] although the biomes occupied by the peoples who left sites such as El Inga and San José (Bell 1965; Mayer-Oakes 1986a), Chobshi (Lynch and Pollock 1981), and Cubilán (Temme 1982) are unknown.

Early occupations of diverse forest formations are more abundant. The sequence of the Sabana de Bogotá, in the highlands of eastern Colombia, is the most complete and well-documented regional sequence available in the northern Andes, covering from some 12,000 years ago until settled farmers appear in the record 3,000 years ago (for example, Correal and Van der Hammen 1977; Correal 1981, 1986). There are records of substantial and sustained occupation of the Porce River valley, in Antioquia, and of the area collectively known as the Middle Cauca (Aceituno 2002). There is also evidence in southwestern Colombia (upper Calima and upper Cauca River valleys) of early human occupation in mountain forests dating to late Pleistocene times. In San Isidro, the best-documented site, a vast array of bifacial, unifacial, and grinding tools has been found in association with charred macrobotanical remains (Mora and Gnecco 2003).

Although evidence indicates that the lowlands have been peopled since the end of the Pleistocene (Correal 1977), the adjacent upper elevations appear to have been settled later. Santiago Mora (2003) has documented a 9,000-year-old settlement in Peña Roja, in the middle Caquetá River valley in the Colombian Amazon, with unifacial and grinding tools used to process vegetal resources in a rainforest ecosystem. William Barse (1990) found in the center of the Orinoco watershed an occupation dated to the early Holocene that occurred in the savanna-forest ecotone. The research carried out by Carlos López (1999) in the arid middle Magdalena River valley has uncovered substantial occupation dated to the late Pleistocene, including points with narrow stems (figure 5.2C). The rest is noncontextual evidence based on surface finds that may or may not belong to the late Pleistocene, although they probably do. Broad Stemmed (figure 5.2E) and Restrepo points are thought to be of late Pleistocene age, but they have not yet been securely dated. This is also the case for the "Fishtail" points (figure 5.2D) (for example, Correal 1983; Jaimes 1999) found in the area. If the dates from southern South America can be extended to the rest of the subcontinent, then these bifacial point forms could be placed right at the end of the Pleistocene (Flegenheimer 1987; Bird 1988a; Politis 1991; Miotti 2003a).

Space: Colonization and Meaning

The archaeology of the early colonization of northern South America has experienced a conceptual shift in the past two decades, from a narrow and dogmatic ontological essentialism to a dynamic and active conception of culture. The new approach views the late Pleistocene colonists of northern South America as impacting, altering, and symbolically appropriating a variety of ecosystems and turning them into humanized landscapes. The early hunter-gatherers from northern South America affected the natural distribution of resources beginning in the late Pleistocene, developing territorial patterns that are essential for understanding how these people built and gave meaning to the

Figure 5.2. Late Pleistocene and early Holocene bifacial point types of South America: (A) El Jobo; (B) Clovis-like; (C) Narrow Stemmed; (D) Fishtail; (E) Broad Stemmed. Tools are not at the same scale.

landscape. Such a territoriality was related to restricted mobility and the focalized use of resources; these factors were the source of the definite structural transformation of most neotropical ecosystems.

Northern South America is not a homogeneous geographical area. The Ecuadorian Andes form a continuous, although diverse, mountain chain (with high inner valleys, *jalcas*, and *páramos*) flanked at both sides by lowlands covered with rainforests. In southwestern Colombia, the Andes split into three branches of different geological origin, forming inter-Andean valleys much wider than the narrow valleys of the central Andes and even Ecuador. Between the three cordilleras, there are two low river valleys: the Magdalena and the Cauca. On both sides, as in Ecuador, there are two lowland areas covered with tropical rainforests: the narrow Pacific strip and the Amazon basin. To the north of the latter extend large plains covered with grasses and forested along the rivers. The rest of the area is made up of rolling savannas along the Colombia Caribbean and the arid strip of the Atlantic coast of Venezuela. These geographical variants at the equator produce dramatic climatic changes along the altitudinal gradient. Differences in insolation and solar exposure, rainfall, and soils make a mosaic of markedly different and narrow tiers, except in the Amazon and the eastern plains, where the ecosystems are substantially wider.

When humans coming from northeastern Asia entered and eventually populated the Americas, the world was experiencing rapid and dramatic environmental changes. In a matter of decades (a few centuries at most), the composition of environments changed in response to changing rainfall and temperature patterns. The climatic changes occurring during the terminal Pleistocene (10,000–13,000 BP) and early Holocene (9,000–10,000 BP) affected animal and plant species differentially, creating biomes with no contemporary counterpart. To account for these phenomena, Russell Graham (1990: 57) proposed that an individualist model (that is, biomes are not highly coevolved systems but collections of species more or less randomly distributed throughout environmental gradients) has to be favored over a collective model (that is, biomes are stable groups of species, tightly linked and highly coevolved, that react uniformly to environmental fluctuations) to explain "nonharmonic" species distributions. The individualist model accounts for the existence of Pleistocene and early Holocene biomes with no contemporary analogues.

The coexistence during late Pleistocene times (10,000–13,000 BP) of now-allopatric species, currently distributed in different climatic regions, has also been accounted for with the equability model, which holds that the basic climatic variables responsible for the distribution of plants and animals were caused by seasonal shifts, not by annual averages (Graham and Mead 1987: 371; Graham 1990: 57). Thus, the current distributions in tropical biomes are possibly the result of reduced Holocene seasonality. Barbara Leyden (1984:

4858) found in the lowlands of Guatemala evidence of seasonality during the late Pleistocene; temperature and precipitation patterns were more marked than nowadays. Leyden also documented less-pronounced seasonality toward the beginning of the Holocene. A similar pattern has been registered for El Valle, in Panama (Piperno et al. 1991: 209–10). The contemporaneous example discussed by Dolores Piperno and colleagues (1991: 215) regarding the effects of reduced precipitation upon plant associations in the Caribbean watershed of Panama (caused by a long dry period triggered by El Niño between 1982 and 1983) is a good illustration of what may have happened during the Pleistocene-Holocene transition. If precipitation and temperature were drastically reduced in the tropics during that time, as seems to have been the case (see Wijmstra and Van der Hammen 1966: 80; Van der Hammen 1974: 21), then the composition of vegetal associations may have resulted from decreasing seasonality. If this was so, then it is not surprising that late Pleistocene/ early Holocene biomes have no contemporaneous analogs. Although no data have been found to suggest a global pattern of that kind, data from Australia have been interpreted in this same vein (see Kershaw 1995: 673).

Humans only added to this ongoing dynamism. The presence of now-allopatric species in late Pleistocene/early Holocene pollen sequences may also be used to argue that useful species were transported from their traditional habitat to other locations (and perhaps were even cultivated). The "odd" association of certain species, not necessarily domesticated, may well be an indication of human transformation of the distribution and structure of plant (and animal) resources.

Space I: Transformations

Data from northern South America indicate human manipulation of plant (and possibly animal) resources since at least 11,000 years ago, including forest clearing and/or use and maintenance of naturally created clearings by burning, as well as the cultural selection of useful species through tending and planting. The region exhibits an early pattern of what David Rindos (1984: 176) termed "agrilocality," that is, a region where human groups are responsible for specialized domestication and where spatiotemporal patterns are evident that would have allowed for the emergence and development of agroecologies. Implicit in these concepts of agrilocality and agroecology is the human manipulation and transformation of ecosystems. Evidence from San Isidro suggests exactly that, as early as 10,000 BP; pollen data from the site include secondary vegetation, as herbaceous plants and weeds—Gramineae, Cyperaceae, and two colonizer species of open spaces of the genera *Plantago* and *Trema*—appear among a majority of mature or primary forest species. This suggests the existence on the site or in its surroundings of an open or partially open space during the time of human occupation. The prevalence of mature forest species, however, shows that the documented phenomenon was not a total forest clearing or deforestation but the existence of a space open enough to permit the growth of pioneer species. We cannot say whether this open space was naturally or humanly created, but that this palynological evidence derives from an archaeological site is probably not coincidental. The dominance (92 percent) of remains of the genus *Lagenaria* from San Isidro (figure 5.5A) and palm (more than 99 percent) from Peña Roja could simply represent dietary preferences or high natural availability, as in the "resource islands" reported by Darrell Posey (1984: 117) for the Amazon. Alternatively, these high percentages of a single plant taxon may indicate a humanly induced concentration of preferred resources. Favored species may have required planting and tending, including forest clearing, weeding, and maintenance of naturally opened spaces—which, in turn, may have lured animals.

In the premontane humid forests of northwestern Colombia, in the valleys of the rivers San Eugenio and Campoalegre (Middle Cauca) and Porce, archaeological sites have been found (El Jazmín, Antojo, Guayabito, and Campoalegre) with occupations from about 9,500 years ago, indicating humanization of the space based on circumscribed mobility in redundantly visited and exploited areas. The principal material items of those sites are stone tools and debris, mostly indicative of knapping, cutting, scraping, and grinding; polished adzes have also been found (Aceituno 2002). In El Jazmín, forest species diminish from the earliest Holocene occupation of the site, dated to 9020 ± 60 BP in its lowest levels (Beta 95061); at the same time, there is an increase in pioneer (Compositae, Melastomataceae, Sapindaceae) and forest-edge plants (Rubiaceae, Cecropiaceae), grasses (*Andropogon* sp., *Bambusa* sp., *Dioscorea* sp.), low bushes (Araceae, Piperaceae, Plantaginaceae, Sphagnaceae), and palms (*Astrocaryum* sp., *Bactris* sp., *Geonoma* sp., *Scheelea* sp., *Socratea* sp.); such associations are characteristic of secondary forests and intervened areas (figure 5.3). That inverse correlation and the human imprint on the site (stone tools and charred botanical remains) suggest that those early colonists were impacting and transforming the areas around the site. Principal component analysis (figure 5.4) indicates that the group formed by weeds, pioneers, forest-edge species, and palms is removed from that of grasses and cultivars and those of forest elements and ferns. The strong correlation between the associations indicates some kind of intervention. The high figures of mature-forest species in both dimensions mean that their distribution correlates with the increase of the other associations.

Palms, fruits, tubers, and Gramineae were identified in the pollen columns recovered at the sites. Palms, the most numerous group, are represented by

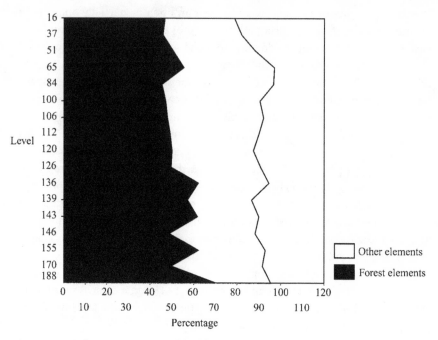

Figure 5.3. Pollen composition from El Jazmín.

the genera *Bactris, Geonoma, Astrocaryum, Scheelea,* and *Socratea;* palm phy-toliths were recovered from a grinding base from level V at El Jazmín. Fruits belong to the genera *Solanum* and *Passiflora,*[2] while tuberous plants belong to the genera *Dioscorea,*[3] *Manihot,*[4] and *Xanthosoma.*[5] *Amaranthus* and *Zea mays* belong to Gramineae. The use of *Manihot* and *Dioscorea* was determined by starch grains recovered from grinding tools from El Jazmín (Aceituno 2002). Charred *Persea* seeds from San Isidro (the longest being 6 centimeters) are very likely from a cultivar (figure 5.5C), as they are larger than average for a wild population (see Smith 1966, 1969); the same can be said of *Erythrina edulis* specimens (figure 5.5B). *Maranta* phytoliths found in grinding tools from San Isidro may well belong to a known cultivar, perhaps *M. arundina-cea.* Phytoliths of *Lagenaria siceraria* were recovered from Peña Roja. This information, along with the recorded transformation of the landscapes, points to the hypothesis that those early colonists manipulated plant groups in ar-eas impacted and transformed by human imprints. The abundance of useful wild plants increases in humanized landscapes (Piperno 1989; see also Politis 1996b). This is analogous to what Rindos (1984) called "coevolution."[6]

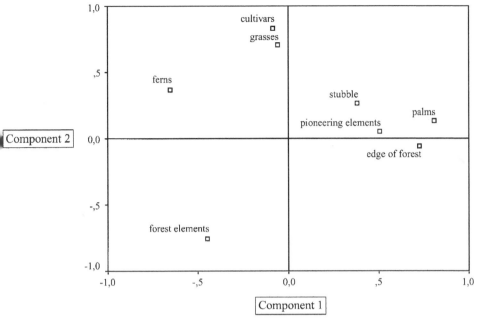

Figure 5.4. Principal component analysis of pollen from El Jazmín: group 1 (forest elements) and group 2 (other elements, including pioneer and forest-edge plants, low scrub, grasses, and palms).

Space II: Early Territories, Humanized Spaces

Much has changed in the interpretation of the early colonists of South America since the pioneering efforts of Carl Sauer (1944), Samuel Lothrop (1961), and Gordon Willey (1971). Yet many archaeologists still think that the varied strategies used to exploit and give meaning to different tropical biomes in late Pleistocene times were followed by a mostly Holocene pattern of decreased mobility and zonal settlement, linked to the appearance of new technologies geared to the processing of previously ignored resources. According to a well-known theoretical formula, resources giving less return to labor investment would have been exploited only when more productive resources were depleted (Hayden 1981). This theoretical formula is meaningless, however, if not linked to well-documented diachronic trajectories. Increasing stylistic diversity through time has been interpreted as an epiphenomenon of decreased mobility. The most frequently invoked rationale in support of this idea is that resource scarcity may have resulted in fringe survival and/or economic competition between groups. If groups were previously bound by interaction

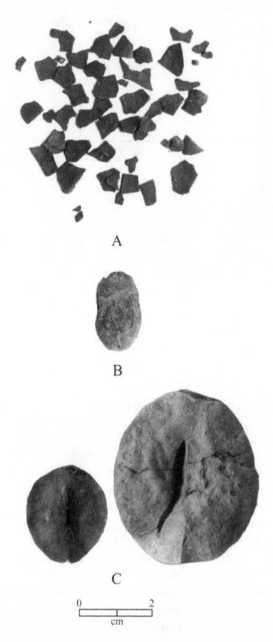

Figure 5.5. Macrobotanical remains from San Isidro: *A*, fragments of *Lagenaria siceraria*; *B*, fragment of *Erythrina edulis*; *C*, two fragments of *Persea americana*.

mechanisms, then competition may have severed them, eventually leading to stylistic differentiation. The latter has been monitored diachronically through reduced spatial distribution of archaeological horizons.

The pattern of the North American Paleoindian record most widely used for arguing for a rapid, directional colonization followed by a settling-in process is the initial existence of a pancontinental style followed by a late Pleistocene plethora of regional styles (Tankersley 1990; Anderson 1996). This pattern has also been noted for Europe by Douglas Price (1991: 200), who sees several changes in lithic bifaces during the Pleistocene-to-Holocene transition. Specifically, the geographical distribution of bifaces decreases and the number of zones with distinctive bifacial forms increases through time. This very pattern was imposed in South America during a time when very little evidence was available. Willey (1971) proposed a demic spread of mobile, directional hunters (his Big Game Hunting Tradition), giving way to more "settled" hunters (his Andean Hunting Tradition), then to horticultural experimentation via territorial constriction and sedentism (his Archaic). Yet no clear pancontinental style was then at hand. Juan Schobinger (1973) attempted to fill in the void; he proposed the existence of an early horizon characterized by Fishtail points. Although their distribution was and is still poorly known outside the Southern Cone, Schobinger did not hesitate to portray the Fishtail points as a pancontinental style spreading, north to south, along the Andes and the eastern foothills.

No clear pattern can be discerned in South America comparable to that of North America and Europe; we are not yet in a position to trace a clear areal extension of the early "horizons." One exception to this lack of data is Abriense, a unifacial industry of hastily made tools so far, limited to the Sabana de Bogotá (Correal 1986). El Jobo points, once thought to have been limited to northwestern Venezuela, are now credited as having had a wider distribution: three fragments of lanceolate points stated to be "similar" to the typical El Jobo were found in Monte Verde, in southern Chile, where they also date to circa 13,000 years BP. Despite the similarities in form, technology, and age between the specimens from southern Chile and those found in Venezuela (Collins 1997: 426; Arturo Jaimes, personal communication 2000), we still lack a secure stylistic assessment of the El Jobo form. This lack stems from the essentialist approach to unit creation that has dominated the late Pleistocene archaeology of the Americas. The significant variation[7] (formal for sure, and very likely also temporal) exhibited by El Jobo bifaces has been all but ignored, resulting in an almost total disregard of crucial variables, especially chronology.[8]

In 1876 Charles Rau (cited by Dunnell 1986: 159) wrote a typical statement of an essentialist ontology: "North American Indians of the same tribe . . .

arm their arrows with stone points of different forms, the shape of the arrowheads being a matter of individual taste or convenience." A century later, José Cruxent (1979: 79) explained the differences observed in El Jobo points from Venezuela in terms of idiosyncratic variation, that is, noise: "El Jobo points present a certain diversity within the same type category. This phenomenon of variation is tentatively explicable, considering that a society that has at its disposal a common intellectual and traditional basis acquired by inheritance will attain some diversification of its artifact types, thanks to the inventive talent of certain individuals."

A similar situation occurs with the Fishtail point "horizon" (Willey 1971; Schobinger 1973), which is supposed to span most of Andean South America. Yet we are not even sure whether the few examples of Fishtail points found in northern South America (Correal 1983; Jaimes 1999) are similar to specimens from the Southern Cone. Furthermore, the characterization of the horizon—as with Clovis, Folsom, and El Jobo—rests entirely in the bifaces, to the exclusion of other tools and debitage. The associated tool inventory varies so greatly from site to site (compare Bird 1988a: 134–79; see also Menghin 1952; Emperaire et al. 1963: 203; Cardich 1978; Flegenheimer 1987: 148; Nami 1987: 90) that the interpretative weight lies on the bifaces. This would not necessarily be a problem, since archaeology has long made use of types or isolated traits in time-space systematics. It becomes problematic, however, when a cultural interpretation is made to rest on single items that are used to characterize cultural distributions and even cultural dynamics with archaeological units that are the building blocks of time-space systematics.

Moreover, the bifaces have been only partially investigated. Morphological studies have been attempted for Fishtail points (Bird 1969; Politis 1991), indicating stem similarity and blade and size variability, but the technological characteristics cited by Junius Bird (1969: 55–56) and Gustavo Politis (1991: 297) are too general to be useful in the adequate construction of a horizon or even in the determination of its supposed pancontinentality. Bird (1969: 55), for instance, noted that Fishtail points were manufactured from flakes slightly thicker than the finished piece; this would separate them from any known bifaces of the North American Paleoindian (but see Morrow 1995). Although that generalization is wrong, given that some North American Paleoindian points were made following the same pattern noted by Bird (for example, Haynes 1980: 116; Hofman 1992: 201; Morrow 1992: 2), it has been repeated time and again (for example, Bray 1980: 169; Rovner 1980: 167; Bonnichsen 1991: 317–18; Politis 1991: 297). As a result, the definition of the type is still loose, and identifications are difficult to make. For instance, though the Madden Lake points from Panama have been classified as Fishtail points, excepting one classified as Clovis-like (Bird and Cooke 1978: 267; Ranere and

Cooke 1991: 238), William Mayer-Oakes (1986b: 149) thinks that their stems are not "eared" enough to classify them as Fishtail points. Instead, he prefers to identify them as El Inga Broad Stemmed (EIBS), after his identification of that type in the Ilaló complex from Ecuador (see Mayer-Oakes 1986b: 66). EIBA, fluted or unfluted, have broad, tapered stems and blades with straight edges. Yet Madden Lake bifaces have slightly convex blade edges, making them more similar to EIBA than to Fishtail points, although lacking the "eared" stem. So, what is more diagnostic of Fishtail points—the blade or the stem? What is clear from Bird's original description of the type (Bird 1969: 56–57) is that blade form was not considered, although an important feature was noted: rounded shoulders. *Shoulders* is the term that lithic typologists use when stem and blade are clearly separated, as in the case of Fell I and Palli Aike Fishtail points (compare Bird 1969). Having this in mind, and knowing that some North American archaeologists recognize a waisted Clovis variant (or, at least, late Pleistocene Paleoindian bifaces) with expanding, proximal ears, such as the Barnes type from the Great Lakes region (see Storck 1991: 154) and Simpson and Suwannee types from Florida (Dunbar 1991: 187, fig. 2), Bird and Richard Cooke (1978: 267) followed the cautious road, identifying one of the Madden points (Bird and Cooke 1978: fig. 2-a) as a Clovis-like specimen (in this case, a waisted Clovis). But the remaining are neither Clovis, Fishtail, nor EIBA. The majority of Madden Lake bifaces belong, from a morphological point of view, to a distinctive type exhibiting tapered stems, slightly convex edge blades, and rounded shoulders. Yet there is no agreement in defining a different type, because differences have been accorded a minor role in interpretation.

The situation is even more extreme regarding fluted Restrepo points, of which there are a handful of examples, limited to Colombia. Although they may well date to the late Pleistocene, they have nearly all come from the surface. The only specimen found in excavation, at Cueva de los Murciélagos (Correal 1983), in the Gulf of Urabá, had no cultural or chronometric associations. Paiján points from the coast of Peru belong to the late Pleistocene (Chauchat 1975) but have been found only on the surface in the Magdalena Valley (López 1999). Yet, as is the case with El Jobo and Fishtail points, we do not know whether they can be surely identified with Paiján, because identification has been based on gross morphology.

Thus, there is inadequate spatiotemporal resolution and ontology for tracing the chrono-topological extension of early projectile point/knife styles in the subcontinent. This situation makes the drawing of conclusions regarding cultural affiliation difficult to impossible. In this regard, it is illustrative to note that Anthony Ranere and Cooke (1996: 71) proposed that a late Paleoindian deme "occupied the tropical forests that stretched from Chiapas through Central America and down the Andes to Ecuador (but excluding the eastern Andes of Colombia)." This latter exclusion is attributable to the fact that Abriense assemblages, clearly belonging to the terminal Pleistocene, pose an uncomfortable reality: a simple, unifacial technology does not fit the bifacial idea of mobile colonizing hunters. Thus, data from northern South America are inconclusive regarding decreasing spatial extension of stylistic horizons from late Pleistocene times onward.

Quite another picture emerges, however, if we consider stylistic differentiation,[9] which is evident in the area by at least 11,000 BP; bifacially flaked, elongated El Jobo points, and unifacial, simple Abriense artifacts are securely dated to this time period. Other assemblages—including Fishtail, Madden, Paiján, fluted Restrepo, and Broad Stemmed points—likewise may well date to this time period or slightly later. Even Clovis-like points (figure 5.2B) were found in the Paraguaná peninsula of Venezuela (Jaimes 1999), but little is known about them. In some assemblages, grinding tools may have been prominent; their presence in San Isidro is well documented (Gnecco and Mora 1997).

To this inconclusive evidence of pancontinental styles we must add the interpretation about early territoriality, which can be deduced through several lines of evidence at San Isidro. The degrees of curation (*sensu* Shott 1996) of a lithic assemblage are informative of mobility: high mobility demands high curation. Highly curated assemblages (that is, assemblages with artifacts that are abandoned only when their potential utility has been realized) have been explained with three basic arguments: (1) transporting of artifacts between sites in anticipation of their continued use (Binford 1977), (2) time budgeting (Torrence 1983), and (3) limitations in raw material availability (Bamforth 1986) owing to absolute scarcity or to cultural behaviors restricting access to the sources. Douglas Bamforth (1986: 39) identified four variables of tool manufacture and use that have been associated with curation: portability, versatility, reshaping, and recycling. Those variables can be examined in the lithic assemblage from San Isidro to determine its degree of curation. Although portability is a relative criterion, a weight below 20 grams and a size of less than 10 centimeters in the maximum dimension can be used as the limit between portability and nonportability (that is, between portable and not-as-portable). Those figures seem adequate for the hunter-gatherers at issue, that is, those with no animal or vehicular transportation.

Most of the tools from San Isidro do not exceed 10 centimeters in their longest dimension, and few tools weigh more than 10 grams. The tools exceeding these parameters (grinding and knapping tools) could not have fulfilled their role weighing less—and, therefore, measuring less—than they do. Moreover, their use must have occurred in specific locations (as in the places where plant material needing processing was collected or where raw material was knapped). Thus, that they were transported from place to place is very unlikely. Evidence of versatility comes from multifunctional tools (4.2 percent of the sum total of artifacts). The generalized morphology of these specimens permits their use in at least two different functions, with some tools capable of being used in three or more functions. Some bifaces were also used in more than one function. Although their form suggests that they were used as projectiles, use-wear analysis revealed that some were used for butchering and scraping. In the San Isidro assemblage, the percentages of rejuvenation and recycling are modest: only three broken bifaces were recycled, while rejuvenation could be determined in only one biface (rejuvenated while still hafted) and perhaps in five retouched but unused tools. Other possible evidence of rejuvenation—abrupt and invasive retouch—will be explored shortly. Thus, even excepting the always-problematic variable of portability, the results indicate low curation.

One implication of Bamforth's (1986) idea on the relationship between high curation and raw material scarcity is obvious: artifacts made of scarce materials would be more curated than artifacts made of abundant materials. To facilitate evaluation of this implication, the assemblage from San Isidro was discriminated by raw materials—scarce (obsidian) and abundant (chert)—according to the criteria of versatility, recycling, and retouch; the latter was taken to represent the degree of reshaping and was divided into three analytical categories (unretouched, marginal retouch, and invasive retouch). No clear segregation in raw materials was identified: artifacts made with chert and obsidian (the most popular raw materials used at the site) experienced a similar degree of curation. But this is true only in absolute terms; considered in relative terms, the relation in the San Isidro assemblage between obsidian and chert artifacts is 1:10, and when the relations between the variables are analyzed, yielding 1:3 for versatility and 1:2.4 for recycling, these ratios indicate that the artifacts made with obsidian were more curated than those made with chert. Thus, although the degree of curation in the assemblage is low, the artifacts made with the scarce raw material experienced higher curation. To this distinction we must add that the use of obsidian was maximized, a fact evident in the relationship between artifacts and debris (1:74 for obsidian tools and 1:49 for chert tools) and in the size of debitage (only 5 percent of the debitage is more than 1 centimeter in length), in which case the use of chert was clearly wasteful. Regarding diversity, the analysis of the ethnographic record of hunter-gatherers (Shott 1986: 20–27) indicates that as mobility diminishes, diversity in tool function increases. Thus, a high diversity in tool function in the San Isidro assemblage, coupled with low curation and higher curation of scarce materials, suggests a situation of restricted mobility and territoriality.

Raw material procurement also suggests territoriality. Data from northern South America (table 5.2) show reliance on local sources. The use of sources

Table 5.2. Provenience of Raw Material in Late Pleistocene Sites from Northern South America

Site	Local raw material (%)	Nonlocal raw material (%)
Taima-Taima	100	
El Vano	100	
El Abra	99	1
Tibitó	99	1
Tequendama	99	1
Sueva	100	
Sauzalito	100	
San Isidro	100	
Peña Roja	100	
El Inga	100	
OGSE-80	100	
OGSE-201	100	
Cubilán	100	

that are extremely difficult to locate, such as very small buried obsidian flows in the valley of Popayán in southwestern Colombia, demonstrates a detailed knowledge of territory. Raw material was divided into the categories of local (sources located within a radius of 50 kilometers from the site) and foreign (sources outside the 50-kilometer radius).[10] The results point to use of predominantly local raw materials. A good example of how local raw material dominated tool manufacture can be seen in the case for two stemmed points found in surface deposits at La Elvira in Colombia (Gnecco 2000) and at Imbabura in Ecuador (Mayer-Oakes 1986b: 4–6) some 400 kilometers to the south. These presumed late Pleistocene–age bifaces (large specimens about 18 centimeters long) are virtually identical, sharing not only the same form but also technological features such as platform preparation. Both were manufactured with high-quality obsidian, yet both were made with obsidian procured in local sources as determined by neutron activation analysis (Gnecco 2000).

From the point of view of territoriality, the emergence of agrilocalities appears, alternatively, as its consequence and as its cause: as its consequence because restricted mobility and the development of territoriality would have forced agrilocalities into existence through pressure on the resource base, and as its cause because certain social demands, such as intra- and interpolity competition, could have required strategies to maximize resources beyond their natural productivity, resulting in zonal settlements that made previous mobility patterns obsolete. Territoriality and its associated aspects (for example, social competition and the emergence of alternative strategies of occupation), the exploitation of focal resources (as along the southern coast of Peru [Keefer et al. 1998; Sandweiss et al. 1998], in San Isidro [Mora and Gnecco 2003], and in Peña Roja [Mora 2003]), and the alteration and manipulation of vegetal and animal resources may have occurred from the very beginning of initial colonization and occupation and not as an incidental result of the crisis of previous patterns. Thus, the early hunter-gatherers in northern South America may have been moving in a highly occupied space: a humanized space. Archaeological evidence from northern South America shows that as early as 11,000 years ago, the first colonists were humanizing the landscape through their actions on the environment. Humans, plants, and animals were transformed through the process of coevolution. The early colonists gave territorial meaning to a landscape they intimately knew. While some locations, raw materials, plants, and animals were favored, others were not. Over the long term, coevolutionary trends produced nonreversible changes. The evolution of neotropical ecosystems thus resulted from ecological and historical relationships between human beings and the space they peopled with symbolic meaning.

Notes

1. There are problems with the stratigraphic integrity of two of the most publicized sites: El Inga (Bell 1965; Mayer-Oakes 1986b) and Chobshi (Lynch and Pollock 1981). Although El Inga has been treated as Paleoindian because of the presence of fluted and nonfluted Fishtail points among a varied tool inventory (which includes other types of fluted bifaces), considerable mixing of the deposits is evident there (compare Bell 1977), and no secure Pleistocene dating has ever been obtained. The shallow deposits of Chobshi Cave in the Andes south of Quito were mixed (Lynch and Pollock 1981: 97). Therefore, the only Pleistocene date of 10,010 BP cannot be securely associated to a human event. The pre–Las Vegas evidence (OGSE-80), dated to shortly before 10,000 BP, is so meager as to have been labeled by its excavator as "an unknown culture" (Stothert 1988: 58).

2. In the area currently grow the wild species *S. hirtum* and *S. mammosum* (Pérez 1956: 710). The genus *Passiflora* comprises a large number of widely distributed species, such as *P. mollisima, P. vitofolia, P. pinnatistipula*, and *P. quadrangularis* (Pérez 1956: 614).

3. One of the principal cultivars in the tropics today, *D. trifida*, belongs to this genus; other edible species are *D. convolvulacea, D. dodecaneura*, and *D. trifoliata* (Piperno and Pearsall 1998: 117).

4. Bitter manioc (*M. mollisima*), which belongs to the genus *Manihot*, is (along with palms) one of the most important economic resources in the tropics.

5. To this genus belongs *mafafa*, a starch-rich tuber widely consumed by many groups in the frontier lands of northern South America.

6. "Coevolution is an evolutionary process in which the establishment of a symbiotic relationship between organisms, increasing the fitness of all involved, brings about changes in the traits of the organisms" (Rindos 1984: 99).

7. The hundreds of fragments and complete pieces found in the Falcón and Lara

states have no homogeneous form, nor were they made using the same technology: some are bipointed, others have rounded bases, others are almost cylindrical or flat, others are lanceolate, and others have proximal projections.

8. At El Vano, also in northwestern Venezuela, Jaimes (1999) dated El Jobo bifaces to circa 11,000 BP.

9. By stylistic differentiation we mean the differences lying in all aspects of the continuum from raw material procurement to abandonment of artifacts.

10. The figure of 50 kilometers (assuming that the site is located at one end of the territory) produces an area of 2,500 square kilometers, similar to or larger than those known ethnographically (see Kelly 1995: 112–15).

6

Fluted and Fishtail Points from Southern Coastal Chile

New Evidence Suggesting Clovis- and Folsom-Related Occupations in Southernmost South America

LAWRENCE J. JACKSON

Junius Bird's early work at Fell's Cave in Chile drew the world's attention to the presence of Early Paleoindian peoples in southernmost South America. The site produced a convincing association of deep stratified deposits and distinctive lanceolate projectile points, known as "Fishtails," later ^{14}C-dated by Bird to the same period as North American Paleoindian sites. However, the fluting of South American Fishtails has always been something of an enigma, with the absence of true fluted points indicating the possibility of a completely different South American Paleoindian sequence. Careful attention to the ^{14}C dating of Fell's Cave and Fell's Cave–type Fishtails at other sites in Chile and Argentina strongly suggests an age range of about 10,200 BP to 10,800 BP, with an average age of about 10,500 BP, coeval with the Folsom complex of North America (Taylor et al. 1996). Surface finds of true fluted points with clear Clovis morphological affinities from a growing number of sites in southern coastal Chile reinforce the suggestion that we are only now beginning to see the earliest evidence for Paleoindian occupancy of South America and that Fishtails may represent a unique late development from a Clovis-like culture base.

Bird's work at Fell's Cave in 1936 and 1937 in southern Chile established the presence of Early Paleoindian peoples in southernmost South America. This was a remarkable accomplishment at a time when Clovis and Folsom sites had only recently been discovered in the North American Southwest and were beginning to be identified east of the Mississippi (see Roberts 1940; Shetrone 1936). Characterized by "Fishtail" fluted points, rather than the true fluted points of North America (see Morrow and Morrow 1999), the early South American site of Fell's Cave provided convincing evidence of an early occupation that was later securely ^{14}C-dated.

In the six decades since Bird's pioneering research, Fishtail fluted points— also known as Fell's Cave I or Fell's Cave Stemmed—have been documented in a scattered distribution throughout Central America and Andean South America from Ecuador to southern Chile and neighboring Argentina (Bird 1938a, 1938b, 1969; Bird and Cooke 1978; Flegenheimer 1987; Mayer-Oakes 1986b; Nami 1987; Snarskis 1979). Best known from a handful of excavated South American sites, such as Fell's Cave in Chile (Bird 1988a) and El Inga in Ecuador (Mayer-Oakes 1986b), Fishtail points have now also been recorded in a number of stratified and ^{14}C-dated sites in Argentina and Chile. Important new sites include Cerro la China (Flegenheimer 1987), Cueva del Medio (Nami 1987), Piedra Museo (Miotti 1995), Tres Arroyos (Massone 1987), and Cueva del Lago Sofia (Prieto 1991)—all in southern Chile and Argentina.

Deliberately fluted points are made primarily on bifacial preforms with relatively wide bases and narrow parallel-sided blades. They are distinctly different from Fishtail points with facially thinned, broad blades and slender stems made largely on flakes. Fishtail points have been found in every Central American country, including Belize, Costa Rica, Guatemala, Honduras, Mexico, and Panama (Aschmann 1952; Bird and Cooke 1978; Coe 1960; Hester et al. 1981; Snarskis 1979). Their distribution overlaps significantly with that of Fishtail fluted points and Fishtail variants such as those from Madden Lake in Panama. This distributional overlap implies that distinct cultural entities may be represented. The general scarcity of true fluted points in South America, however, is puzzling. Although William Mayer-Oakes does present a few examples from El Inga, the rest of South America has been markedly lacking in examples of fluted points, suggesting the possibility of a regional isocline beyond which true fluted points do not occur. However, one of the most vexing problems in South American archaeology is the vast geographical area represented and the relative scarcity of well-excavated Paleoindian sites or even published surface finds. Some recent developments suggest that this may well be a major impediment to understanding the Paleoindian record.

The chronology of South American Paleoindian cultures is immensely important in understanding Paleoindian origins and dispersal in the New World. Publication of a stone, bone, and wood artifact assemblage from the MV-II layer at the Monte Verde site in Chile is associated with ^{14}C dates ranging from 11,790 ± 200 to 13,565 ± 250 (Dillehay and Pino 1997: 44, table 3.1; see also Fiedel, this volume) yet begs the question of Clovis origins and relationships with Fishtail assemblages fully 2,000 years later (Bird 1988a; Dillehay 1997a; Lynch 1990). The temporal position of unfluted, parallel-flaked, lanceolate points (in many morphological respects comparable to Late Paleoindian projectiles in North America) is also largely unresolved.

Well-defined regional sequences for late Pleistocene and early Holocene point types are rare in South America. We must rely on a handful of well-dated South American sites (only a few with stratified deposits) and the distribution of typologically identical points to establish the general framework of Paleo-indian culture history. The vague definition, yet remarkably broad geographic and age distribution, of El Jobo lanceolate points in South America is a good example of this problem. El Jobo lanceolate points have been assigned ages ranging from as early as 17,000 BP to as recent as 10,000 BP in diverse Central and South American contexts (see Bryan 1991). Use of the type as a cultural and temporal marker is almost impossible since there is no formal definition comprehensively documenting its attributes and range of variability (Jackson 1999).

Gordon Willey (1971) observed that Bird's ^{14}C dates for Fell's Cave placed Fishtail points in the Straits of Magellan at about 11,000 BP—coeval with North American Paleoindian occupations. Although the stratified Fell's Cave deposits have yielded a broad range of dates, there has been a tendency to assume that this is a Clovis-age phenomenon and, further, since Clovis-like materials were absent from the deposits, that this is a uniquely divergent South American Early Paleoindian development.

Recent evidence from coastal Chile (see L. Jackson 1995; Jackson and Massone n.d.) brings the issue of typology and age into clearer focus when North American Paleoindian materials are used for comparison. Following discussion of the ^{14}C dating of Fell's Cave components in South America, I will present multiple surface finds of apparent true fluted points and explore their possible cultural implications.

Fishtail Points and Radiocarbon Dates

Bird's work provided several uncalibrated ^{14}C dates for the Fell's Cave Fishtail deposits. These include a date of 11,000 ± 170 BP on a Layer 20 hearth, 10,770 ± 300 BP on a Layer 19 hearth, and 10,080 ± 160 BP on Layer 18 (Bird 1988a). A span of 1,000 ^{14}C years is suggested, from about 11,000 to 10,000 BP. However, if Fishtail points are a single technological tradition, a one-millennium span is larger than is currently known for any other Paleoindian-period point type. Critical evaluation of these statistical estimations is needed.

Statistician Albert Spaulding used a very simple procedure to assign proportionately higher values to dates with less variance (Spaulding, personal communication 1985; see Jackson 1986 for formulae and details of application). When his method is used, the three Fell's Cave dates actually average about 10,539 ± 220 BP—coeval with early Folsom in the American Southwest. Ervin Taylor and colleagues (1996) tabulated reliable Clovis and Folsom dates in North America and concluded that Clovis is, in fact, chronologically distinct from Folsom, with an apparent hundred-year separation between the latest Clovis and the earliest Folsom dates. Using Spaulding's method, these reliable dates have a weighted average of 11,209 ± 218 BP for Clovis and 10,654 ± 225 BP for Folsom.

In southern South America, ^{14}C dates for Fell's Cave Fishtail components are available from seven sites—Fell's Cave, Palli Aike Cave, Cueva del Medio, and Tres Arroyos in Chile and Cerro la China, Cueva del Lago Sofia, and Piedra Museo in Argentina. Bird (1988a) recorded three dates from Fell's Cave (discussed above) and one date of 8639 ± 450 BP from Palli Aike Cave—a date he regarded as too young. Mauricio Massone (1987) recorded three dates from Tres Arroyos, ranging from 10,280 to 11,880 BP, with variance of 110 years on the former and 250 years on the latter date. The site of Cueva del Medio provides a large series of dates, recorded by Hugo Nami (1994) and Nami and Toshio Nakamura (1995), with a broad range from 9595 to 12,290 BP and variances ranging from 70 to 250 years. The largest variances tend to be associated with the earliest dates, such as 11,040 ± 250 BP. From Piedra Museo, Laura Miotti (1995) recorded a date of 10,400 ± 80 BP (Component 2), and Miotti and Gabriela Cattáneo (1997) recorded a date of 12,890 ± 90 (Component 1). Miotti and Monica Salemme (2004: 180) have reported new dates on two separate components: Component 1 provides four new dates, ranging from 10,390 ± 70 to 11,000 ± 65 (see table 6.1); Component 2 provides three new dates, ranging from 9230 ± 105 to 10,400 ± 80. Alfredo Prieto (1991) notes two early dates of 11,570 ± 60 BP and 12,990 ± 241 BP from Cueva del Lago Sofia, as well as four dates ranging from 10,020 to 10,840 BP. Nora Flegenheimer (1986) recorded a series of dates from Cerro la China I, II, and III that range from 10,430 to 11,285 BP, with variances of 75 to 180 years. This sample of fifty-four ^{14}C dates is useful for estimating the span and average age of Fishtail fluted point occupations in Chile and Argentina.

Radiocarbon dates are imprecise because there are a number of problems with both statistical estimation and ^{14}C time scales (Hajdas et al. 1995a; Lotter 1991). A simple graph plot of the one-sigma ages offers another perspective (figure 6.1). Of the fifty-four dates plotted, thirty-two (59.2 percent) are between 10,000 and 11,000 BP at the one-sigma level. One-sigma ranges for twenty dates (37 percent) are between 10,200 and 10,800 BP; two (3.7 percent) are between 10,800 and 11,000 BP; five (9.2 percent), including Palli Aike, are less than 10,000 BP; and seven (12.9 percent) are entirely above 11,000 BP. The majority of dates lie between 10,200 and 11,000 BP (thirty-four out of fifty-four dates, or 62.9 percent), with a few outliers younger than 10,200 and older than 11,000 BP.

Two pieces of stratigraphic evidence from Fell's Cave also help bracket the maximum possible age range. A date of 11,000 BP for the lowest Fell's Cave level suggests a maximum age, because the only associated Fishtail point was found on the surface of the level. Similarly, a date of 10,080 BP for an upper

Table 6.1. Radiocarbon Dates on Fell's Cave Components

Site	Lab number	Technique	Date	Source
Fell's Cave	I-5146		10,080±160	Bird 1988a
	W-915		10,720±300	
	I-3988		11,000±170	
Cueva del Medio	PITT-0244	Standard	9595±115	Nami 1994, 1996b, 1997;
	Beta-40281	Standard	9770±70	Nami and Nakamura 1995
	Gr-N 14913	Standard	10,310±70	
	Beta-52105	Standard	10,350±130	
	Beta-52522	Standard	10,430±80	
	NUTA-1734	AMS	10,430±100	
	NUTA-1735	AMS	10,450±100	
	Gr-N 14911	Standard	10,550±120	
	NUTA-1811	AMS	10,710±100	
	NUTA-2332	AMS	10,710±190	
	NUTA-1812	AMS	10,850±130	
	Unknown	AMS	10,860±160	
	NUTA-2330	AMS	10,960±150	
	Beta-39081	Standard	10,930±230	
	NUTA-1737	AMS	11,120±130	
	NUTA-2197	AMS	11,040±250	
	PITT-0343	Standard	12,290±180	
Tres Arroyos	Dic 2732		10,280±110	Massone 1983, 1987, 2003;
	Dic 2733		10,420±100	Massone et al. 1998
	Beta 20219		11,880±250	
	Beta 101023		10,600±90	
	Beta 113171		10,580±50	
	OxA-9245		10,575±65	
	OxA-9246		10,630±70	
	OxA-9247		10,685±70	
	OxA-9666		10,130±210	
	OxA-9248		11,085±70	
Piedra Museo Component 1	AA-20125	AMS	12,890±90	Miotti 1995;
	AA-27950		11,000±65	Miotti and Cattáneo 1997;
	OxA-8528		10,925±65	Miotti and Salemme 1999;
	OxA-8527		10,390±70	Miotti and Salemme 2004
	OxA-9249		10,400±80	
	AA-8428	AMS	10,470±65	
Component 2	GRA9837		9710±105	
	LP 859		9230±105	
	LP 949		12,900 ±105	
Cueva del Lago	PITT-0684		11,570±60	Prieto 1991
Sofia	OxA-8635		10,710±70	Borrero 1999
	OxA-0319		10,780±60	
	OxA-9504		10,310±160	
	OxA-9505		10,140±120	
	PITT-0939		12,990±241	
Palli Aike	C-485		8639±450	Bird 1951
Cerro la China I	AA-8954		10,525±75	Flegenheimer 1987;
	AA-8952		10,745±75	Flegenheimer
	AA-8953		10,804±75	and Zarate 1997
	I-12741		10,730±150	
	AA-1327	AMS	10,790±120	
Cerro la China II	AA-8956		10,560±75	Flegenheimer
	AA-8955		11,150±135	and Zarate 1997
Cerro la China III	AA-1328		10,610±180	Nami 1996b; Flegenheimer and Zarate 1997

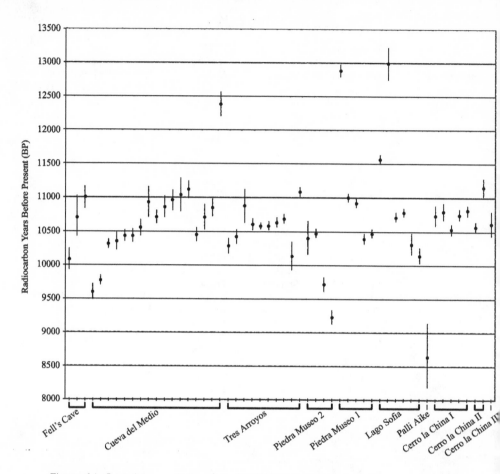

Figure 6.1. One-sigma variance plot of Fishtail component dates from seven sites in southernmost South America (data derived from table 6.1).

transitional level is associated with a shift in projectile point form and suggests a minimum age. Overall, ^{14}C evidence for Fishtail components strongly suggests that this is not a Clovis-age phenomenon. A majority of dates support an age range between 10,200 and 10,800 BP. Large variances with some of the dates between 10,800 and 11,000 BP may indicate a skewed statistical effect or a second subset of early dates.

Fell's Cave Stratigraphy and Dating

One of the reasons for regarding Fell's Cave as an 11,000 BP site is that Bird believed his 10,720 BP date to be more than 11,000 years old, because the 5,568-year half-life was used. However, despite a corrected 5,730-year half-life standard, most ^{14}C laboratories still use the 5,568-year half-life as a matter of convention (Murray Tamers, personal communication 1997). Consequently, Bird's dates can be evaluated in the context of other Fell's component dates. A second reason to regard the Fell's Cave Fishtail component as dating to 11,000 BP is the apparent lack of any known Clovis antecedents in the area. (This supposition is addressed in the final section of this chapter.) A third reason to regard Fell's as a Clovis-age site is the association of the lowest cave levels with extinct fauna, notably ground sloth and native American horse. However, there are reasons to question some of these associations and to consider the more abundant and clear associations with guanaco, which survived the terminal Pleistocene and was more significant to Paleoindian peoples (Jackson 1989; see chapters by Borrero and by Johnson and colleagues in this volume).

Subsequent excavations of Fell's Cave by Henri and Annette Emperaire revealed a somewhat different picture than that suggested by Bird's excavations (Emperaire et al. 1963). Bird had grouped fine stratigraphic layers into general divisions in a successful attempt to develop a regional cultural chronology. The Emperaires' excavations revealed that the deepest cave layers were culturally sterile but had associated extinct fauna. Careful examination of the results of both excavations shows that extinct fauna occurred well out of context in upper cave layers as well. They are found in Bird's Layer 17 with a radiocarbon date of 9030 ± 230 BP. Bird also noted that some horse bones in the cave were still articulated, suggesting natural death. Evidence of the butchering of horse and ground sloth is actually quite limited; many bones show carnivore modification (see Borrero, this volume). Evidence of guanaco butchering was much more extensive and convincing in the early levels. Bird also described how the Paleoindian hearths had been dug into earlier levels, suggesting the distinct possibility that some extinct fauna from deeper levels were accidentally introduced into hearths. Finally, John Fell noted in a communication to Bird that the Emperaires' excavations revealed a stratigraphic profile in which a fire had burned down through all the layers, suggesting an alternative explanation to human consumption for at least some of the extinct fauna (Jackson 1989).

Even if the association of a Fell's Cave component at 11,000 BP with extinct fauna is accepted without question, there are other reasons to question such an early age for Fishtail points. Most significant is the absence of Fishtail points from the deepest layer, Layer 20. Layers 18 and 19 were quite clearly associated with Fishtail points. However, only one such point was found on the surface of Layer 20 (the 11,000 BP level of the cave). An alternative explanation is that there may well have been a Clovis-age occupation of Fell's Cave and that it is not associated with Fishtail points. During Bird's excavations, a bone "flaker" was recovered in the lowest stratum of Bird's generalized Level 5, which is most likely associated with Layer 20. This tool resembles bone "foreshafts" recovered from North American Clovis sites and raises the distinct possibility of a Clovis-age cave occupation by people who used bone points and foreshafts and left no fluted or Fishtail stone points. A similar bone tool is reported from the deepest levels of Cueva del Medio (Nami 1987).

Fishtail Points and Fluting

Another reason to question a very early age (that is, older than 11,000 BP) for Fell's Cave Fishtails is the nature of the fluting on these stone points. One of the most diagnostic features of the true fluted point is the channel flake, created by the removal of a longitudinal flake struck from the base of a point using a prepared striking platform. Channel flakes, the by-product of this removal, are ubiquitous at most North American fluted point sites where there are activity areas of biface production. However, channel flakes, with their distinctive isolated and ground basal platforms, are not reported from Fell's Cave or any other Fishtail point site in southern South America (Jackson 1989). Although no channel flakes are reported from El Inga, bifacial preforms with prepared basal platforms, or nipples, are present (William Mayer-Oakes, personal communication 1997). The only reason for the preparation of such platforms is to allow fluting of the bifaces by the removal of channel flakes. Thus, detailed examination of El Inga debitage might actually produce this missing evidence.

Why are channel flakes absent in South America? The fact that these highly diagnostic parallel-sided by-products of fluting are missing from South American assemblages could be attributable to recovery methods or simply to their not being recognized by archaeologists. Sites where fluted points were manufactured—where channel flakes would be recovered—are scarce in the South American record. My examination of the Fell's Cave collections at the American Museum of Natural History did not reveal any channel flakes. A majority of Fishtail or Fell's Cave–type fluted points do not show typical fluting, but rather large areas of facial thinning, often at an angle to the base. Excellent examples of basal thinning and fluting variability, as well as effects of resharpening, are provided by a series of complete points from Fell's Cave (figure 6.2).

How do we define fluting, and does it identify a Paleoindian culture marker? Chris Ellis and Brian Deller (1988) describe the specialized pressure flaking required to prepare a fluted preform base from an isolated central platform. This isolated area is ground and bevelled before being struck, and a longitudinal channel flake (or flakes) is removed from one or both faces of the preform. Careful examination of Fell's Cave Fishtails typically reveals large facial flakes removed for facial thinning at various oblique angles, rather than centered longitudinal fluting. Since retouch of marginal areas tends to preserve a channelled appearance in the facially thinned areas near the point base, we might

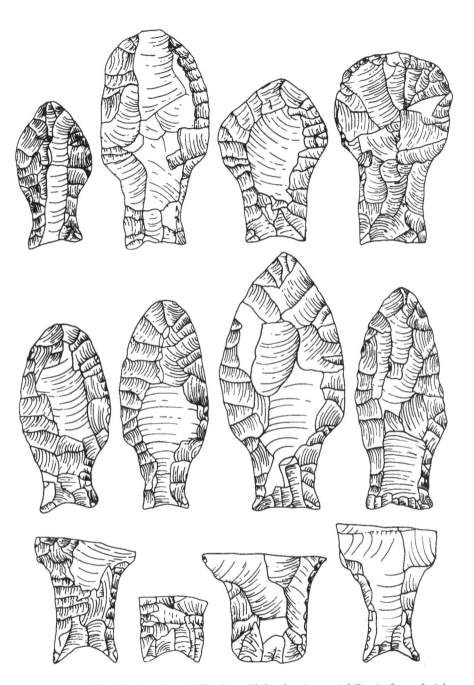

Figure 6.2. Fishtail points from Fell's Cave, Chile, showing variability in form, facial flaking, and fluting (redrawn by J. E. Morrow from sketches made by L. Jackson from specimens in American Museum of Natural History, New York, 1989).

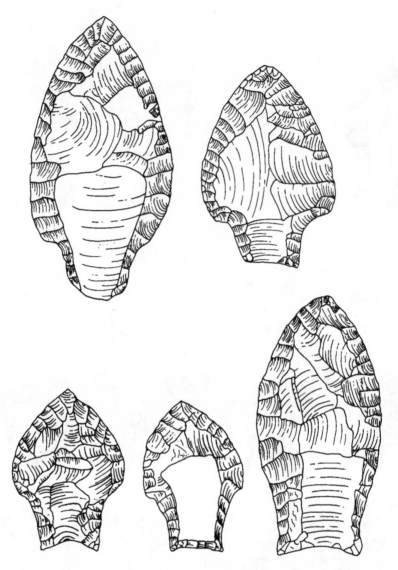

Figure 6.3. Fishtail and fluted points from Madden Lake, Panama (redrawn by J. E. Morrow from sketches made by L. Jackson from specimens in American Museum of Natural History, New York, 1989).

infer stylistic or functional adherence to a fluted appearance even if the technological basis differs. Although not all researchers agree on the intentionality of fluting on Fishtail points, the technology of Fishtail point production quite clearly differs markedly in this respect from North American fluted points (Morrow and Morrow 1999; Nami 1997). Overall point morphology and metrics are also different. Fishtail points tend to have very broad, excurvate blades, while North American fluted points are narrower and more parallel sided. Fishtail bases are also much narrower below the blade (stemmed), are delicately incurvate along the stem margins, and often are markedly concave.

A further complication is that, even allowing for morphological changes attributable to the resharpening of many specimens, several varieties of Fell's Cave Fishtail points exist. Terms such as Fell's Cave Type 1 and Type 2 (Nami 1987) are commonly used to specify particular types of Fishtail points. In parts of Central America, such as Madden Lake in Panama, variability is so pronounced as to suggest that many examples are not even correctly classified as Fishtails (figure 6.3). If Fishtail points persisted over a period of six hundred or more years, as suggested by radiocarbon chronology, then technological changes and style drift should be expected. We should be looking for such changes at stratified sites.

The lumping of fine stratigraphic levels at Fell's Cave into Bird's generalized "Layer V" has likely obscured aspects of morphological change in this point type. Considerable variability in the Fishtail points recovered from the site exists, and undoubtedly a temporal progression of small changes in discrete and continuous variables could be tracked. The obsidian quarry site of El Inga shows enormous variability in the types of Fishtails and other points present, from characteristic Fell's Cave Fishtails to more traditional fluted specimens, but good radiocarbon-dated sequences are lacking (Mayer-Oakes 1986b). More promising are some of the newly discovered stratified cave sites in Chile and Argentina, which have yielded reliable radiocarbon dates.

Technological comparisons suggest both intriguing similarities and differences between North and South American Paleoindian traditions. However, comparisons are severely limited because of the scarcity of nonquarry, bifacial tool production sites in South America (which would give important clues to technological production sequences) and the highly curated and reworked nature of much of the extant South American Fishtail fluted material.

True Fluted Points in South America

Although some may disagree with use of a term such as *true fluted point*, this distinction has validity in South America for differentiating between "Fishtail fluted" points that do not appear to share the distinctive North American

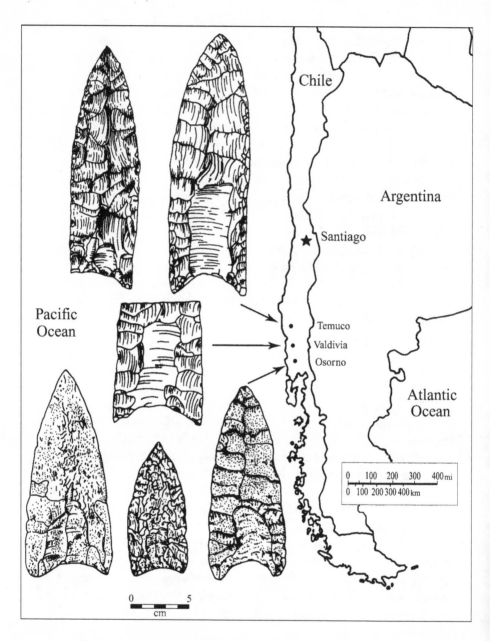

Figure 6.4. Clovis-like fluted points from southern coastal Chile (redrawn from illustrations in Jackson and Massone, n.d. [*top row*]; Jackson 1995 [*middle row*]; Seguel and Campana 1975 [*bottom row*]). Scale: 5 mm = 1 cm.

technological tradition of fluting and specimens that more closely resemble those from North American Clovis sites. Fluting alone does not necessarily define the Early Paleoindian tradition. Douglas Bamforth (1991) has noted, for instance, that up to 30 percent of points on Great Plains Folsom sites are unfluted. In conjunction with other morphological and metric traits, however, fluting does help identify most Clovis and Folsom sites. One observation that may be important in understanding the position of Fishtails in South American cultural sequences is that, although finds of Clovis-like points are reported at sites such as El Inga, Folsom-like points (other than Fishtails) are not.

A rapidly increasing body of South American evidence suggests the broad presence of a Clovis-like fluted point tradition. Although dated or stratified sites with such specimens are, so far, scarce, a strong body of data from deflated surface sites should be given very close attention. This discussion is restricted to a small number of Clovis-like fluted points recorded from coastal Chile in southern South America (figure 6.4).

Zulema Seguel and Orlando Campana (1975) record three distinctive Clovis-like points with parallel flaking, concave bases, and short flute scars. Found in the provinces of Osorno and Valdivia, these specimens are in periglacial zones frequented by late Pleistocene mastodon and other fauna. Two of the points are from the Nochaco site in Osorno province, excavated by Jorge Silva in 1960 and 1962. The third point is from a glaciofluvial terrace of the Pilmaiquen River (5 kilometers from Trumao). The three lanceolate points are made of basalt, obsidian, and a siliceous material (*silex* in Spanish). The authors note that the river terrace is connected to a series of fossil lagoons. They suggest that these sites fill a major gap in knowledge of cordilleran population movements, linking Tagua-Tagua in the north and the southern sites of Patagonia.

An obsidian projectile point with Clovis affinities was collected by Americo Gordon in the Puerto Saavedra region of coastal Chile many years ago. Casts of this specimen made by Bird are curated with the American Museum of Natural History in New York and with the Chilean Museum in Santiago (John Hyslop, personal communication 1988; Fransisco Mena, personal communication 1995). I recorded key measurements and attributes on this specimen and reported it as a good Clovis analog (L. Jackson 1995). This is a surface find, but an intriguing aspect is that the coastal area in which it occurs is one of fossil lagoons and relict lakes. The find location is not far from Lago del Budi, where mastodon remains have also been found (Oliver 1935). The Puerto Saavedra point is parallel sided, has a very distinct and centered longitudinal flute on each face, and has basal finishing typical of Clovis in the Great Lakes region (see Roosa 1965).

The Puerto Saavedra point is clearly different from Fishtail points and from Folsom, except for its pronounced basal concavity (which is also a common Clovis trait). Its location on the southern Pacific coast of Chile raises intriguing questions about coastal migration. Around Lago del Budi, the landscape is comparable to the Clovis-age playas of the North American Southwest and periglacial pondings associated with Gainey phase fluted point sites in the Great Lakes region.

In Jackson and Massone n.d., another new Clovis-like point from Arauco province in Chile is recorded. Parallel sided and concave based, this surface-collected basalt specimen has short, but distinctive, flute channels (which are common to Clovis); it was found in 1995, 7 kilometers southwest of the city of Canete near the Reputo River. The authors record key measurements and attributes that suggest close similarity to Clovis. (Illustrations of all of the above-described specimens are provided in Jackson and Massone n.d. and in figure 6.4.)

Quite clearly, there are coastal Chilean sites that provide evidence of Clovis-like fluted specimens and that are almost certainly Paleoindian in age. None of these sites, however, has been shown by excavation to be a Paleoindian habitation or kill site. However, such sites must surely exist, and I predict that a strong Clovis-age Paleoindian occupation will soon be documented in coastal Chile. Indeed, while I was writing this paper, Howard Bowe and Persis Clarkson (personal communication 2002) forwarded illustrations of recently discovered concave-based lanceolate points with apparent fluting from the northern Chilean altiplano. Additionally, they included a photo of a nicely fashioned spurred trianguloid end scraper—quite typical of Paleoindian assemblages in North America.

Since no known later culture in southern South America has produced fluted points, we might quite reasonably assume that a Clovis-age culture is represented by the fluted, non-Fishtail specimens found in coastal areas. The dating of Fishtails only as early as perhaps 11,000 BP further suggests that these Clovis-like specimens can only predate them, since none has been found in the deposits that have produced Fishtails.

What is the relationship of presumably early Clovis-like specimens to Fell's Cave Fishtails? Clovis-like points must predate a Folsom-age phenomenon, since the notion of Fishtails appearing suddenly in southernmost South America at 10,800 BP or 11,000 BP begs the question of the preceding 500 or 600 years of known Clovis development elsewhere. A Clovis-age presence might also be inferred from the very existence of even earlier south Chilean sites, such as Monte Verde, which supposedly represent occupations at 12,500 BP. The fluting variability of Fishtails, the absence thus far of Folsom-like fluted points in South America, and the principal dating of Fishtails circa 10,500 BP in the latest Pleistocene suggest a Middle Paleoindian phenomenon, which likely had a regional base in earlier Clovis-like technologies. As noted by Juliet Morrow and Toby Morrow (1999), about 700 radiocarbon years separate the earliest dates for North American Clovis from the earliest dates for South American Fishtails.

Summary and Overview

Acceptable radiocarbon dates for Fell's Cave Fishtail components at a number of sites in southern South America strongly suggest Folsom age-equivalence at about 10,500 BP. The consistent radiocarbon dating of Fell's Cave Fishtail points between about 10,200 and 10,800 BP appears to confirm a Middle Paleoindian phenomenon lasting about 600 years. The existence of some relatively late but not necessarily anomalous dates for Fishtail components suggests that style and cultural changes over time need to be examined within the Fishtail tradition. Different varieties of Fishtails are recognized, not only within regions but also at single sites, such as Fell's Cave Types 1 and 2.

Radiocarbon dates of 10,310 BP at Cueva del Medio and 10,080 BP for Layer 18 at Fell's Cave are reminiscent of late dates for Folsom at some sites in the American Southwest. Although variance values and sample uncertainty must always be considered when evaluating ^{14}C ages, both averaging of relatively large samples of dates and overlapping of one-sigma ranges for individual dates appear to confirm a Folsom-age phenomenon. A significant subset of Fishtail dates in the range of 10,800 to 11,000 BP may be attributable, in part, to statistical variance effects. The Fell's Cave stratigraphy clearly suggests that dates older than 11,000 BP are unlikely. Extremely old dates, such as those at Cueva del Lago Sofía, appear anomalous and probably do not accurately date Fishtail occupations.

New data, principally from coastal Chile (in the form of surface-collected Clovis-like fluted points), strongly suggest an antecedent cultural tradition dating to sometime earlier than 11,000 BP and overlapping in time with North American Clovis. Multiple sites and specimens, only recently recognized, provide clear evidence of a non-Fishtail fluted point occupation in southernmost South America. The presence of similar specimens at sites such as El Inga appears to support a broad Early Paleoindian culture base extending throughout Andean South America and is likely linked with similar Central American developments.

Much work will be needed to establish regional Paleoindian sequences in South America. More ^{14}C dates on Fell's Cave Fishtail components, excavation, and dating of sites with Clovis-like lithic assemblages, extensive regional surveys to establish site distributions for different cultural periods, and stratigraphic data to aid the development of projectile point seriation are all needed. A focus on the Early Paleoindian occupation of southernmost South America—specifically, coastal Chile—in the first decade of the twenty-first century will likely be extremely helpful in understanding how Paleoindian peoples arrived in South America, whether they had an antecedent regional culture base, and the impacts of terminal Pleistocene faunal extinctions and environmental change on Paleoindian peoples. Junius Bird did the pioneer work at Fell's Cave. It is our job, six decades later, to find the missing pieces of the puzzle.

III

Perspectives from the North

7

New Radiocarbon Dates for the Clovis Component of the Anzick Site, Park County, Montana

JULIET E. MORROW AND STUART J. FIEDEL

In this chapter we report and interpret three new high-precision ^{14}C dates on samples of antler and human bone from the Anzick site (24PA506), located near Wilsall, Montana. Anzick is the only known burial of the Clovis culture and thus is among the most important archaeological sites documenting the early settlement of continental North America. The new dates confirm that circa 13,000 cal BP, a Paleoindian infant was buried here with the largest assemblage of finely crafted, red ochre-covered Clovis stone and antler tools ever discovered.

Site Setting

The Anzick site (24PA506) is located in an intermontane basin just east of the Rocky Mountain front (figure 7.1). The burial site lies within the eroded talus slope of a Cretaceous-age rock outcrop (elevation at 5,160 feet above sea level), which is the most prominent topographic feature at the north end of the Shields basin. The Bridger Mountains to the west, the Belt Mountains to the north, and the Crazy Mountains to the east encircle the Shields basin. The Shields River, Flathead Creek, and numerous smaller drainages converge like the spokes of a wheel on the visually striking outcrop. Because of its high elevation and its central location within the valley at the nexus of several perennial waterways, this outcrop was probably an important landmark for Clovis people and later inhabitants of this region. According to local informants, post-Clovis remains in this area include a bison kill of indeterminate age, late precontact tipi rings, and historic Native American eagle traps.

History of Discovery and Archaeological Investigations

The Anzick Clovis burial was discovered accidentally in the spring of 1968 during mechanized removal of weathered sandstone/shale talus and fine-grained sediments from a north-facing outcrop (Taylor 1969). The excavators, Ben

Figure 7.1. Locations of selected Early Paleoindian sites mentioned in text: (1) Broken Mammoth; (2) East Wenatchee; (3) Anzick; (4) Indian Creek; (5) Simon; (6) Drake; (7) Blackwater Draw Locality 1; (8) Lehner; (9) Aubrey (glacial margins after Dyke, Moore, and Robertson 2002).

Hargis and Calvin Sarver, were mining the angular talus for use in a septic system drain field. Archaeologist Dee Taylor (1969) attempted to relocate the physical context of the skeletal remains and the artifacts. Larry Lahren and Robson Bonnichsen (1974) reported more specifically on the inferred function of osseous artifacts from the artifact assemblage. However, details of the site's discovery and the subsequent archaeological excavations conducted by numerous professionals to recover contextual information have never been published in a comprehensive site report. Because the Anzick site was found accidentally by nonprofessionals using heavy equipment, the original context of the artifacts and human skeletal remains could not be reconstructed (Taylor

1969). Nevertheless, several studies of the Anzick artifacts have been published (Lahren and Bonnichsen 1974; Wilke et al. 1991), and two samples of human bone have been dated using the accelerator mass spectrometry (AMS) ^{14}C technique (Stafford 1994). Subsequent to the original reports of the site and its contents (Lahren and Bonnichsen 1974; Taylor 1969), the artifacts found in association with the human remains were divided into three collections. On the advice of local archaeologist Larry Lahren, the owners (Faye Hargis-Case, Calvin Sarver, and the Anzick family) of the three collections loaned the materials to the Montana State Historical Society (MSHS) in Helena from 1988 to 2001 (Lahren 2001). After they were catalogued as artifacts on permanent loan, a number of researchers—including this chapter's senior author—conducted analyses of the stone tools and foreshafts (Jones 1996; Wilke et al. 1991). Under Bonnichsen's supervision, Scott Jones (1996) completed a descriptive study of the Anzick artifact assemblage for his master's thesis at Oregon State University. More recently, Douglas Owsley and David Hunt completed an analysis of the human skeletal remains (Owsley and Hunt 2001).

When initially reported, it was thought that two Paleoindian children had been buried in the same grave (Lahren and Bonnichsen 1974; Taylor 1969). Two fragmentary juvenile crania (one "bleached" white and the other covered with red ochre) were included in the collection, and both were originally reported as having been associated with the Clovis artifacts. However, AMS ^{14}C dating revealed that the skulls were of very different ages (Stafford 1994). The "bleached" cranium, not stained by red ochre like its ostensible companion, yielded an average date of 8610 ± 90 BP. Although no artifacts of corresponding age were recovered in association, this date alone suggests the presence of a spatially and temporally separate burial of a six- to eight-year-old child (Owsley and Hunt 2001) of the Late Paleoindian period. In a 1999 interview at the site, Calvin Sarver (one of the two original site discoverers) affirmed the vertically and horizontally separate proveniences of the "bleached" cranium and the ochre-covered skull fragments (Owsley and Hunt 2001: 117).

Three independent lines of evidence (eyewitness testimony, ^{14}C assays, and presence of red ochre) indicate that the red ochre–covered cranial vault, belonging to a one to two-year-old child, was originally associated with the assemblage of 115 ochre-covered Clovis chipped stone and osseous artifacts.[1] Because of previous dating of numerous sites of the Clovis complex (Haynes 1992), investigators anticipated a date of circa 11,000 BP. Thomas Stafford's AMS dating of purified amino acids derived from the cranium supported this estimate, although he reported a wide range of rather late dates: 10,240 ± 120 (AA-2978) on aspartic acid, 10,370 ± 130 (AA-2982) on alanine, 10,710 ± 100 (AA-2980) on hydroxyproline, 10,820 ± 100 (AA-2979) on glutamic acid, and 10,940 ± 90 BP (AA-2981) on glycine (Haynes 1993: 221; Stafford 1994: table

4). Another assay (CAMS-35912) by Stafford produced a much earlier date of 11,550 ± 60 BP on the XAD fraction of a sample of ochre-stained bone from the Anzick site (Dixon 1999: 121; Owsley and Hunt 2001).

The Clovis Burial Assemblage

Jones and Bonnichsen (1994) have suggested that the Anzick artifacts may represent a mixed set of heirlooms and utilitarian tools that were provided by the dead child's relatives for use in the afterlife. The 115-piece tool kit consists of complete and fragmentary bifacially flaked cores and projectile point pre-forms (n = 84), unifacial cutting/scraping tools (n = 6), fluted projectile points (n = 8), shatter from biface reduction (n = 2), and antler foreshaft fragments (n = 15) (Morrow 2001a). The flint used to manufacture the tools and preforms was derived from at least six different sources. Several of the flint types are macroscopically identical to types from known quarries in Montana and Wyoming. Some of the lithic resources exploited by the Clovis group that visited the Anzick site are macroscopically identical to porcellinite from northeastern Wyoming (southeast of the site); Montana City Chert from near Helena, Montana (northwest of the site); and Shirley Basin Jasper from south-central Wyoming (south of the site).

Anzick is unique among known Clovis sites both for the abundance of artifacts and for their association with preserved human remains. The Anzick assemblage—like the known Clovis caches such as East Wenatchee/Richey-Roberts (Gramly 1993), Drake (Stanford and Jodry 1988), and Simon (Woods and Titmus 1985)—contains bifacially flaked artifacts representing a continuum of all stages of fluted point production, from large, early-stage bifacial cores to fluted preforms (see Morrow 1995) and finished fluted projectile points (figures 7.2 and 7.3). Figure 7.3 shows maximum length versus maximum width for all of the complete bifaces that could be accurately measured. As in the known Clovis caches, the majority of the Anzick bifaces bear traces of transport abrasion: rounding and polish of prominent flake scar crests and spots of polish on the interiors of flake scars. Differential patination, percussion marks, and fracture patterns imply that some of the stone tools may have been broken before interment, perhaps even "ritually killed," as has been suggested for the foreshafts (Lahren and Bonnichsen 1974). Other tools appear to have been damaged during the 1968 excavation or afterward. Detailed use-wear analysis of the entire assemblage could help address questions regarding raw material procurement and individual tool function in the Clovis era. The Anzick artifacts are preforms and tools that were curated and repeatedly used prior to their interment. They constitute a functional Clovis stone tool kit, not a specially created mortuary collection. One can only speculate about the ex-

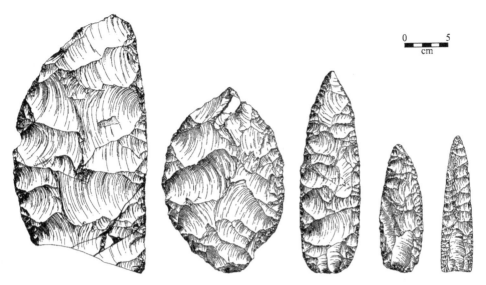

Figure 7.2. Clovis bifaces associated with two-year-old child at Anzick site. *Left to right*: broken early-stage biface/bifacial core; complete early-stage biface/bifacial core; middle-stage biface; middle-stage end-thinned biface; finished fluted point.

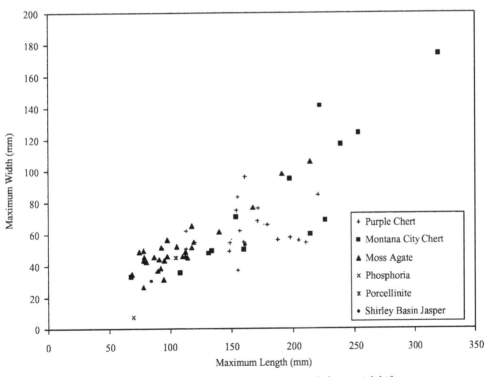

Figure 7.3. Plot of maximum width versus maximum length for Anzick bifaces.

Table 7.1. Metric Attributes of Antler Foreshafts from the Anzick Site

Specimen number	Portion	No. of fragments	Maximum length (mm)	Maximum width (mm)	Maximum thickness (mm)	Wei (gr
88.68.13 (24PA506/95 and 24PA506/123)	Beveled end	2 (conjoined)	128	19.9	13.4	26
88.68.14 (24PA506/94)	Beveled end	1	133	19.8	12.6	35
L88.07.37 (24PA506/37)	Beveled end	2 (conjoined)	132	18	12.3	28
L88.07.38 (24PA506/38 and 24PA506/122)	Medial	2 (conjoined)	97.5	20	13.6	30
L88.07.39 (24PA506/39)	Beveled end	1	54	17.4	12.3	10
L88.08.10 (24PA506/67)	Complete (single bevel)	2 (conjoined)	227	15.5	13.8	48
24PA506/118+119[a] (no MSHS No.)	Complete (double bevel)	4 (conjoined)	280	17.4	14.6	75
24PA506/120 (no MSHS No.)	Medial	1	92	19	11	12
Total		15				264

a. Sample submitted for ^{14}C dating.

traordinary ritual or social status of the infant whose untimely death triggered the disposal of so many still-usable tools.

Associated with the human skeletal remains and flaked stone artifacts were fifteen fragments of worked osseous material (table 7.1; figure 7.4). These conjoin to form as many as (but no more than) eight roughly cylindrical foreshafts. It may not be coincidental that this is also the number of points and point fragments recovered. Only two foreshafts in the Anzick assemblage are complete: one is beveled on one end; the other is beveled on both ends. The beveled ends of the foreshafts typically exhibit incisions executed in a cross-hatching pattern (figure 7.4). Similar artifacts have been recovered from other Clovis contexts across North America, including the East Wenatchee site in Washington (Gramly 1993) and Blackwater Draw in New Mexico (Hester 1972) (see figure 7.1). They have been variously interpreted as having functioned as spear foreshaft components, fleshing tools, sled runners, and haft-tightening devices (for example, Frison 1991b; O'Brien and Lyman 1999; Pearson 1999).

The Anzick foreshafts have long been assumed to be made of bone. However, the senior author's comparison of the Anzick foreshaft fragments (using a stereoscopic microscope at 10× to 40×) with archaeological and modern reference specimens (elk antler, white-tailed deer antler, mastodon bone, and mammoth bone) indicated that the Anzick specimens had been manufactured from antler—specifically, elk antler.[2] This identification was supported by an independent assessment of the foreshafts by Illinois State Museum faunal specialists Jeff Saunders, Bonnie Styles, James Oliver, and Terry Martin.

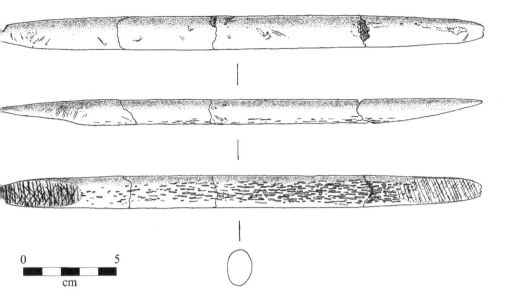

Figure 7.4. Anzick foreshaft #118/119. Longest medial segment sampled for ^{14}C assay.

Despite the frequent use of antler as a raw material for tools in European Up-per Paleolithic industries, antler artifacts had never previously been reported from a Clovis assemblage (G. Haynes 2002: 130). The overall dimensions of the foreshafts (average length of 253 millimeters, n = 2; average width of 18.4 millimeters, n = 8; average thickness of 13.0 millimeters, n = 8), the thickness of the cortical material, and late Pleistocene species distributions implicate elk (wapiti, *Cervus elaphus*) as the most likely source of the worked antler. The al-ternative derivation of the antlers from elk-moose (*Cervalces scotti*) is unlikely but cannot be excluded. Recent dates of circa 11,400 BP from Illinois indicate the persistence of this cervid into the Clovis era, although it did not survive into the early Holocene. However, the westernmost limit of its known range in the terminal Pleistocene is about 1,000 kilometers east of Anzick (Schubert et al. 2004). *Cervus elaphus*, although ubiquitous in North America during the Holocene, is very rare and poorly dated in late Pleistocene contexts, south of the glacial margin (FAUNMAP Working Group 1994). Along with moose, brown bear, and several other species, the elk may have emigrated from Berin-gia only after deglaciation (Pielou 1991). The Anzick site provides the earliest evidence of elk migration southward from Alaska, where *Cervus elaphus* is well represented in late Pleistocene cultural deposits; an elk bone from Broken Mammoth, a campsite of the Nenana culture, has been directly dated to 11,060

Table 7.2. Summary of Amino Acid Racemization Results of Anzick Samples

	BETA laboratory number	Racemization results		Concentration ratios		
		D/L Asp	D/L Ala	Asp/Glu	Ser/Glu	Ala/Glu
Published values				0.68	0.47	1.51
Reference values				0.68	0.47	1.53
Antler tool #122	1395	0.06	0.006	0.62	0.44	1.69
Antler tool #122	1395	0.07	0.010	0.61	0.43	1.70
Percentage of standard				90	93	112
Human rib bone	1396	0.06	0.004	0.46	0.41	1.83
Human rib bone	1396	0.06	0.007	0.46	0.41	1.82
Percentage of standard				68	87	121

Note: D/L Asp = racemization of Aspartic acid; D/L Ala = racemization of Alanine. Concentration ratio analysis compares Aspartic acid, Serine, and Alanine concentrations to Glutamic acid in the sample (Asp/Glu, Ser/Glu, Ala/Glu).

± 90 BP (CAMS-7204) (Holmes 1996). The presence of well-preserved amino acids in the Anzick foreshafts (table 7.2) indicates that they may contain DNA that could verify the species identification.

The identification of the foreshaft material as antler of elk (*Cervus elaphus* or *C. canadensis*) in this context is very significant for three reasons. As the first known evidence of the use of antler for Clovis tools, it provides another link to the Eurasian Upper Paleolithic industries, in which antler was a preferred material for projectile tips. It is the earliest dated occurrence of elk (wapiti) in North America south of the former ice sheets. Elk is not a native species, having immigrated from Beringia at the end of the Pleistocene. The oldest elk remains previously recovered from an archaeological context were the antler tools found in the Folsom component (circa 10,600 BP) of the Agate Basin site in eastern Wyoming (Frison 1991a: 58). Bones of butchered elk are common in the Marmes phase component (dated circa 10,000 BP) of the Marmes Rockshelter in Washington (Hicks 2004: 137–38), and early Holocene elk skeletons are known from natural deposits in Ohio. The presence of elk antler at Anzick implies either that the Clovis hunters had arrived recently from Alaska, where modified wapiti bones, directly dated to 11,060 BP, occur in a cultural context at the Broken Mammoth site, or that elk were procured locally, which implies that the species had already successfully migrated from Alaska, through the ice-free corridor, prior to 13,000 cal BP. If elk could make it through the corridor on dry land at that date, so could people.

Additionally, the antler foreshafts allow inferences to be drawn about the diet of the elk at that date, with further implications for human diet.

New Radiocarbon Dates

Sarah Anzick, owner of the human skeletal remains and foreshafts, gave permission to the senior author to date the three samples: two antler foreshaft pieces and a human rib fragment.[3] The Anzick antler pieces were photographed, illustrated, weighed, and measured. Because the red ochre–encrusted rib fragment had been analyzed and reported on previously (Owsley and Hunt 2001), it was not photographed or illustrated but was weighed. Anzick bone and antler samples were then sent to Beta-Analytic Laboratories, where small samples were removed from each specimen for AMS ^{14}C assay. All samples underwent pretreatment that included collagen extraction with alkali. The measured ^{14}C ages were corrected for observed ^{13}C fractionation; the corrected conventional ages as well as the calibrated ages are presented in table 7.3.

Foreshaft #118/119, from which material was extracted for the Beta-168967 date, is demonstrably different from foreshaft #122, which provided the sample Beta-163832. The precise agreement of the dates for two distinct artifacts is remarkable and probably indicates that both dates are accurate.

The calibrated dates reported by Beta-Analytic are derived from the 1998 INTCAL program (Stuiver et al. 1998). However, the latter is primarily based on a data set from the Cariaco basin varves that was significantly revised in 2000 (Hughen et al. 2000). When the revised calibration set (Hughen et al. 2000; Reimer et al. 2004) is used, both antler samples date to circa 12,900 to 13,050 years (±55) cal BP. The rib dates to circa 12,800 to 12,850 cal BP. The child's rib yielded a conventional age of 10,780 ± 40 BP, a date that overlaps at two-sigma with the 10,680 ± 50 BP average of Stafford's bone dates for the same individual (excluding the 11,550 ± 60 outlier). The obvious difference between these apparently consistent dates for the child's bones and the slightly older ages of the antler pieces requires comment and explanation. The use of different dating protocols cannot account for the difference between the two sets of dates. All of the Beta-Analytic dates, both for the antler and for the human bone samples, were on gelatin extracted from collagen. Stafford's dates were on XAD-purified amino acids. Nevertheless, the Beta date for the rib falls squarely within the range established previously by Stafford. Recent dating by Stafford of late glacial faunal material resulted in discrepancies of approximately 150 ^{14}C years between dates for gelatin and XLA-purified samples from the same specimens; in one case, the XLA dates are older, but in the other, they are younger. The direction of the difference appears to be related to the differing chemistry of the sediment matrices in which the bones were deposited (Schubert et al. 2004).

There are five plausible explanations, which need not be mutually exclusive, for the discrepancy between the Anzick antler and bone dates.

Table 7.3. Summary of AMS Radiocarbon Dates on Anzick Samples

Material dated	Laboratory number	$^{13}C/^{12}C$ ratio	^{13}C corrected radiocarbon age (BP)	Calibrated intercept (cal BP)	1-sigma calibrated date 68% probability (cal BP)	2-sigma calibrated result 95% probability (cal BP)
Antler #118/119	Beta-163832	-22.5 o/oo	11,040±60	13,010	13,160 to 12,900	13,170 to 12,880
Antler #122	Beta-168967	-18.2 o/oo	11,040±40	13,010 to 12,900	13,150 to 12,890	13,160 to 12,890
Bone (rib)	Beta-163833	-21.2 o/oo	10,780±40	12,880 to 12,910	12,960 to 12,800	12,980 to 12,910
					12,740 to 12,650	12,740 to 12,640

1. The bone date is too young because of contamination of the collagen with more recent carbon. Testing of the amino acid ratios of the dated specimens (table 7.2) indicated that the rib differed more from modern reference samples than did the antler pieces; this result implies probable diagenetic alteration of the bone. This is the most likely cause of the younger bone dates.

2. The antler tools were heirlooms that had been used by the infant's family for several decades prior to their interment in the infant's grave. However, their retention in active use for 60 to 150 years, over the course of three to six human generations, seems improbable.

3. The elk that yielded the antler had somehow (for example, by habitual eating of plants growing near a geothermal vent in the nearby Yellowstone region) tapped into a reservoir of old, ^{14}C-depleted carbon, which in turn made the elk's collagen appear too old. In view of the nearly identical ^{13}C content of the bone and antler samples, this seems unlikely.

4. The feature was created by two discrete depositional episodes; the artifacts were buried first, then, perhaps decades later, the child was interred (fortuitously or deliberately) near them. Although this sequence seems improbable, the proximity of the other, much later child's skull to the Clovis deposit, together with the lack of provenience documentation during the initial burial discovery, requires some consideration of this scenario.

5. The apparent age difference is only an artifact of ^{14}C fluctuations during the terminal Pleistocene.

At other Clovis sites (for example, Lehner), dates of circa 11,000 and 10,700 BP have been derived from the same contexts. This may reflect sharp, rapid fluctuations of atmospheric ^{14}C associated with deglacial climatic events, particularly the Intra-Allerød Cold Period at circa 13,200 cal BP (Andresen et al. 2000; Goslar et al. 1999) or the Younger Dryas onset at circa 12,940 cal BP (Fiedel 1999a, 2002). The new Anzick dates appear roughly contemporaneous with dates of circa 11,050 BP for German trees that were buried by Laacher See tephra (LST) 190 years before the onset of the Younger Dryas (that is, circa 13,130 cal BP or alternatively circa 12,880–12,916 cal BP if one calculates LST age using the later Greenland Ice Core Project [GRIP] ice-core date for YD onset) (Baales et al. 2002; Baales and Street 1996; Friedrich, Kromer, Kaiser, et al. 1999; Friedrich, Kromer, Spurk, et al. 1999; Hajdas et al 1995a; Kaiser 1989; Kromer et al. 2004; Litt et al. 2003). On the basis of tree-ring data presented by Bernd Kromer and colleagues (2004) (see figure 2.1, this volume), the antler artifacts would date to circa 13,100–13,250 cal BP, while the rib would date to circa 12,950 cal BP.

It is even possible that all the Anzick bone and antler dates are too young, as there may be a tendency for collagen dates to underestimate true age (Rutherford and Wittenberg 1979; Taylor 1992). However, antler-based ^{14}C dates from other ancient contexts (most notably, for a barbed antler point from England dated to 11,100–11,500 BP; Sheldrick et al. 1997) generally have been precise, internally consistent, and within expected ranges.

Inferences from 13C

As a standard procedure for carbon dating, in addition to ^{14}C, the amount of a stable carbon isotope, ^{13}C, is also measured. Beta Analytic Laboratories performed this measurement for the three Anzick samples. The ^{13}C offset (delta ^{13}C) for the infant rib was recorded as -21.2 per mil. One of the antler artifacts has a delta ^{13}C of -18.2 per mil; the other is -22.5 per mil (see table 7.3).

Since the dates determined for the two artifacts are identical and they came from the same depositional context, the notion that variable contamination by exogenous carbon caused these very different readings is improbable. Comparison of data for much larger late Pleistocene mammal samples (Bocherens et al. 1996; Coltrain et al. 2004; Drucker and Henry-Gambier 2005; Feranec 2004; Guthrie 2004; Hoppe 2004; Matheus 1995; Matheus et al. 2003; Stuart et al. 2004) shows that only rarely do contemporaneous individuals of the same species vary by more than 1 per mil. At the Hudson-Meng bison kill site in Nebraska, bison bone collagen had a range of more than 6 per mil (-15.6 to -21.9 per mil), but this unusually wide variation is ascribed to differential postdeposition diagenetic changes (Jahren et al. 1998). However, a fairly wide range of variation also can be seen in a few of the samples of red deer (*C. elaphus*) antler and bone that were dated by the Oxford AMS facility, as reported in *Archaeometry* from 1994 to 2000. These are of particular relevance because they belong to the same species as the Anzick samples. Nine antler samples from Stonehenge, all approximately coeval, ranged from -20.4 to -23.9 per mil (with a mean of -22.0). The mean for twenty-seven antler samples from various other sites was -21.7; the mean for twenty bone samples was -20.4. The minimum measurement for antler was -19.9 per mil, but seven of the bone samples (mainly late Pleistocene specimens) measured between -18.0 and -18.9 per mil.

If diagenetic (postdepositional) change is not responsible, then the nearly 4 per mil difference between the Anzick elk antler specimens must be attributed instead to the individual animals' differing diets and/or habitat characteristics. The -22.5 per mil animal could have incorporated more browse in its diet. If it frequented parkland on the edges of forested patches, it may have eaten plants with exaggeratedly negative carbon isotopes attributable to the "canopy effect" that has been observed in wooded areas. Alternatively, the -18.2 per mil animal may have lived some distance to the south of the -22.5 elk. In that case, its diet would have included a higher proportion of C4 plants, with less-negative isotope values; the proportion of C4 plants in the plains increases toward the south, and delta ^{13}C values of vegetation and soils are strongly correlated with latitude. Altitude can also affect isotope values, so the differences might be indicative of animals living in plains versus montane habitats.

Nursing infants are analogous to predators with respect to a "carnivore enrichment effect"; their delta ^{13}C may be as much as 1 per mil higher than their mothers' (Richards et al. 2002). As a result, the Anzick infant's mother may have been in the range of about -21.2 to -22.2 per mil. In a purely C3 ecosystem, there is generally a 0.8 to 2 per mil enrichment from herbivores to the carnivores that prey upon them (Drucker and Henry-Gambier 2005) and a 3 to 6 per mil enrichment from grass to herbivore collagen. The northern plains seems to have been a C3-dominant system at 11,200 BP. Glen Fredlund and Larry Tieszen (1997) determined the average late Pleistocene delta ^{13}C of soil humates in the Black Hills of South Dakota as -24.7 ± 0.6 per mil, indicative of "nearly exclusive C3 vegetation." This sets a lower limit on the delta ^{13}C for the grazing mammals of that region during the late Pleistocene; pure grazers should have had collagen values of about -22.3 to -18.1 per mil. From the other direction, assuming that the Anzick infant's mother did not depend heavily on nuts, seeds, or freshwater fish (which seems a safe assumption for an environment that, according to Fredlund and Tieszen, resembled the plains of modern Alberta), we can calculate that, during the year before her infant died, she often consumed flesh of a grazing mammal with a delta ^{13}C value of about -22 to -24.2 per mil. Bison of Younger Dryas age (circa 10,200–10,600 BP) from the Carter/Kerr-McGee and Agate Basin sites in Wyoming have produced bone collagen ^{13}C values of -18.18, -17.72, -18.53, and -16.62 per mil (Lovvorn et al. 2001). Most of the tested Hudson-Meng bison bones, dating from 9500 BP, were in the same range (for example, -16.56, -17.23, -17.20, -16.98, -19.25 per mil) (Jahren et al. 1998). Beringian bison of late glacial age ranged between about -20 and -20.7 per mil (Matheus et al. 2003). These relatively high numbers, even allowing for latitude differences, would seem to indicate that bison were not the predominant constituent in the Anzick mother's diet. In California, ground sloth and horse of late glacial age averaged about -21.4, while coeval camel, bison, and mastodon averaged about -20.6 per mil (Coltrain et al. 2004). Only a few of the Alaskan and Yukon mammoth samples reported by Dale Guthrie (2004) exceeded -23 per mil, and most of those were older than 35,000 years. However, a specimen dated to 11,500 ± 160 BP (the most recent of the large sample) had a delta ^{13}C of -22.9 per mil. For comparison, a study of collagen and soft tissues from West Beringian (Yakutian) megafauna obtained values from -23.1 to -21.4 per mil for mammoth, -22.7 to -21.4 per mil for horse, -19.3 for bison, -19.9 for musk ox, -19.6 for lion, and -20.1 for wolf. A Yakutian domestic dog (said to be of late Pleistocene age but of unspecified provenience) had a value of -22.8 per mil (Bocherens et al. 1996).

Unfortunately, the suspicion of minor contamination by exogenous carbon precludes confident interpretation of the Anzick infant's isotopic data. Nevertheless, the reading seems at least to be compatible with a mother's diet consisting largely of mammoth, perhaps supplemented by meat of elk, horse, and domestic dog (Fiedel 2005). Given the frequent association of Clovis artifacts with mammoth carcasses, this result should not be a surprise. There are only two approximately contemporaneous (circa 10,700 BP) human specimens from the Americas for which ^{13}C values are published. Buhl Woman, found near the Snake River in southern Idaho, was dated to 10,675 ± 95 BP (Green et al. 1998). Despite the similarity in apparent age to the Anzick infant, the association of a stemmed biface suggests Buhl's affiliation with the post-Clovis Windust phase. The reported delta ^{13}C value for Buhl Woman is -19.5 per mil, which Thomas Green and colleagues (1998) suggest indicates a diet of meat supplemented by anadromous fish. The higher value, relative to Anzick, may reflect not only consumption of fish but also the absence of recently extinct mammoth and horse from Buhl Woman's diet. The much-publicized Kennewick Man from Washington is much more recent than Anzick and Buhl (8410 ± 40 BP, or about 9400 cal BP before correction for inferred marine reservoir effect). This individual's delta ^{13}C is reported as -12.6 per mil, clearly indicating a diet rich in marine or anadromous fish (which is why the reservoir correction of the date to about 8300–9200 cal BP was necessary) (Taylor et al. 1998). Peñon Woman from central Mexico dates to 10,775 ± 75 BP (Gonzalez et al. 2003). Her delta ^{13}C is -11.6 per mil. This falls within the range of values obtained for Mexican mammoths, from -14 to -11 per mil, which reflects the effect of latitude on C3/C4 grass ratios.

If one had to guess where the infant's mother had been living before her band arrived at Anzick, it would appear more likely that she came from the north (a pure C3 grassland) rather than the more southern plains, where the mixture of C3 and C4 grasses produced a higher (less negative) delta ^{13}C in the resident fauna (as is evident in the Wyoming bison bones as well as delta ^{13}C of mammoth teeth from Blackwater Draw, Miami, and Dent [Hoppe 2004]).

Implications

The location of the Anzick site (south of the embouchure of the ice-free corridor that has long been assumed to be the most likely route of Paleoindian entry from Beringia), as well as the technology and form of the bifaces, would suggest that this might have been one of the first places visited by migratory Clovis bands as they explored North America (Morrow and Morrow 1999). The date of 11,550 ± 60 BP for the Anzick bones (Owsley and Hunt 2001) lends support to this supposition. The antiquity of Anzick seems to equal that of the Aubrey Clovis site in Texas, where two dates on charcoal average circa 11,550 BP (Ferring 2001). However, the Aubrey dates could reflect inherent age of old wood or perhaps do not relate directly to Paleoindian activities at the site (see Roosevelt et al. 2002). The new dates from Anzick undermine the credibility of the 11,550 BP date for the Clovis burial assemblage. If one provisionally accepts as accurate both the Aubrey dates and the new Anzick dates, then Anzick, evidently later than Aubrey by at least 200 calendar years, cannot represent initial Clovis arrival out of the north. Instead, the date of circa 11,040 BP fits well with other evidence of Clovis entry (from an undetermined point of origin) into the northern plains and Northwest around 11,000 BP—synchronous with Clovis expansion throughout North America. At Indian Creek, Montana, an Early Paleoindian assemblage dates to 10,980 ± 110 BP and overlies a deposit of Glacier Peak tephra, dated in this area to 11,125 ± 130 BP (Davis and Baumler 2000). At East Wenatchee in Washington, the large cache of Clovis bifaces lay directly on Glacier Peak tephra. The consensus age of the tephra, based on several dated occurrences in lakebed cores, is circa 11,200 BP (Foit et al. 1993; Mehringer et al. 1984; Mehringer and Foit 1990). Tentative correlation of the Northwest pollen sequence with other deglacial records suggests that the tephra fell during the brief, unnamed warm period (Greenland Interstadial 1a in ice cores) between the Intra-Allerød Cold Period and the onset of the Younger Dryas. This would indicate a calibrated age of circa 13,100 cal BP for the tephra and also provides a likely *terminus post quem* for Clovis occupation of Montana.

Acknowledgments

This research was conducted through the cooperation of the Montana State Historical Society Museum, the Anzick family, Faye Hargis-Case, and Calvin Sarver. Bonnie Styles, Jeff Saunders, Terrence Martin, and James Oliver of the Illinois State Museum kindly examined fragments of all but one of the Anzick foreshafts; their expertise helped narrow down the possible range of taxa. We also gratefully acknowledge the financial support of this research from Patty Jo Watson and the dean of Arts and Sciences of Washington University–St. Louis, Tom and Shirley Townsend of the Missouri Archaeological Society, and Larry Lahren. We thank Toby Morrow for rendering figures 7.2 and 7.3 and Chris Wardlow for scanning and perfecting figure 7.1. Patty Jo Watson, C. Vance Haynes, David Anderson, Ruthann Knudson, Toby Morrow, Robert

Taylor, and two anonymous reviewers provided editorial comments that collectively improved the original manuscript. We take full responsibility for any potential errors or omissions herein.

Notes

1. An exact total of the artifacts recovered from the Anzick site has not yet been published. Numerous authors have referred loosely to the discovery of over 100 stone and bone artifacts in association with the two juveniles. Based on Morrow's personal experience analyzing the collection from 1999 to 2002, the Anzick assemblage actually comprises 117 recovered stone artifacts. This total includes all fragments. Conjoinable fragments allow for downward adjustment of the total number of stone artifacts to 100. Additional refitting may be possible and would yield a still lower and more accurate estimate of the total number of stone artifacts originally placed in the infant's grave.

2. The interior of only one of the foreshafts (Specimen L88.08.10 currently on exhibit at the MSHS in Helena) was not available for examination, owing to its having been refitted and glued, possibly for the purpose of the original casting. The exterior surface of this specimen appears morphologically similar to the other foreshafts.

3. The Anzick materials, because of the date and circumstances of discovery, remain the private property of the landowners. Thus, the regulations concerning treatment of human remains found on federal or tribal lands or curated in federally funded facilities are not applicable in this case. To date, we are unaware of claims of affiliation or requests for repatriation made by any Native American group in the thirty-seven years since the Anzick site was discovered. We are grateful to Sarah Anzick and the Anzick family for permitting analyses of the Anzick skeletal remains and artifacts and to Larry Lahren, whose supervision and support made these analyses possible.

8

The Rancholabrean Termination

Sudden Extinction in the San Pedro Valley, Arizona, 11,000 BC

C. VANCE HAYNES JR.

What follows is a hypothetical scenario based on a limited number of facts acquired by geological and archaeological investigations in the San Pedro Valley over three decades. Other interpretations may be just as valid as those presented here, and subsequent findings most likely will require revisions.

The San Pedro River in southeastern Arizona starts in Mexico and flows northward for 227 kilometers to join the Gila River at Winkelman, Arizona (figure 8.1). About half a million years ago, after nearly two million years of net aggradation, the ancestral San Pedro began to entrench the valley fill, exposing Plio-Pleistocene alluvium and playa lake deposits (figure 8.2a) of the Saint David Formation (Gray 1967), containing several Blancan and Irvingtonian vertebrate fossil localities that have enhanced the scientific literature (Johnson et al. 1975; Lindsay et al. 1990). The paleomagnetic chronology of the Saint David Formation shows that it is essentially the same age as the hominid-bearing beds of Olduvai Gorge in East Africa and of similar lithology but without primate remains, much less hominid remains.

Gravel strath terraces at various elevations in the inner valley (figure 8.2a) represent former positions of the San Pedro channel left high and dry as the river cut to a lower level (Haynes 1987). In the Old World, gravels of similar ages contain Lower and Middle Paleolithic archaeology. In the San Pedro Valley, these gravels of the Nexpa Alloformation (Qne) are devoid of artifacts but contain scattered remains of the late Pleistocene Rancholabrean fauna, that is, mammoth, horse, camel, bison, and others.

The Millville Alloformation (Qmi) of fine- to coarse-grained terrace alluvium (figure 8.2a) represents net aggradation after a long period of net degradation. Alluvium of this age (approximately 40,000 to 100,000 BP) in the Old World contains Middle Paleolithic archaeology and bones of *Homo neanderthalensis*.[1] In the San Pedro Valley, it contains Rancholabrean fauna but no archaeology. At the Murray Springs Clovis site on Curry Draw (figure 8.2b and 8.3b), the Millville is unconformably overlain by late Pleistocene mudstone and marl, lake beds, of the Murray Springs Alloformation (Qso and Qco) containing a rich Rancholabrean fauna and no archaeological evidence. As the glaciers to the north retreated after 18,000 BP, water tables in the San Pedro declined, reaching their lowest levels in over 30,000 years by 12,000 BP. The drop may not have been unidirectional, but fluctuations probably matched the climatic swings revealed by ice core studies (Mayewski et al. 1993) and resulted in a net decline. In the West and Southwest, late Pleistocene records of lake levels show similar declines in level from high stands about 18,000 BP to lowest levels or complete desiccation between 14,000 BP and 11,000 BP (Benson et al. 1997).

As the late Pleistocene lakes of the San Pedro Valley dried up between 14,000 and 13,000 BP, small spring-fed creeks wended their way to the San Pedro River across dry lake beds. The drainage channels contained sandy streambeds forming the Graveyard Gulch Allomember (Qgr of figure 8.2b) of the Lehner Ranch Alloformation (figure 8.3c). The verdant riparian habitat that attracted the abundant big-game animals (Saunders 1983) was beginning to wither after 11,500 BP because of a drought that exacerbated the trend (C. V. Haynes 1991). This period correlates with the Allerød warm period of northern Europe (Wohlfarth 1996). The Clovis drought ended with the sudden appearance of the cold, dry conditions of the Younger Dryas event (figure 8.4). In the San Pedro Valley, this correlates precisely with the deposition of a black algal mat that blanketed the Clovis landscape (figures 8.3c and 8.3d) soon after the Clovis people and the megafauna were gone. By "soon" I mean within days or weeks because mammal skeletons and artifacts on the Clovis occupation surface show little or no dispersion, as would be expected by scavenger activity and attrition (G. Haynes 1991), and the Graveyard sand shows no evidence of pedogenes or bioturbation other than well-preserved foot impressions of mammoth and bison. The valley floors of the Clovis landscape went underwater, hosting blue-green algae (Rogers 2006) that created the "black mat" and preserved bones and artifact clusters.

Clovis in the Valley

During the drought, humans entered the San Pedro Valley for the first time, as far as we know. A band of Clovis people seem to have come from the north, having found colorful jasper in what is now Petrified Forest National Monument (figure 8.5). Farther south they found shiny black nodules of obsidian (figure 8.6a) in Cow Canyon (Shackley 2006) on the southern edge of the Blue Range (figure 8.5), from where they may have followed the Gila River to the San Pedro or the San Simon River. A Clovis point found at the northeast edge of Willcox Playa suggests that they may have left the San Simon Valley and passed between the Pinaleño and Dragoon mountains and entered the San

Pedro Valley via Texas Canyon, where another Clovis point has been found (Di Peso 1953). On the Post Ranch near Benson, they found a source of white translucent chalcedony (figures 8.1 and 8.5) before moving upriver to Curry Draw and finding Murray Springs, a well-used watering place for game animals (figure 8.3e). What follows is a fanciful interpretation based on the limited facts as presently known.

About 11,000 BP, a small herd of bison, desperate for water, moved off and watched as the Clovis people constructed a semicircular enclosure of brush across the drainage a short distance above a water hole (figure 8.3e). After the people moved away, the thirsty bison returned to the water hole, only to be ambushed from three sides by hunters armed with spears tipped with sharp Clovis points (figure 8.6b) and propelled by spear throwers (atlatls). The experienced hunters brought down at least a dozen bison (Haynes 1976; Hemmings 1970) (figure 8.3f). During butchering, tools were sharpened and modified on the spot (figure 8.3g). Processing the meat and hides took time, so the people established a temporary camp (figures 8.3h and 8.3b) on the flat ground of the old lake beds between Curry Draw, which they named Bison Kill Creek, and a tributary called Wolf Creek because of some dire wolves that were attracted by the blood and gore (figure 8.3i).

While the women were drying meat and preparing hides, the men repaired their spears by discarding broken Clovis point bases (figure 8.6c) and replacing them with new ones fashioned at the campsite (figures 8.3h, 8.6d, and 8.6f) (Agenbroad and Huckell 2006; Haynes 1979). An impact flake from the bison kill area fits the impact fracture of a broken Clovis point abandoned in the camp 80 meters away (figure 8.6e), and another impact flake from the campsite fits the impact fracture on a Clovis point in the bison kill area 150 meters away (Huckell 2006).

A week later while packing up to move farther south, some young scouts came in with the news that there was a small group of female mammoths heading their way. The Clovis band hurriedly moved downstream to be downwind and waited until the mammoths, obviously under stress, were thoroughly engaged in finding water by scraping and deepening the water hole (figure 8.3e), which was all but dry. The hunters broke into teams of four so that each team could attack a single mammoth. As two on one side propelled spears aimed for the rib area, two on the other side attacked with atlatl-propelled spears. This was kept up until one mammoth was obviously in trouble, whereupon all of the hunters concentrated their attention on her until she fell (figures 8.7a and 8.7b). Another escaped with at least two Clovis points in her chest and died 2 kilometers to the east at the Escapule site (figure 8.7c), on the left bank of Horsethief Draw (Hemmings and Haynes 1969).

Already well stocked with bison jerky, the band butchered only the limbs,

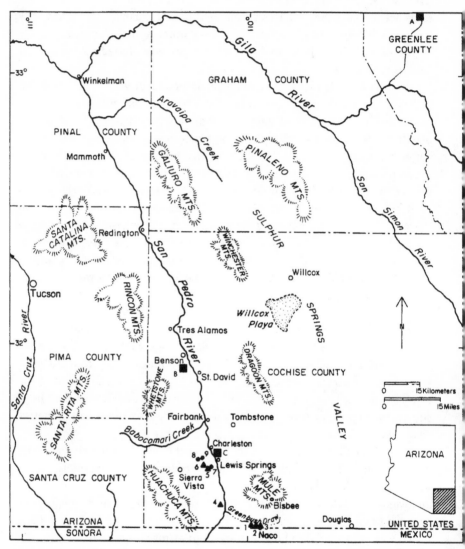

Figure 8.1. Map of the San Pedro from the border with Mexico to the Gila River at Winkelman, Arizona. Stratified Clovis sites (black triangles) are (1) Naco, (2) Navarrete, (3) Leikem, (4) Lehner, (5) Escapule, and (6) Murray Springs. Other Clovis-age mammoth bone localities (black circles) are (7) BLM V500 mammoth and two other Horsethief Draw localities, (8) Schaldack locality with bones of at least two mammoths and another approximately 100 meters downstream, and (9) Donnet mammoth skeleton. Lithic source areas (black squares): A, Cow Canyon obsidian; B, Post Ranch chalcedony; and C, Escapule Hill black silicified limestone.

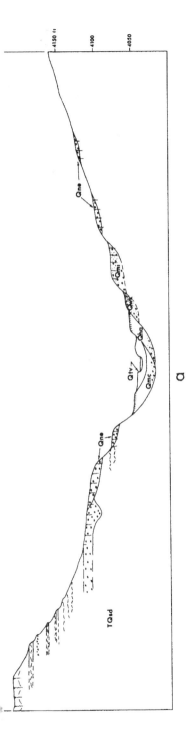

a

Figure 8.2a. Generalized geologic cross section of the inner San Pedro Valley near Lewis Springs, showing gravel straths of the Nexpa Alloformation (Qne) perched on dissected Saint David Formation (TQsd) and former positions of the river channel abandoned as the San Pedro degraded during net lowering of base level throughout the middle Pleistocene. The Millville Alloformation (Qmi) forms an alluvial terrace inset against Saint David Formation. Horizontal distance, approximately 3 kilometers.

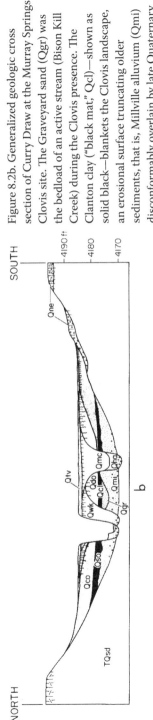

b

Figure 8.2b. Generalized geologic cross section of Curry Draw at the Murray Springs Clovis site. The Graveyard sand (Qgr) was the bedload of an active stream (Bison Kill Creek) during the Clovis presence. The Clanton clay ("black mat," Qcl)—shown as solid black—blankets the Clovis landscape, an erosional surface truncating older sediments, that is, Millville alluvium (Qmi) disconformably overlain by late Quaternary Sobaipuri pond mud (Qso) and Coro marl (Qco). All later units (Qwk, Qha, Qmc, and Qtv) are Holocene alluvia. Horizontal distance, approximately 400 meters.

a

b

c

d

e

f

g

h

i

Figure 8.3. Photo plate of San Pedro Valley sites. *a*: Playa and alluvial deposits of the early and middle Pleistocene Saint David Formation exposed at the Curtis Ranch faunal locality. *b*: Aerial view down Curry Draw (Bison Kill Creek during Clovis time) from the Murray Springs Clovis site, at the junction with the East Swale (Wolf Creek during Clovis time), to the San Pedro River. Areas 6 and 7 of the Clovis campsite are on the interfluve between Curry Draw and the East Swale. The saddle in the hill just across the river is the source area of black silicified limestone used by the Clovis people. *c*: Arroyo wall exposure of the Clovis-age channel sand (Qgr = unit F_1) of Wolf Creek buried by the "black mat" (Qcl = units F_{2a} and F_{2b}), overlain by the Donnet silt (Qdo = unit F_3) at the Murray Springs site. *d*: The algal "black mat" exposed in the headcut of Curry Draw of the Murray Springs Clovis site blankets the Clovis occupation surface that truncates older deposits exposed in the arroyo wall. *e*: The Clovis-age water hole in Area 1 of the Murray Springs Clovis site, thought to have been excavated by mammoths during the Clovis drought of 11,000 BP (circa 13,000 years ago). The numerous depressions are believed to be mammoth tracks. *f*: The rib cage of an extinct *Bison antiquus* in Area 4 of the Murray Springs site has been exposed by dental pick removal of the crumbly "black mat" crumb by crumb. *g*: A pile of bifacial thinning flakes lay on the Clovis occupation surface relatively undisturbed for 13,000 years until exposed by careful removal of the "black mat." *h*: Area 7 of Murray Springs is the middle of the Clovis hunters' campsite, on the left bank of Wolf Creek, where meat was processed and tools were repaired. *i*: A lower jaw of a dire wolf in Area 3 at Murray Springs reveals the presence of natural predators and suggested the name of Wolf Creek for the ancient tributary of Bison Kill Creek (Curry Draw today).

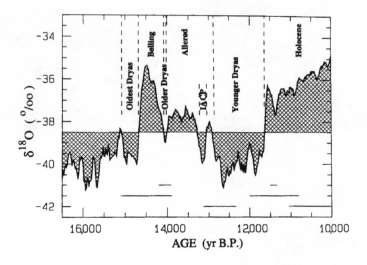

Figure 8.4. Correlation of the oxygen isotope paleoclimatic record of the Greenland ice core (GISP2) with the European pollen zone boundaries. The radiocarbon ages are in calibrated years. (Reprinted with permission from Stuiver et al. 1995.)

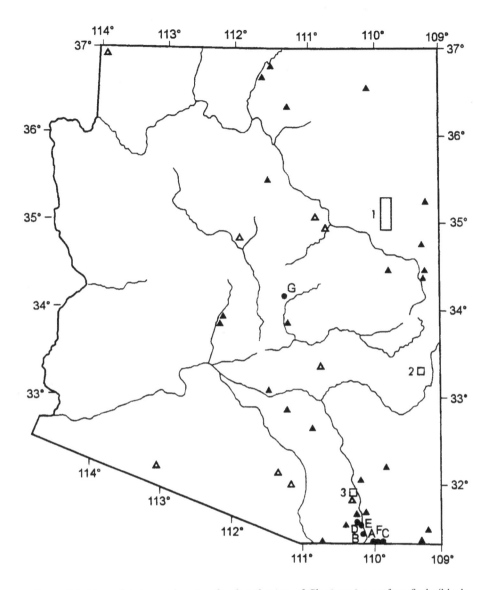

Figure 8.5. Map of Arizona showing the distribution of Clovis point surface finds (black triangles) in relation to the known stratified Clovis sites (black circles) and lithic source areas (open quadrangles) represented in the Clovis sites of the upper San Pedro Valley. Stratified Clovis sites: *A*, Naco; *B*, Lehner; *C*, Leikem; *D*, Murray Springs; *E*, Escapule; *F*, Navarrete; and *G*, Silktassel. Lithic source areas: (1) Petrified Forest National Monument; (2) Cow Canyon obsidian; (3) Post Ranch chalcedony; and Escapule Hill black silicified limestone (at the *E*). Clovis point distribution is updated from Huckell 1982 by including those of Anonymous 1989, Crownover 1994, Downum 1993, Geib 1995, Phillips and others 1993, and Roth 1993. Open triangles mark localities of Clovis points believed not to be in their original findspot.

8.6 a

Figure 8.6. Photo plate of artifacts. *a*: Obsidian nodules and flakes from Areas 1 and 3 of the Murray Springs site were found on the Clovis occupation surface immediately under the "black mat." The obsidian source is in Cow Canyon at the south end of the Blue Range in eastern Arizona. *b*: Clovis artifacts from Areas 4 and 5 at Murray Springs consist of projectile points damaged in the hunt and tools used to butcher the downed bison. *c*: Clovis artifacts from the Clovis campsite (Areas 6 and 7) at Murray Springs include discarded projectile point bases, knives, and scrapers used in processing meat and hides and in preparing weapons damaged in the hunt. *d*: Chert flakes produced by the manufacture of bifacial tools such as Clovis points and knives were found in all Clovis occupied areas at Murray Springs. These, with many conjoining or refitting, are from the mammoth kill of Area 3. *e*: Two impact flakes were found to conjoin with two Clovis points. The flake on the left, found in the bison kill of Area 4, refits the Clovis point with missing base found 73 meters away in the campsite of Area 6. The flake on the right, found in the campsite of Area 7, refits the Clovis point found 140 meters away in the bison kill of Area 4. *f*: A match between natural stripes in tan chert of one of the Naco Clovis points (*right*) and bifacial thinning flake (*top center*) at Murray Springs suggests that some of the tan chert Clovis points from Naco and Lehner (points on the left) were made at Murray Springs. *g*: The occurrence of eight essentially complete Clovis points with the partially articulated skeleton of a single mammoth at Naco with no other evidence of human presence suggests that this mammoth got away from the Clovis hunters, possibly at the Lehner site. The Clovis point on the left is 1.16 centimeters long. *h*: In total, forty-three Clovis points are from the stratified Clovis sites of the upper San Pedro Valley. The two at the top are from the Escapule site. In the next line down, the point on the right is from the Leikem site, whereas the other eight were with the Naco mammoth. The next thirteen are from the Lehner site. The rest are from Murray Springs.

8.6 b

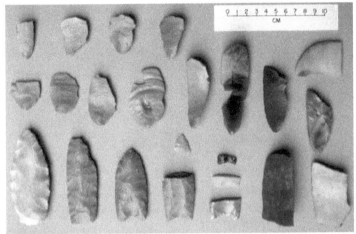

8.6 c

8.6 d

8.6 e

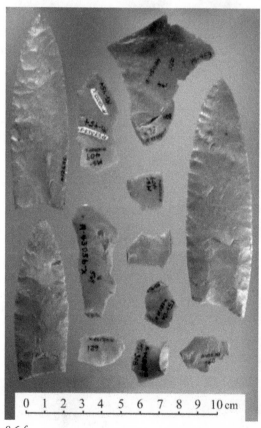

8.6 f

8.6 g

8.6 h

8.7 a

Figure 8.7. Photo plate of San Pedro Valley Clovis sites. *a*: In Area 3 of Murray Springs, the upper surfaces of the bones of a female mammoth ("Big Eloise") were stained dark brown by contact with the "black mat" (unit F_2). Clovis tools in and around the skeleton lay upon an ancient erosional surface (Z_{1-2}) preserved by deposition of the "black mat." *b*: A swath of mammoth-foot-sized depressions, believed to be mammoth tracks, covered the Clovis-age surface (Z_{1-2}) around the water hole (Figure 8.3e) and between it and the skeleton of "Big Eloise" (*top center*). *c*: The Escapule Clovis site, directly covered by the "black mat," was partially exposed by erosion of the surface. *d*: Beneath the mammoth tracks at Murray Springs, between the water hole and the skeleton of "Big Eloise," a shaft wrench made from a mammoth long bone was found partly in contact with the "black mat"; a segment of the broken handle occurred 1–2 centimeters below it (photo by B. Burns). *e*: At the Lehner Clovis site, the bones of at least twelve mammoths occurred in contact with the base of the "black mat" and partly embedded in the top of the Graveyard sand and gravel of the fossil channel of Mammoth Kill Creek shown here in the west wall of Trench 2 (1965 photo). *f*: Among the bones of twelve mammoths at the Lehner site were thirteen Clovis points. Two are shown here among mammoth ribs in the channel sand of Mammoth Kill Creek. *g*: At the Naco Clovis site in 1952, in the left bank of Greenbush Draw, five Clovis points were found within the rib cage of a single mammoth, while three others were with other parts of the skeleton. Here the "black mat" was represented by light- and dark-gray laminations of pond mud. *h*: The Leikem mammoth occurred 700 meters upstream of and in the same stratigraphic position as the Naco find. In 1964, back dirt—from the exploratory trench (*lower right corner*) that revealed the mammoth skeleton—contained a single Clovis point (figure 8.6h). *i*: Mammoth bones and nondiagnostic artifacts at the Navarrete site approximately 40 meters upstream of the Naco find appear to have been exposed by prehistoric erosion before the recent exposure that led to their discovery in 1983. Bank height is approximately 3 meters.

8.7 b

8.7 c

8.7 d

8.7 e

8.7 f

8.7 g

8.7 h

8.7 i

8.8a

Figure 8.8. Photo plate of San Pedro Valley sites. *a*: The Clanton clay ("black mat") in the bison kill area (Area 5) at Murray Springs is unusually thick because of persistent wet soil conditions during the early part of Donnet silt (Qdo = Unit F_3) deposition. The crenulations at the base are believed to be bison tracks exposed in cross section. Bank height is approximately 4 meters. *b*: The water hole was preserved by a thin blanket of the "black mat" and its thick facies of white marl alternating with incipient "black mat" stringers that, all together, filled the water hole and mammoth-track impressions in Area 1 of Murray Springs. *c*: A mammoth rib on the Clovis occupation surface is preserved by the "black mat" where exposed in the right bank of the north branch of Curry Draw at Murray Springs. This is the type of exposure that led to the discovery of the terminal Pleistocene faunal localities and Clovis sites in the upper San Pedro Valley. *d*: At the Donnet locality, 3.5 kilometers north-northwest of the Murray Springs site, the postcranial skeleton of an adult mammoth occurred under the "black mat" and at the top of channel sand of the Graveyard Gulch Allomember (Qgr = unit F_1). The skull and lower jaw had been eroded away by the time of discovery, but dispersed charcoal provided a radiocarbon age of 10,530 ± 520 BP (AA-320). There was no evidence of human presence. *e*: The partially exposed skeletal remains of two young adult mammoths at the Schaldack locality, 3 kilometers northwest of the Murray Springs site, lay on the Clovis occupation surface and directly under the "black mat" but without any associated artifacts. *f*: The occurrence of a mammoth tooth directly under the "black mat" in the left bank of Horsethief Draw 500 meters downstream from the Escapule Clovis site led to the discovery of an adult mammoth skeleton (the BLM V500 mammoth) on the Clovis occupation surface, but no artifacts were found. Scale bar is 12 centimeters long. *g*: The lower jaw and teeth of a young mammoth were exposed by erosion of the "black mat" about 500 meters downstream from the BLM mammoth, and a similar find occurred on the opposite bank (*right*) of Horsethief Draw, all without artifacts. *h*: An eroded area near the Lindsay Ranch House on the east side of the San Pedro River revealed the teeth of a small Pleistocene horse (*Equus asinus*) in anatomical position directly under the Clanton clay "black mat" and resting on an erosional surface forming the truncated top of the late Pleistocene Coro marl. No Clovis artifacts were found in this area. *i*: The 1975 archaeological excavations at the Lehner Clovis site revealed a Clovis roasting pit containing the charred and broken remains of a baby mammoth, black bear, and jackrabbit. The 5.5 centimeters of flagging (*upper right*) provides scale.

8.8b

8.8c

8.8d

8.8e

8.8f

8.8g

8.8h

8.8i

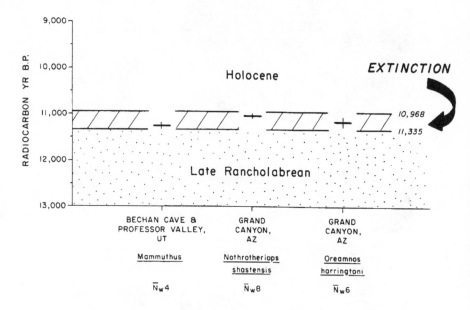

Figure 8.9. Graph of the minimum age of the Rancholabrean termination of the Colorado Plateau (reprinted with permission from Agenbroad and Mead 1989, p. 863 figure 2).

disjointing two and taking parts of them back to the camp for a feast (Hemmings 1970). The next day they recovered sinew as well as thick segments of a long bone for making bone tools. They had lost a mammoth bone shaft wrench (figure 8.7d) and needed to replace it (Haynes and Hemmings 1968).

A few days later the band moved down Curry Draw to the San Pedro River, which was barely a trickle. After they left, some mammoths returning to the water hole investigated the skeleton of their fallen family member. The Clovis band, while camped by the river and exploring the area around Lewis Springs, discovered a hill made of black silicified limestone (figures 8.3b and 8.5). They fabricated some stone knives and choppers of the black stuff before moving upriver. Mammoth spoor indicated that a herd had recently gone up Mammoth Kill Creek, a small spring-fed tributary, so up it they went and again successfully brought down several mammoths (figures 8.7e and 8.7f) at what is now known as the Lehner Clovis site (Haury et al. 1959). Among those that got away, one with eight Clovis points in him went up Greenbush Draw, only to die at the Naco site (figures 8.7g, 8.6g, and 8.6h), 18 kilometers east of the Lehner site (Haury et al. 1953). Another, the Leikem mammoth, which died half a kilometer farther up the draw, probably suffered the impact of at least one

Clovis point (figure 8.7h). Lehner became the site of several successful hunts, as a black bear and a rabbit in addition to a baby mammoth were roasted in a shallow pit (figure 8.8i). At the Navarrete site (Huckell 1974) in Greenbush Draw (figure 8.7i), less than 100 meters above the Naco site, the band scavenged bone from another mammoth carcass before moving up the San Pedro Valley and into Mexico in search of better watering places.

At the height of the drought, it suddenly turned glacially cold. A deep freeze developed and lasted for nearly a week. The few watering places that remained froze solid, and none of the large animals could quench their thirst. The Clovis folk survived, though in reduced numbers. By the time the water table rebounded, the Rancholabrean megafauna had vanished, thus terminating the Pleistocene epoch. Under the cool climate of the Younger Dryas period (Berger 1990), early Holocene water tables emerged in the shallow valleys, forming wet meadows, ponds, and marshes (cienegas) along the San Pedro and its tributaries (Haynes 1993). These are in evidence today by the organic black clay deposits, or "black mats" (figures 8.3d and 8.8a), of the Clanton Ranch Allomember and its white pond marl facies, the Earp Allomember (figure 8.8b), that precisely covered the Clovis landscape, preserving the Clovis site and the skeletons (figure 8.8c) of the last remnants of the terminal Pleistocene megafauna. Remains of at least nine other mammoths are known in this stratigraphic position.

Five kilometers north of Murray Springs, the Donnet mammoth (figure 8.8d), with a healed broken rib, died in the dry bed of a tributary to Woodcutter Draw, and a kilometer farther west up Woodcutter, two more mammoths (one a young adult female) died on the right bank, at the Schaldack locality (figure 8.8e). Scattered and weathered remains of two more mammoths occurred on the opposite bank downstream about 50 meters. Along the left bank of Horsethief Draw, an adult mammoth died about 500 meters downstream from the Escapule site (figure 8.8f). Another young mammoth lay dead on the left bank, 500 meters farther on (figure 8.8g); scattered and weathered remnants of another mammoth occurred opposite it on the right bank of Horsethief Draw. At Lindsay Ranch on the east side of the San Pedro River, teeth of a small horse (*Equus asinus*) occurred in anatomical position between the "black mat" and the eroded surface of Coro marl (figure 8.8h). All of these were on the Clovis occupation surface but without artifacts and were directly covered by the "black mat" at essentially the same time.

At most of these localities there are, in addition to mammoth remains, the scattered remains of horse, donkey, camel, tapir, dire wolf, coyote or dog, and bison. So far, only at Murray Springs were bison definitely a Clovis prey species. At the Lehner site, the camel, horse, bison, and tapir remains were not in clear association with Clovis artifacts. However, the occurrence of burnt bear and rabbit bone fragments in a roasting pit (figure 8.8i) suggests that they were components of a Clovis meal (Haynes 1982).

Multiple Causes of Extinction

The widespread yet sudden demise of the megafauna circa 10,950 BP in the upper San Pedro Valley with only 40 percent of the localities bearing evidence of the Clovis people suggests a cause for extinction that was not solely attributable to predation by humans. Drought is clearly in evidence at Murray Springs and elsewhere in western North America at some time between 11,000 and 11,200 BP, and warmer temperatures during this period are probable (C. V. Haynes 1991). Edward F. Lehner, discoverer and former owner of the Lehner Clovis site, was the first to suggest to me the idea of a sudden and prolonged freeze. In 1978 for several days the upper San Pedro experienced a deep freeze that damaged riparian vegetation along the draws as a sustained flow of heavy subfreezing air gravitated down the valleys. Many of the mesquite trees on Ed Lehner's place died and recovered in subsequent years only by sprouting from the roots. The question Ed raised is, what would happen to the megafauna if a freeze such as this lasted a week or more?

Multiple ^{14}C ages for the Clanton clay ("black mat") indicate that its deposition began shortly before 10,800 BP and ended at 9600 BP, exactly the same ^{14}C age as the Younger Dryas deposits of Scandinavia (Wohlfarth 1996). With the sudden onset of Younger Dryas cooling (figure 8.4) (Fiedel 1999a; Mayewski et al. 1993), the possibility of a prolonged deep freeze becomes more interesting. Maybe what could happen is what did happen circa 11,000 BC (circa 11,000 BP; Stuiver and Reimer 1993) to terminate the Rancholabrean fauna so suddenly (figure 8.9).

Acknowledgments

This research, performed over more than thirty years, has been supported at various times by the National Geographic Society, the National Science Foundation, the University of Arizona Departments of Anthropology and Geosciences, the former Geochronology Laboratories, and the Arizona State Museum. The participation and contributions of colleagues include D. P. Adams, L. D. Agenbroad, J. L. Betancourt, B. Burns, P. E. Damon, G. C. Frison, C. A. Gifford, H. Haas, E. W. Haury, E. T. Hemmings, R. Hereford, C. M. Hoffman, Bruce B. Huckell, A. E. Johnson, G. Kelso, J. E. King, G. E. Lamer, John F. Lance, E. H. Lindsay, A. Long, P. S. Martin, J. I. Mead, P. J. Mehringer Jr., R. N. Rogers, J. J. Saunders, E. B. Sayles, M. S. Shackley, T. L. Smiley, R. H. Thompson, L. C. Todd, S. Velastro, W. W. Wasley, M. Wilson, and S. L. Woodward.

Avocational archaeologists played a major role in the discovery of the San Pedro Valley Clovis sites and faunal localities. The periodic monitoring of Greenbush Draw by Fred and Marc Navarrete led to the discovery of the Naco and Navarrete Clovis sites. Edward F. Lehner, discoverer of the Clovis site that bears his name, not only participated in the excavations but also, with his wife, Lyn, hosted the scientific personnel and guided tours for local schoolchildren for many years. Louis Escapule and his wife, Jackie (discoverers of the Escapule Clovis site), conducted the initial excavations only after professional geoarchaeologists, including the author, had neglected to conduct test excavations on the mistaken belief that most of the site had eroded away. Many of the mammoth localities of the upper San Pedro Valley were discovered by the Escapules.

Chief Warrant Officer Stanley Hurley and his wife, Ursula, discovered the pre-Clovis Hurley mammoth on Fort Huachuca and participated in the Murray Springs excavations. Phil Van Strander and John C. McMahon discovered a pre-Clovis mammoth.

On November 18, 1988, much of the upper San Pedro riparian area was designated as a national conservation area that is managed by the Bureau of Land Management (BLM): it includes the Murray Springs, Lehner, and Escapule Clovis sites. BLM archaeologists Gay Kincade, John Herrin, and Jane Pike Childress as well as area manager Jesse Juen and local manager William Childress have been very helpful in permitting additional geoarchaeological research in the valley and are developing plans for the public display of the Clovis sites. The Friends of the San Pedro, a volunteer group of citizens, have been very helpful in developing walkways at the Murray Springs site. Glen R. Loftis of Sierra Vista has scouted the area for many years and has reported other fossil finds, as has Grady Cook, also of Sierra Vista. Joseph Cracciola and his late father, Andrea, kindly provided access to the Murray Springs site via their leased state land. This chapter was first presented orally at the International Conference on Mammoth Site Studies, March 1998, at the University of Kansas in Lawrence. Jo Ann Overs of the Geosciences Department and Barbara Fregoso of the Department of Anthropology at the University of Arizona provided expert word processing. Carol A. Gifford provided expert technical editing.

Notes

1. Unless otherwise indicated, radiocarbon dates cited in this chapter are uncalibrated.

9

Paleoindian Archaeology in Florida and Panama

Two Circumgulf Regions Exhibiting Waisted Lanceolate Projectile Points

MICHAEL K. FAUGHT

This chapter compares the Paleoindian and Early Archaic records of Florida and Panama, two regions with waisted lanceolate Paleoindian projectile points. Clearly the early chipped stone industries in Florida (and the greater southeastern United States) and Panama (and greater Central America) are derived from the North American fluted point tradition. But are the similarities attributable to contemporaneous related groups, diffused styles shared by visiting wanderers, convergent behaviors shared by technological or economic needs, or some combination of these factors? To address these complicated questions, we need accurate chronologies and appropriate theory about the relationships of artifact attributes. In both regions, there is evidence for arrival by Clovis peoples at the beginning of the Younger Dryas climatic episode (YD) and lasting into the early Holocene. However, the magnitude of occupations in each region—based on numbers of artifacts, findspots, and sites—is dramatically different. Another finding of this research is that several attributes of artifacts found at sites in Central America are similar to Folsom points from the Great Plains of North America.

Hypotheses about ancestor/descendant relationships based on technological and stylistic attributes of chipped stone artifacts, while at times controversial, are necessary to ascertain and reconstruct human adaptations to changing natural and social environments. In theory, similarities between artifacts derive from a shared cultural-historical heritage, borrowed attributes resulting from interactions between groups, convergent behaviors, or combinations of the three. Two factors constrain our ability to adequately interpret archaeological data, however: one is accurate control of temporal occurrences, and the other is adequate theory about how artifact characteristics inform about changing functions and social-group affiliation.

Projectile points and chipped stone assemblages in Panama (and greater Central America) and in Florida (and the greater southeastern United States) share characteristics of fabrication and form that indicate fluted point ancestry for both (Faught n.d.b; Ranere and Cooke 1996). But how, when, and from where these people came are new kinds of questions being asked with increasing frequency (Bradley and Stanford 2004; Dixon 2001; Meltzer 2001). I begin this chapter by pointing out that the earliest fluted point sites have been found near the Gulf of Mexico, possibly indicating that populations occurred along the submerged coasts of that paleo-feature. I then describe, briefly, the archaeological records of Florida and Panama: artifacts, sites, site distributions, and temporal controls to investigate possible historical connections. I compare the shapes of points found in both regions by an overlay illustration technique, and I suggest explanations for similarities between artifacts in these two places, including the possibilities of both early and later occurrences of fluted point–related people.

Precise chronology for late Pleistocene, Clovis, and Late Paleoindian material is lacking in the Southeast and in Central America (Haynes 1984, 1992; Taylor et al. 1996). Furthermore, the radiocarbon time frame in which items do begin to show up in dated stratigraphic situations in both regions is difficult to interpret because 500 years of radiocarbon time, from 10,000 BP to 10,500 BP, represents 1,240 years of calibrated time (that is, calibrates to approximately 11,179 cal BP to 12,419 cal BP [Stuiver et al. 1998; Fiedel, this volume]). Consequently, and understandably, researchers in both regions use available ^{14}C data, stratigraphic positioning, and assumptions about biface stylistic evolution (that is, shape and manufacturing sequence) to reconstruct how the artifacts might be related to each other in time.

A Circumgulf Paleoindian Interaction Sphere

Our understanding of diversity and demography in the New World has undergone some dramatic changes over the past ten years. Some of the earliest sites in the New World are known from South America, at the opposite extreme from where such sites would be expected. Fluted points and fluted point sites are much more prevalent in eastern North America than in the far North and Northwest (Anderson and Faught 2000; Dillehay 2000; Faught 1996; G. Haynes 2002). The well-respected and logical ice-free corridor model has not proven to be the pathway for the earliest sites, and thus coastal migration models are logical and have become more popular (Anderson and Gillam 2000; Dixon 1993, 2001; Erlandson 2001; Fladmark 1979; Josenhans et al. 1997). Finally, the diversity and distribution of early artifact assemblages and early skeletal remains indicate that fluted point–related people were not the only ones expanding across the late Pleistocene landscape of the western hemisphere (Dillehay 2000; Faught 1996; Roosevelt et al. 2002).

Table 9.1. Pooled Mean Averages of Fluted Point Sites with Multiple Radiocarbon Determinations Older than 11,000 BP

Site	Averaged date	Reference
Aubrey, Texas	11,565±70 (average of 2)	Ferring 1995
Blackwater Draw, New Mexico	11,301±236 (average of 3)	Holliday 2000
Lubbock Lake, Texas	11,100±60 (average of 2)	Johnson 1991b
Domebo, Oklahoma	11,040±250 (average of 3)	Haynes 1993
Colby, Wyoming	11,030±120 (average of 2)	Haynes 1992
Hiscock, New York	11,022±39 (average of 4)	Laub et al. 1996; Laub and Haynes 1998

The origin point of the fluted point tradition and technology, the most prolific of Paleoindian groups, remains clouded. The earliest fluted point sites are from the southern plains and Llano Estacado of New Mexico, Texas, and Oklahoma. The three earliest sites with fluted points (or related assemblages) and multiple ^{14}C determinations to average from reliable stratigraphic context include Aubrey and Lubbock Lake in Texas, Blackwater Draw in New Mexico, and Domebo in Oklahoma (table 9.1; Faught 1996, n.d.a). Blackwater Draw is the type-site for Clovis points, and it remains one of the earlier sites, even though it has a large margin of error (Holliday 2000; Roosevelt et al. 2002; Sellards 1952).

The rapid or explosive expansion of Clovis sites is indicated because of the number of sites with ages between 10,900 and 11,000 BP, synchronous with the Younger Dryas climatic reversal described in more detail by Stuart Fiedel in this volume (compare Bonnichsen et al. 1987). Numerous well-dated fluted point sites occur with distance from the southern plains "core" in North and South America (if Magellan is included). Early outliers include Colby in Wyoming and Hiscock in New York, then Lehner Ranch and Murray Springs in Arizona (Haynes et al. 1992), Indian Creek (an early Folsom representative) in Montana (Taylor et al. 1996), Paleo Crossing in Ohio (Brose 1994), Shawnee Minisink in Pennsylvania (Dent 1999), and Fell's Cave in Chile (Bird 1988a; Politis 1991). The latest of the well-dated fluted point sites—those with averaged ages after 10,800 BP—are in far northeastern North America (Anderson and Faught 1998; Ellis et al. 1998; Faught n.d.a).

Proposals of earlier fluted point sites at Topper and Cactus Hill in the eastern United States may change the apparent early cluster of fluted point sites (Ellis et al. 1998), but they will need to be dated with multiple ^{14}C-age precision in reliable stratigraphic context to compare with those presented here. Whether the southern portions of North America turn out to be the "found land" of migrating Clovis groups or just good places to end up remains to be determined (Stanford 1991; Steele et al. 1998). Elsewhere, I have hypothesized that earlier fluted point–related sites will be found on the continental shelves of the Gulf of Mexico or along the Eastern Seaboard and that those sites might better inform about fluted point origins (Faught 1996).

Neither Florida (or the greater Southeast) nor Panama (or greater Central America) has sites with multiple ^{14}C ages in reliable stratigraphic context to compare with these Clovis sites, but both exhibit sites and artifacts with technological and stylistic attributes to compare, and the growing number of ^{14}C ages allows for theorizing about how fluted point–related peoples arrived and survived in both areas.

A Brief Summary of the Panamanian and Greater Central American Record

Paleoindian presence in greater Central America is known from diagnostic artifacts, debitage from bifacial reduction, and diagnostic tools recovered as isolated specimens or from surface expressions and excavated deposits (figure 9.1). Los Grifos, Los Tapiales, and nearby findspots in Guatemala and Belize represent a northern cluster of related sites; while Turrialba, Nieto, Cueva de los Vampiros, and La Mula West and nearby findspots make a southern cluster (Pearson 2002; Pearson and Cooke 2003; Ranere and Cooke 1996; Snarskis 1979).

Three diagnostic lanceolate projectile point types have been described from Panama and greater Central America (Bird and Cooke 1978; Gruhn et al. 1977; Mayer-Oakes 1986b; Ranere and Cooke 1991, 1996; Snarskis 1979). Two are Clovis-like and fluted (one is straight sided and the other is "waisted," or concave sided); the third type is called "Fishtail," as its blade and stem resemble points from sites in South America such as Fell's Cave in Chile, Los Toldos in Argentina, and El Inga in Ecuador (Bird 1988a; Bird and Cooke 1978; Mayer-Oakes 1986b; Politis 1991). Fishtails in Central America are fluted. The Clovis-like points are considered to be earlier than the Fishtail points (Pearson 2002; Ranere and Cooke 1996).

More diagnostic Paleoindian points (Clovis-like and Fishtail) have been found in southern Central America ($n = 22$) than in the north ($n = 14$), and of "possibly earlier" Clovis-like varieties, more are straight-sided ($n = 11$) and more likely to be in the south ($n = 8$). Only three waisted Clovis-like varieties have been found in the northern cluster of sites, while five have been found in the south. The ratio of Clovis-like (both waisted and straight sided) to Fishtail points in all of Central America is nearly even (19 versus 17), and the number of Fishtail points in the northern cluster of sites ($n = 8$) is just about equivalent to the number of Fishtail points found in the southern cluster ($n = 9$). One possible implication of these numbers, combined with the magnitude of oc-

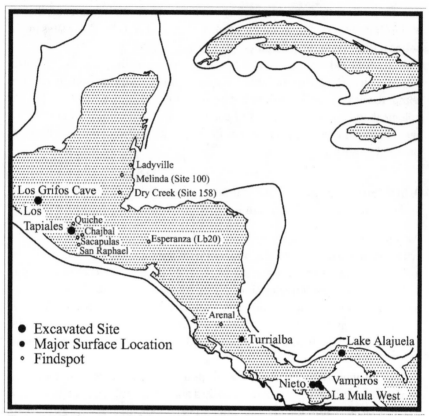

Figure 9.1. Early sites and isolated fluted points in Central America discussed in text (continental shelf estimated from various sources).

cupation apparent in both clusters, is that Panama and the southern cluster were occupied earlier and longer.

Turrialba in eastern Costa Rica is the largest Paleoindian fluted point site in Central America, and it is in the southern cluster (Pearson 2002; Snarskis 1979) (figure 9.1). All three point types were identified from this collection: straight-sided Clovis-like, waisted Clovis-like, and Fishtail. Michael Snarskis proposed a sequence of point styles at Turrialba by noting that Clovis points were found on the older (upper) terraces of the Reventazon River, while Fishtail points were found on lower and more recent terraces (Snarskis 1979). In Panama, two prolific findspots and surface expressions with bifacial flaking, spurred scrapers, and fluted points and fluted point fragments are La Mula West and Madden Lake (also known as Lago Alajuela) (figures 9.1 and 9.2; see also Ranere, this volume). In addition, the Nieto site produced debitage and

Figure 9.2. Fluted points from Madden Lake (Lago Alajuela), Panama. Basal ears are broken off the point 2nd from left. The Macapale Island point, 3rd from the left, has a Folsom-like base.

tool fragments that inform on the sequence of reduction produced by fluted point–related people, and Cueva de los Vampiros has produced stratified deposits in a cave inhabited by fluted point–related knappers (Pearson 2002; Pearson and Cooke 2003).

Radiocarbon ages for fluted points (or fragments) in stratigraphic settings occur at Los Grifos in Mexico, Los Tapiales in Guatemala, and Los Vampiros in Panama. At Los Grifos, a waisted Clovis point and two Fishtail points were found in a layer with two ages of 8930 ± 150 (I-10760) and 9460 ± 150 (I-10761) (Garcia-Barcena 1979, 1982; Ranere and Cooke 1991: 240). Other artifacts found in association with the fluted points at Los Grifos were simple-edged, retouched cutting and scraping tools, but evidently no bifacial debitage, blades, spurred end scrapers, or other artifacts that might better implicate Clovis-related groups were present.

Multiple activities are indicated at Los Tapiales through the presence of one fluted biface (preform?), spurred scrapers and other tools, debitage, and three kinds of stone. Ruth Gruhn and colleagues (1977) have proposed that occupation of Los Tapiales took place at 10,710 ± 170; this conclusion is based on one of three ages derived from charcoal from the lower portions of the sediment matrix (Tx-1631), extracted from 10–20 centimeters above bedrock. The other two ages are also potential associates with the occupation: 11,170 ± 200 (GAK-4889) taken from bedrock and 9,860 ± 185 (GAK-4890) taken from 15–25 centimeters above the bedrock. According to the excavators, there was no evidence for layering or discrete occupation surfaces in this volcanic ash unit; it could, therefore, be a palimpsest of numerous occupations or a bioturbated, disarticulated, single occupation. The excavators do not report where, in this sequence, the fluted point fragment was found. An argument could be made that the *terminus post quem* date of 9860 BP is equally plausible as being representative of the actual age of the artifact assemblage and in agreement with dates obtained from Los Grifos.

In Panama, at Los Vampiros a very early age bulk sample determination of 11,550 ± 140 BP (Beta 167520) came from a "thin occupation floor" below a discrete zone with an age of 8970 ± 40 (Pearson 2002). At La Mula West, Donald Crusoe and J.L. Felton (1974) reported an exposed prepared fire pit producing an age of 11,300 ± 250 BP (FSU-300); at Lake La Yeguada, increased charcoal fragments and pollens from pioneer species plants from sediment cores have led Dolores Piperno to propose that humans had been altering the forests circa 11,050 BP. Anthony Ranere and Richard Cooke report bifacial chipping debris around the lake (Pearson 2002; Piperno et al. 1991). At Agua-dulce Rockshelter, biface debitage was associated with ages of 10,725 ± 80 BP (NZA-10930) and 10,529 ± 184 BP (NZA-9622) on phytoliths (Pearson 2002), and at La Corona Rockshelter, biface debitage was associated with a single ^{14}C determination of 10,440 ± 650 BP (Beta-19105) (Cooke and Ranere 1992a).

Ranere and Cooke (1996) show that stemmed bifacial points of early Holo-cene age and bifacial reduction strategies occur only at sites older than 7,000 years old in Panama, especially in the central region (compare Cooke and Ra-nere 1992a; Pearson and Cooke 2003; Ranere and Cooke 1996). There is no evidence for bifacial reduction strategies in post-7,000-year-old cultural de-posits. This apparent rejection or abandonment of a useful strategy for reduc-ing chipped stone assemblages contrasts with archaeological assemblages in Florida and in most areas of eastern North America, where the production of bifacial objects continued to the time of European contact.

A Brief Summary of the Floridian Paleoindian Record

As in Panama, diagnostic artifacts in Florida are found as isolated finds, as surface expressions with abundance of debris, and from excavations in sealed deposits (figure 9.3). Page-Ladson (and surrounding findspots and surface ex-pressions) is a well-known locality in the northernmost of three large clusters of sites and findspots in Florida, known as the Aucilla region (Faught n.d.b). In addition to having a high frequency of isolated artifacts and surface expres-sions, the Suwannee region includes stratified sites such as Darby and Hornsby Springs on the Santa Fe River, the Bolen Bluff site, and Silver Springs south of Gainesville. The Tampa Bay region includes one of the largest Late Paleoindian and Early Archaic sites in Florida, Harney Flats (Daniel and Wisenbaker 1987), as well as numerous findspots and surface expressions.

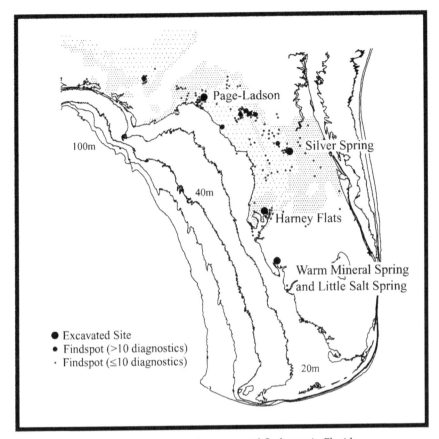

Figure 9.3. Paleoindian and Early Archaic sites and findspots in Florida.

Three kinds of lanceolate Paleoindian projectile points are known from Florida, including fluted points and two kinds of unfluted, waisted lanceolates. In Florida, fluted points are universally classified as Clovis, regardless of whether the base is straight or waisted, or what the basal shape is. The other two waisted lanceolates are classified as Suwannee and Simpson (figure 9.4; Anderson and Sassaman 1996; Bullen 1975; Cambron and Hulse 1964; Justice 1987; Milanich 1994). The emphasis on bifacial reduction along with formal unifacial chipped stone tools of large and small size indicates a fluted point–related heritage (Faught n.d.b; Hemmings 2004).

Isolated finds of Paleoindian points have been inventoried by James Dunbar of Florida's Bureau of Archaeological Research in Tallahassee and by the late Ben Waller of Ocala, Florida, an early avocational diver and collector (Dunbar 1991; Dunbar and Waller 1983). This sample ($N = 543$) was compiled from both private and institutional collections. Suwannee points are by far the most fre-

Figure 9.4. Selected Paleoindian points from Florida. The point in the center is fluted and similar to specimens in Central America; points on the right and left are classified as Suwannee.

quent projectile point type recorded (81 percent); Clovis projectile points are the second most frequently recorded (approximately 14 percent); and Simpson projectile points are the rarest type recorded (5 percent).

Fluted points are frequent in the Suwannee and Aucilla River areas but less so in the Tampa Bay region. Suwannee points occur in each of the three aforementioned clusters in Florida, but they are most frequent in the Santa Fe and Itchetucknee River valleys of north-central Florida. Simpson projectile points are localized in northern Florida around the Chippola River in the panhandle (Chason 1987). The increased sample of Late Paleoindian points (Suwannee) over early points (fluted) indicates evidence of increasing resource catchment range and likely increasing populations.

Remains of late Pleistocene fauna are frequent in Florida in the rivers and other karst features of the northern and western portions of the peninsula (Webb 1974). This fauna comprises larger extinct mammals of genera including *Mamut, Mammuthus, Equus, Bison, Camelops,* and *Eremotherium,* as well as a plethora of smaller animals. Some of the specimens of faunal bone from extinct species have possible butchery cut marks and other evidence for human alteration, but later inhabitants may have altered the old bones well after the animals went extinct (Dunbar and Webb 1996). Some artifacts, however, seem to have unambiguous associations. For instance, foreshafts of ivory have been found in Florida, one of the few places in the New World where such artifacts are found (Dunbar and Webb 1996; Hemmings 1998, 2004).

Although Florida has a rich array of early artifact types and an impressive number of findspots, ^{14}C dates for diagnostic Paleoindian points in sealed stratigraphic contexts remain elusive. A three-part arrangement of Early, Middle, and Late Paleoindian periods has been constructed for the greater Southeast from stratigraphic data, models of stylistic evolution, and limited ^{14}C control (compare Anderson and Sassaman 1996; Dunbar 2002; Ellis et al. 1998). At Little Salt Springs, a "wooden spear" ^{14}C-dated to 12,030 ± 200 BP (TX-2636) and found with "burnt" remains of extinct tortoise dated to 13,450 ± 190 BP (TX-2335) was proposed as the result of human activities (Clausen et al. 1979). However, the ages of these items are not overlapping; the "spear" is more likely a stick, and the tortoise is stained but not burned (Dunbar 2002; Purdy 1991: 146).

At the Page-Ladson site in the Aucilla region, proboscidean digesta, extinct bone specimens, and abundant numbers of Paleoindian and Early Archaic artifacts from several time periods have been found in a thirty-foot-deep sinkhole. The digesta and animal remains indicate that animals were rummaging in the karst depression features when water levels were lower. Sedimentation of proboscidean digesta and faunal bone clusters around 12,300 BP (Dunbar et al. 1988; Webb 2006). Single-blow conchoidal flakes of coarse chert and possible cut marks on a mammoth tusk from this late Pleistocene deposit led David Webb (2006) and James Dunbar (2002) to propose human presence at Page-Ladson before circa 12,000 BP. The working hypothesis is that these features were important locations for fluted point–related Paleoindians and their progeny to find water, chert, wood, and animals (Dunbar 1991; Neill 1964; Watts and Hansen 1988; Watts et al. 1992).

Near Page-Ladson, in a tributary of the Aucilla River, a *Bison antiquus* skull was found with a piece of chert imbedded in the frontal that has been referred to as a projectile point tip until further investigation with X-ray (Mihlbachler et al. 2000; Webb et al. 1984). Other fragments of *Bison* humerus and skull found in the same deposit as the skull returned discrepant ^{14}C ages of 11,170 ± 130 BP (Beta-5942) and 9990 ± 200 BP (Beta-5941), respectively. One of several ivory foreshafts found at Sloth Hole, a site downstream on the Aucilla, near its modern mouth, was dated at 11,050 ± 50 BP (SL2850) (Hemmings 1998, 2004), confirming a Clovis age frame for fluted point diagnostics found at this site.

At Darby Springs, on the Santa Fe River, a Suwannee point was found with mastodon teeth in a calcitic mud in a karst void feature. Radiocarbon assay of this mud indicates an age of 9880 ± 270 BP (no lab number; Dolan and Allen 1961: 35).

Warm Mineral Springs is a well-known site because of the skeletal remains found on a submerged ledge and in a cavern there (Cockrell and Murphy 1978). The earliest ^{14}C determinations in the underwater deposits suggest sedimentation after 10,630 BP, but the majority of ages occur between 10,000 BP and 9000 BP (Clausen et al. 1975; Faught and Carter 1998). The skeletal material from Warm Mineral Springs may be even younger, of middle Holocene age, and therefore these are not necessarily Clovis fluted point–related skeletal remains (Susan Anton, personal communication 2001).

The only occurrence of Clovis artifacts in stratigraphic context in Florida is at Silver Springs in central Florida (Hemmings 1975; Neill 1958). Fluted point fragments were found at the base of a deep sequence of dune deposits. There are no recorded stratigraphic occurrences of fluted points with Suwannee points to securely place them within a specific time period. There are, however, several examples of Suwannee points occurring immediately below Early Archaic Bolen diagnostic artifacts (and related tool kits) in stratified settings, including the Bolen Bluff site, Hornsby Springs, and Harney Flats (Bullen 1958; Daniel and Wisenbaker 1987; Dolan and Allen 1961; Neill 1958). Suwannee projectile points also co-occur with Early Archaic notched points in surface contexts, both terrestrially and underwater. Suwannee lanceolates and notched points commonly co-occur in local collections. This evidence suggests that Suwannee is closer in time to early Holocene Bolen than to late Pleistocene Clovis. Perhaps the more important implication is that co-occurrences of these diagnostic projectile point/knife types, and the stratigraphic record, represent strong evidence for survival from fluted point–related Paleoindians to Early Archaic cultures in Florida.

Lanceolate points undergo extreme waisting and other morphological changes resulting in side- and corner-notched points in the greater Southeast. In addition to Suwannees in Florida, Paleoindian waisted lanceolate projectile points known from the greater Southeast include Dalton and Greenbriar (Anderson and Sassaman 1996). These waisted lanceolate varieties occur slightly lower stratigraphically than the fully notched points such as Bolen, Big Sandy, and Taylor, which show up with dates at and after 10,000 BP (Bullen 1975; Cambron and Hulse 1964; Coe 1964; Driskell 1996; Faught et al. 2003; Justice 1987). In Florida and the greater Southeast, notched projectile points mark the transition from Late Paleoindian to Early Archaic adaptations, but the tool kit retains the fluted point characteristics of bifacial reduction (including use of fluted preforms) and formal unifacial tools that indicate technological and stylistic continuity with fluted point Paleoindian technology (Faught n.d.b).

Currently, the most stratigraphically secure ^{14}C control for stylistic diagnostic artifacts of early human occupation of northwestern Florida comes from the "Bolen surface" at Page-Ladson. At this site, Early Archaic Bolen diagnostics were found in sealed stratigraphic contexts from which six ^{14}C determinations have been made, averaging 9958 ± 40 BP (Dunbar et al. 1988, 1989; Faught 1996: 248; Faught et al. 2003). The artifacts include side- and corner-notched beveled projectile points, antler and bone tools, and other biface tool fragments (possible adze bits, but not use-worn). Confirmation of the early date of notched points also comes from ^{14}C determinations in stratigraphic contexts at LE2105 near Tallahassee, with an average of three points at 9870 ± 40 BP (Faught et al. 2003); the association includes both side- and corner-notched points, unifacial tools including Hendrix scrapers, unifacial adzes, and fluted preforms. Dust Cave in Alabama confirms this age with notched points dating to circa 9900 BP (Driskell 1996).

Projectile Points, Tools, and Reduction Strategies

Figures 9.5 and 9.6 compare and present a selection of projectile points from Florida and Panama. In figure 9.5, the points are shown separately and the provenience of individual artifacts is presented. Figure 9.6 shows the types superimposed. The regularities and variance of the formal categories are obvious. Of course, evaluating the shape of an artifact alone does not allow consideration of the fabrication characteristics of the artifact, which I discuss below.

North American Clovis points were prepared from biface preforms, using both overshot and collateral flaking, with flutes driven off well before the end of the fabrication process (Morrow 1995; also see Ranere, this volume). These are characteristic indicators of Clovis technology in North America. Classic examples of Clovis points are carefully shaped and do not have extreme basal concavities (Morrow and Morrow 1999). The two type specimens are straight and slightly excurvate (Hester 1972), but points from other Clovis sites include waisted and straight-sided varieties (see Anderson and Faught 1998; Bradley 1993; Freeman et al. 1996; Howard 1990; Morrow 1995; Morrow and Morrow 1999; Sellards 1952 for various descriptions).

The fragments of fluted point bases from La Mula West have straight sides and flutes driven off well before the end of the fabrication process. These items were made from a white, fine-grained, crypto-crystalline agate, which would be expected for Clovis points. These characteristics support the interpretations of Ranere and Cooke (1996: 58) for Clovis-age occupation or possible early exploration of Central America by early fluted point–making people. By contrast, Michael Snarskis has proposed that some of the straight-sided fluted points from Los Tapiales may be fluted preforms (1979: 129). Fluted biface preforms are also known from sites in North America, including Kentucky

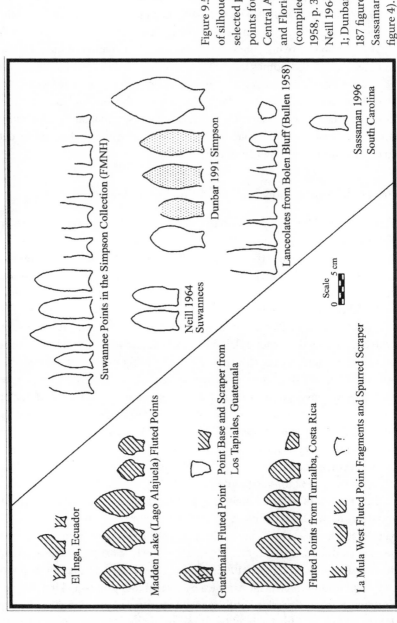

El Inga, Ecuador

Madden Lake (Lago Alajuela) Fluted Points

Guatemalan Fluted Point   Point Base and Scraper from
Los Tapiales, Guatemala

Fluted Points from Turrialba, Costa Rica

La Mula West Fluted Point Fragments and Spurred Scraper

Suwannee Points in the Simpson Collection (FMNH)

Neill 1964
Suwannees

Dunbar 1991 Simpson

Lanceolates from Bolen Bluff (Bullen 1958)

Sassaman 1996
South Carolina

Scale
0   5 cm

Figure 9.5. Comparison of silhouettes of selected projectile points found in Central America (*left*) and Florida (*right*) (compiled from Bullen 1958, p. 39 plate 1; Neill 1964, p. 22 figure 1; Dunbar 1991, p. 187 figures 1 and 2; Sassaman 1996, p. 79 figure 4).

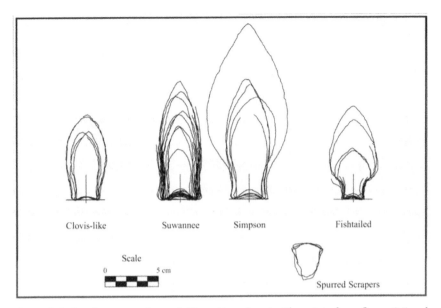

Figure 9.6. Overlay comparison of silhouettes of projectile points from figure 9.5 and spurred end scrapers from Los Tapiales and La Mula West. The outlines were digitized at scale from various publications, and drawings were made in AutoCAD.

(Freeman et al. 1996) and Missouri (Martens et al. 2004; Morrow 1995). Some Central and South American fluted "points" may be products of this reduction stage and not finished points, possibly representing later-age occurrences rather than early-end Clovis.

Waisted fluted points in greater Central America include the San Rafael point (Coe 1960), three points from Turrialba (Snarskis 1979: 128–29, figures 2 and 3b), the Ladyville fluted point (Kelly 1993: 212; figure 5), the Arenal fluted point (Sheets 1994), and the Macapale Island fluted point from Madden Lake (figure 9.2 and 9.5) (Bird and Cooke 1978: 265). Interestingly, the Arenal, Ladyville, and Turrialba fluted points are virtually identical in fabrication and detailed morphology to fluted points from Florida, one of which is illustrated here (figure 9.4, center). The waisted nature of the stem and the radial pattern of light, soft hammer percussion (or possibly pressure) retouch around the margins of these points are distinctive. Determining the significance of these shared attributes depends on a more precise understanding of the age of these specimens, but they may represent contemporaneous occurrences and evidence for low-scale circumgulf interactions.

Fishtail points in Central America were made differently than the fluted points (Bird and Cooke 1978; Ranere and Cooke 1996). The Fishtail points of Central America were made on large thin flakes, or thin biface preforms, with shaping flake scars that tend to meet in the middle of the biface. Pressure flaking or very light, soft hammer percussion was used to shape margins. The "flute" can be the concave portion of the original flake surface (on the exterior, dorsal side of the preform flake) or a basal flake taken off before final finishing. The resultant basal shapes are identical to bases of some Folsom points, and the stem widths maintain a uniform size, as do Folsom points.[1] The technology of shaping around flutes taken off during preform shaping is similar to Folsom technology as well. The "Hartman" fluted point from Costa Rica, reported by James Swauger and William Mayer-Oakes in 1952, is one of these technologically distinctive types, as are two points from Turrialba (Snarskis 1979: figs. 2a and 2b) and the majority of points found in the Chagres River valley at Madden Lake (Lago Alajuela), including some of the most aesthetic (figure 9.2). These all share technological characteristics with Folsom and other Late Paleoindian projectile points, such as Cumberland, Barnes, and Redstone in North America (Justice 1987); the Fishtail types known from Fell's Cave (Bird 1988a); and the points from El Inga in Equador (Mayer-Oakes 1986). Point styles similar to these do not occur in Florida.

The occurrence of spurred scrapers (figure 9.7) in Panama (and greater Central America) is also congruent with Folsom diagnostics. These scrapers have come from La Mula West (Cooke and Ranere 1992a: 255) (figure 9.7), Los Tapiales (Gruhn and Bryan 1977: 274, fig. 12), and Turrialba (Snarskis 1979: 132). Together, these Folsom-like characteristics suggest interaction, reticulation, or both.

Suwannee points do not resemble any of the Central American points in published accounts, except perhaps in the continuation of waisted stems and basal concavities. Ripley Bullen has described the points as "unusually large and fairly heavy, lanceolate shaped, slightly waisted . . . with concave base, basal ears, and basal grinding" (Bullen 1975: 55). However, Albert Goodyear and colleagues (1983) and Randy Daniel and Michael Wisenbaker (1987) have detailed one production sequence of these points that were made on bladelike flakes, with the bases thinned laterally in many cases. It is my impression that Suwannee points were made from biface preforms *and* large bladelike flakes, but no data have been compiled to confirm this hypothesis.

While some Simpson shapes do resemble the Fishtail varieties in Central America by having constricted waists and broad blades, the method of manufacture is different. Simpson points are "wide bladed, relatively narrow waisted, fairly thin, concave based, medium to large sized points with grinding apparent in the haft area, basal ears, but not as developed as in the Suwannee point, and basal thinning occurs but is also not as well developed as the Suwannee" (Bullen 1975: 56). Some Simpson projectile points are extremely waisted and

Figure 9.7. Spurred end scraper from La Mula West, Panama.

broad bladed—unequivocally "Simpson." Other examples, however, tend toward shapes that might as well be described as Suwannee points with broad blades. The concentration of these point forms in the Chippola River in the panhandle of Florida distinguishes them from other point forms.

A functional characteristic of both Suwannee from Florida and Fishtail points from Central America is that they are worked down by resharpening, often resulting in an ever-reduced appearance (figure 9.6). This seems to be a frequent characteristic in Late Paleoindian and Early Archaic assemblages in the circumgulf region in the early Holocene, with such points as San Patrice, Dalton, and Greenbriar (Justice 1987). The similarity of tool maintenance and reduction strategies may imply a knifelike function for these implements, as well as similar manipulation strategies for local resources. Large unifacial scrapers are also characteristic of early Holocene circumgulf resource manipulation activities occurring in Dalton, Suwannee, and other Late Paleoindian assemblages. These artifacts are known variously as Clear Fork gouges, Dalton adzes, and Aucilla adzes (Gerrell et al. 1991; Morse and Goodyear 1973). These indicate early Holocene manipulation of wood resources, although what items were being made of the wood is unknown. Large scrapers or scraper-planes are also known from Central America, including the Lago Alajuela collections, Turrialba (Snarskis 1979: figs. 9.6–9.8), and Los Tapiales (Gruhn and Bryan 1977: figs. 19 and 20). Specimens in Panama exhibit step fractures diagnostic of woodworking use-wear (Keeley 1980). These tools support Piperno's hypothesis that human manipulation of plants was earlier and more complex than previously thought (Piperno and Pearsall 1998).

Conclusions

I began this chapter with the observation that the earliest fluted point sites occur near the Gulf of Mexico, indicating where populations may have been along the now-submerged paleo-gulf coastline. These now-inundated paleo-landscapes were utilized by early peoples, and today they can be considered and sampled by underwater archaeologists (Faught 1996, 2004). The extent of the continental shelves of Central America and Florida is shown in figures 9.1 and 9.3, respectively. Florida is well known for underwater Paleoindian and Early Archaic sites, and my underwater research on the western continental shelf of Florida has produced sites of Late Paleoindian and Early Archaic age, as well as Middle Archaic materials reflecting later coastal occupations (Faught 1988, 1996, 2004). Artifacts are also known from underwater contexts in Panama. Junius Bird and Richard Cooke (1977) reported that materials were dredged from forty- to fifty-foot depths off Balboa from a "muck" layer that yielded a temporally mixed assemblage of pieces of chipped agate, a biface, and a polished stone adze. This discovery substantiates the idea that some of the early archaeological record is obscured by Holocene sea level rise in Panama, just as it is in Florida. Known sites in Panama are concentrated near drainages that go to Pacific, into Parita Bay, rather than to the Gulf of Mexico.

In both regions, isolated projectile points are found in surface and shallow buried contexts, and stratigraphic and ^{14}C control associated with diagnostic artifacts in secure contexts is weak. However, Paleoindian and Early Archaic artifacts and sites are significantly more abundant in Florida than in Panama. This is true in agency-curated collections (such as the Smithsonian Tropical Research Institute, the Florida Museum of Natural History, and so forth) as well as in private collections. So, what are the reasons for these differences? There are obvious differences in the amount of academic interest and research attention over the years (that is, more attention has been focused on Florida than Panama). There are also differences in geologic preservation potentials of both regions. Florida's karst geology is one of the primary reasons for the numerous discoveries of Paleoindian and Early Archaic remains because of both abundant natural resources and preservation potentials.

In the end, however, the differences in magnitude are most likely the result of differences in population size at the end of the Pleistocene and in the early Holocene. In Central America, a lower population density probably produced a sparse archaeological record, as Ranere and Cooke have noted (1996). In Florida, there are both high population and apparent long-term occupation in Late Paleoindian and Early Archaic times.

Gordon R. Willey proposed a model of Clovis origins that described the southward proliferation of fluted point makers from northeast Asia, out of the ice-free corridor, through Central America, and into South America—first to El Inga and then to the Straits of Magellan (Willey 1966). This scenario is untenable today because the progressive distributions of Clovis sites do not come through the ice-free corridor (Dillehay 2000; Faught n.d.a; Meltzer 2001). The earliest Clovis sites discovered so far are in the southern plains, and there are sites in many places in the western hemisphere after that. One alternative model that may have merit, if sites of appropriate age accrue, is that the earliest fluted point–related people came along a western coastal route by way of Panama into the Gulf of Mexico across the isthmus (Faught and Anderson 1996). The possibility that Los Vampiros at 11,550 BP or Los Tapiales at 11,170 BP dates the initial occupation of the region may also support this hypothesis, but not by any unambiguous contextual associations or multiple ^{14}C estimates or through artifact abundance indicating population concentrations.

I agree with Cooke and Ranere's proposal of a sequence of stylistic developments in which waisted Clovis fluted points occurred after the straight-sided Clovis fluted points and were followed by Fishtails (Ranere and Cooke 1991: 241). Their sequential model views both waisted and lanceolate fluted point forms (those made from biface preforms) as earlier than the Fishtails (often made on flakes).

Willey also had ideas with regard to the origins of the Fishtail point style. One is that Fishtail points derived from the Clovis (Llano) tradition of North America and diffused south, while the other suggests that these were derived from El Jobo or Lerma convex-based (stemmed) point assemblages in South America and diffused north (Willey 1966: 68). Lynch proposed a similar scenario suggesting that the Fishtail point series—in which he included Magellan, Toldense, and El Inga—had ancestor/descendant relationships with stemmed point traditions such as Ayamptin, Paijan, and Chobshi (Lynch 1983). Fishtail points and other Magellan industry artifacts in southern South America are as early as Folsom at Fell's Cave at 10,840 ± 100 BP (average of three dates) and Cerro la China at 10,760 ± 100 BP (average of two dates) (Faught 1996; Politis 1991: 290). These dates put the South American sites in the early centuries of fluted point colonization in North America and contemporaneous with Folsom in the plains. The Fishtail point shape in Central America may best be explained as a result of reticulation (sharing, interacting) between different populations, but more temporal control and studied collections are needed to address these proposals more definitely. Similarities between Folsom and Fishtail in Central America imply at least contact between individuals, if not contacts between demes. These similarities include bifacial reduction strategies for the manufacture of projectile points, stem morphology and size, and the presence of spurred end scrapers and other flake tools with spurs like Folsom in the plains. Reticulation is indicated again because these similarities include a crossing over of traditional and technological attributes.

The evidence for the Paleoindian to Early Archaic period transition in Florida is unequivocal—stratigraphically, technologically, and by reoccupation of the same locations. However, occupation of the Floridian peninsula by fluted point progeny is continuous only to the end of the early Holocene, perhaps around 9000 BP, based on stratigraphic lacunae above and low frequencies of later (Kirk) diagnostic artifacts and sites in Florida (Faught n.d.b; Faught and Carter 1998). Reappearance of sites and artifacts indicates growing populations after 8500 BP with changes in settlement pattern and in artifact technology and style, and with new burial practices, calling into question any attribution of later populations having direct ancestry to fluted point–related Paleoindians.

In Panama, Piperno's evidence for human interference in plant distributions at Lake La Yeguada is well argued, and because the evidence is continuous throughout the early Holocene sediment column, continuity of occupation by active human beings is logical. However, bifacial reduction strategies were replaced by unifacial and expedient tool reduction strategies, apparently without a clear sequence of evolving behaviors through the intervening time, as might be expected. Replacement groups may have come in from South America later and subsumed (or never saw) the previous fluted point–related people (Cooke and Ranere 1992a: 263). Based strictly on the differences in the two chipped stone assemblages, replacement seems a more parsimonious alternative.

It is important to address these issues of continuity and relationship. Cooke and Ranere have shown that the people who made post–7,000 BP unifacial and other expedient chipped stone tools and edge-ground cobbles were the ancestors of the Chibchan-speaking social groups encountered at contact (Cooke and Ranere 1992a: 262; Greenberg 1987). If the hypothesis of early Holocene to middle Holocene continuity is correct, then their language and biology would have evolved from those of the people who made fluted points. Elsewhere, and on the basis of different archaeological and linguistic data, I have proposed that fluted point–related Paleoindians of the East (particularly the far Northeast) spoke a proto Macro-Algonquin language that is a pre-Penutian or pre-Gulf language stock (Faught 1996; see also Greenberg 1987; Haas 1958; Willey 1958). Chibchan and Algonquian are not even distant relatives in any linguistic models (Greenberg 1987). So Cooke and Ranere's (1992a) proposal that Clovis people settled in Central America and evolved into Chibchan speakers known at contact creates alternative models, lively debate, and the need for continued research into these details. The same kind of problem arises if the Warm Mineral Springs people are assumed to be Clovis related because of their supposed early age. If they are representatives of middle Holocene replacement populations, then assumption of fluted point affiliation would be wrong. These issues must be addressed to accurately interpret New World microevolution.

Determining ancestor/descendant relationships with enough detail to make accurate historical reconstructions at scales appropriate to discern the evolution of social groups, from Paleoindian to contact and throughout the continents, is a vital part of explaining the process of their adaptations. Most of the proposals expressed in this chapter can best be addressed when the chronology of the colonization process becomes more clear and as our ability to assign cultural, ethnic, and demic identities, in principled ways, to archaeological assemblages increases.

Acknowledgments

This chapter is based on research published by dedicated and productive researchers, including Junius Bird, Richard Cooke, and Anthony Ranere in Panama, as well as James Dunbar and Ben Waller in Florida. In 1997 and 1998, I viewed selected collections firsthand from Lago Alajuela and La Mula West that are curated at the Smithsonian Tropical Research Institute (STRI) and the Museo de Antropologia, both in Panama City, Republic of Panama. I also evaluated collections from the Florida Museum of Natural History in Gainesville and the Bureau of Archaeological Research in Tallahassee. For details of additional sites and artifacts in Honduras, Guatemala, Costa Rica, and Belize, and for additional sites in Florida, I have referred to other published works. My sincere thanks go to Lynette Norr, Richard Cooke, and the personnel of STRI, Anthony Ranere of Temple University, Elise LeCompt of the Florida Museum of Natural History, and James Dunbar of the Bureau of Archaeological Research, Florida Department of State, for their support and cooperation during this investigation.

Notes

1. The mean variation of width of the projectile point base for the Central American sample is 1.89 centimeters. Folsom stem-width variation is narrowly focused. Dan Amick reports a mean of 1.81 centimeters and a median of 1.83 centimeters from a sample of 391 New Mexico Folsom points (Amick 1994: 23). The range for South American examples has not been determined, but no such restriction applies to the Late Paleoindian Suwannee points as seen in figure 9.5.

References

Aceituno, F. J.
2002 Interacciones fitoculturales en el Cauca Medio. *Revista del Area Intermedia* 4: 89–113.

Adams, J. M., G. R. Foote, and M. Otte
2001 Could Pre–Last Glacial Maximum Humans Have Existed in North America Undetected? An Interregional Approach to the Question. *Current Anthropology* 42: 563–66.

Adovasio, J. M., D. Pedler, J. Donahue, and R. Stuckenrath
1999 No Vestige of a Beginning nor Prospect for an End: Two Decades of Debate on Meadowcroft Rockshelter. In *Ice Age Peoples of North America: Environments, Origins, and Adaptations of the First Americans*, edited by R. Bonnichsen and K. L. Turnmire, pp. 416–31. Oregon State University Press, Corvallis.

Agenbroad, L. D., and B. B. Huckell
2007 The Hunting Camp at Murray Springs. In *Murray Springs: A Clovis Site with Multiple Activity Areas in the San Pedro Valley, Arizona*, edited by C. V. Haynes Jr. and B. B. Huckell. Anthropological Papers of the University of Arizona. University of Arizona Press, Tucson. (Forthcoming)

Agenbroad, L. D., and J. I. Mead
1989 Quaternary Geochronology and Distribution of *Mammuthus* on the Colorado Plateau. *Geology* 17: 861–64.

Aguirre, M., and R. Whatley
1995 Late Quaternary Marginal Marine Deposits and Palaeoenvironments from Northeastern Buenos Aires Province, Argentina: A Review. *Quaternary Science Review* 14: 223–54.

Alberti, M. T., L. Miotti, and J. L. Prado
2001 *Hippidion saldiasi* Roth, 1899 (Equidae, Perissodactyla), at the Piedra Museo Site (Santa Cruz, Argentina): Its Implications for the Regional Economy and Environmental Reconstruction. *Journal of Archaeological Science* 28: 411–19.

Alberti, M. T., and J. L. Prado
2004 *Caballos fósiles de América del Sur. Una historia de tres millones de años.* INCUAPA, Olavaria, Agentina.

Amick, D. S.
1994 Technological Organization and the Structure of Inference in Lithic Analysis: An Examination of Folsom Hunting Behavior in the American SW. In *The Organization of North American Prehistoric Chipped Stone Tool Technologies*, edited by P. J. Carr, pp. 9–34. International Monographs in Prehistory 7. University of Michigan, Ann Arbor.

Anderson, D. G.

1990   The Paleoindian Colonization of Eastern North America: A View from the Southeastern United States. In *Early Paleoindian Economies of Eastern North America*, edited by K. Tankersley and B. Isaac, pp. 163–216. Research in Economic Anthropology Supplement 5. JAI Press, Greenwich, Conn.

1991   Examining Prehistoric Settlement Distribution in Eastern North America. *Archaeology of Eastern North America* 19: 1–21.

1996   Models of Paleoindian and Early Archaic Settlement in the Lower Southeast. In *The Paleoindian and Early Archaic Southeast*, edited by D. G. Anderson and K. Sassaman, pp. 29–57. University of Alabama, Tuscaloosa.

Anderson, D. G., and M. K. Faught

1998   The Distribution of Fluted Paleoindian Projectile Points: Update 1998. *Archaeology of Eastern North America* 26: 163–87.

2000   Paleoindian Climate, Dating and Artifact Distributions on a Very Large Scale: Evidence and Implications. *Antiquity* 74: 507–13.

Anderson, D. G., and J. C. Gillam

2000   Paleoindian Colonization of the Americas: Implications from an Examination of Physiography, Demography, and Artifact Distributions. *American Antiquity* 65: 43–66.

Anderson, D. G., and K. E. Sassaman (Editors)

1996   *The Paleoindian and Early Archaic Southeast*. University of Alabama Press, Tuscaloosa.

Andresen, C. S., S. Bjorck, O. Bennike, J. Heinemeier, and B. Kromer

2000   What Do δ^{14}C Changes across the Gerzensee Oscillation/GI-1b Event Imply for Deglacial Oscillations? *Journal of Quaternary Science* 15: 203–14.

Anonymous

1989   Desert Archaeology: New Beginnings, a Look Back. *Archaeology in Tucson* 3: 2.

Anovitz, L. M., J. M. Elam, L. R. Riciputi, and D. R. Cole

1999   The Failure of Obsidian Hydration Dating: Source, Implications, and New Directions. *Journal of Archaeological Science* 26 (7): 735–52.

Antevs, E.

1935   Age of the Clovis Lake Clays. *Academy of Natural Sciences of Philadelphia Proceedings* 87: 304–12.

1953   Age of the Clovis Fluted Points with the Naco Mammoth. *American Antiquity* 19 (1): 15–17.

1959   Geological Age of the Lehner Mammoth Site. *American Antiquity* 25 (1): 31–34.

Anthony, D. W.

1990   Migration in Archaeology: The Baby and the Bathwater. *American Anthropologist* 92: 895–914.

Ardila, G.

1991   The Peopling of Northern South America. In *Clovis: Origins and Adaptations*, edited by R. Bonnichsen and K. L. Turnmire, pp. 261–82. Center for the Study of the First Americans, Oregon State University, Corvallis.

Ardila, G., and G. G. Politis

1989 Nuevos datos para un viejo problema: Investigación y discusión en torno del poblamiento de América del Sur. *Boletín del Museo del Oro* 23: 3–45.

Aschero, C. A.

1979 Un asentamiento precerámico en la Inca Cueva (Jujuy, Argentina): Informe preliminar sobre el sitio Icc4. In *Actas de las Jornadas de Arqueología del NOA*, pp. 77–95. Universidad del Salvador, Buenos Aires.

Aschmann, H.

1952 A Fluted Point from Central Baja California. *American Antiquity* 17: 262–63.

Baales, M., O. Joris, and M. Street

2002 Impact of the Late Glacial Eruption of the Laacher See Volcano, Central Rhineland, Germany. *Quaternary Research* 58: 273–88.

Baales, M., and M. Street

1996 Hunter-Gatherer Behavior in a Changing Late Glacial Landscape: Allerød Archaeology in the Central Rhineland, Germany. *Journal of Anthropological Research* 52: 281–316.

Baker, V. R.

1983 Late-Pleistocene Fluvial Systems. In *Late-Quaternary Environments of the United States*, vol. 1, edited by S. C. Porter, pp. 115–29. University of Minnesota Press, Minneapolis.

Bamforth, D. B.

1986 Technological Efficiency and Tool Curation. *American Antiquity* 51: 38–50.

1991 Technological Organization and Hunter Gatherer Land Use: A California Example. *American Antiquity* 56: 216–34.

Barbetti, M.

n.d. SRT-783 Tree-Ring and Cariaco Varve Data. Australian Government, Australian Institute of Nuclear Science and Engineering. http://www.ansto.gov.au/ainse/prorep2001/R_00_003.pdf (accessed June 28, 2005).

Barrientos, G.

1997 Nutrición y dieta de las poblaciones aborígenes prehispánicas del sudeste de la región pampeana. Ph.D. dissertation, Universidad Nacional de La Plata, La Plata.

Barrientos, G., H. M. Puciarelli, G. Politis, S. I. Perez, and M. Sardi

2003 The Craniofacial Morphology of Early to Middle Holocene Human Populations from the Pampean Region, Argentina: Getting a New Insight into the Morphological Variability of Early Americans. In *Where the South Winds Blow: Ancient Evidence of Paleo South Americans*, edited by L. Miotti, M. Salemme, and N. Flegenheimer, pp. 69–75. Center for the Study of the First Americans, Texas A&M University, College Station.

Barse, W. P.

1990 Preceramic Occupations in the Orinoco River Valley. *Science* 250: 1388–390.

Bartlett, A. S., and E. S. Barghoorn
1973   Phytogeographic History of the Isthmus of Panama during the Past 12,000 years (a History of Vegetation, Climate and Sea Level Change). In *Vegetation and Vegetational History of Northern Latin America*, edited by A. Graham, pp. 203–99. Elsevier Scientific Publishing Company, New York.

Basgall, M. E.
1995   Obsidian Hydration Dating of Early Holocene Assemblages in the Mojave Desert. *Current Research in the Pleistocene* 12: 57–60.

Bayón, C., and G. Politis
1997   Pisadas Humanas en el sitio de Monte Hermoso 1 (Pcia. de Buenos Aires) *Arqueología* 6: 83–115.

Beaton, J.
1991   Paleoindian Occupation Greater Than 11,000 Years B.P. at Tule Lake, California. *Current Research in the Pleistocene* 8: 5–7.

Bell, R. E.
1965   *Investigaciones arqueológicas en el sitio de El Inga*. Casa de la Cultura Ecuatoriana, Quito.
1977   Obsidian Hydration Studies in Highland Ecuador. *American Antiquity* 42: 68–78.

Beltrao, M. C., R. A. Pérez, and M. Locks
1997   Late Pleistocene Archaeological Sites in Brazil and Prior Occupations: Alice Boer (Sao Paulo), Toca da Esperanca (Bahia) and Itaboraí (Rio de Janeiro). Paper presented at the 62nd Annual Meeting of the Society for American Archaeology, Nashville.

Bement, L.
1986   *Excavation of the Late Pleistocene Deposits of Bonfire Shelter, Val Verde County, Texas*. Archeology Series Paper 1, vol. 1. Texas Archeological Survey, University of Texas, Austin.
1993   The Certain Site, Part 2: OU Field School 1993. *Oklahoma Archeological Survey Newsletter* 13 (2): 1–2.
1994   Results of the 1994 Field Season at the Cooper Site. *Oklahoma Archeological Survey Newsletter* 14 (2): 1–2.
1997   *Bison Hunting at Cooper Site: Where Lightning Bolts Drew Thundering Herds*. University of Oklahoma Press, Norman.
2002   Jake Bluff. *Oklahoma Archeological Survey Newsletter* 23 (4): 1–2.

Bement, L. C., and B. J. Carter
2003   Clovis Bison Hunting at the Jake Bluff Site, NW Oklahoma. *Current Research in the Pleistocene* 20: 20–26.

Benson, L., J. Burdett, S. Lund, M. Kashgarian, and S. Mensing
1997   Nearly Synchronous Climate Change in the Northern Hemisphere during the Last Glacial Termination. *Nature* 388: 263–65.

Berger, W. H.
1990   The Younger Dryas Cold Spell: A Quest for Causes. *Palaeogeography, Paleoclimatology, Palaeoecology* 89: 219–37.

Bever, M. R.

1998 The Mesa Site and Paleoindian Technology: Unscrambling the Pleistocene Pre-history of Alaska. Paper presented at the 63rd Annual Meeting of the Society for American Archaeology, Seattle.

Binford, L.

1977 Forty-Seven Trips. In *Stone Tools as Cultural Markers*, edited by R. V. Wright, pp. 24–36. Australian Institute of Aboriginal Studies, Canberra.

1980 Willow smoke and dog tails: hunter-gatherer settlement systems and archaeo-logical site formation. *American Antiquity* 45 (1): 4–20.

Bird, J. B.

1938a Before Magellan. *Natural History* 41 (1): 16–28.

1938b Antiquity and Migrations of the Early Inhabitants of Patagonia. *Geographic Review* 28 (2): 250–75.

1951 The Cultural Sequence of the North Chilean Coast. *Bureau of American Ethnology Bulletin* vol. 2, part 3, pp. 587–94. Smithsonian Institution, Washington, D.C.

1969 A Comparison of South Chilean and Ecuadorian "Fishtail" Projectile Points. *Kroeber Anthropological Society Papers* 40: 52–71.

1970 Paleo-Indian Discoidal Stones from Southern South America. *American Antiquity* 35 (2): 205–9.

1988a *Travels and Archaeology in South Chile*. Edited by J. Hyslop. Iowa University Press, Iowa City.

1988b Early Hunter-Gatherers on the Peruvian Coast. In *Peruvian Prehistory*, edited by R. W. Keating, pp. 41–66. Cambridge University Press, Cambridge.

Bird, J., and R. G. Cooke

1977 Los artefactos más antiguos de Panamá. *Revista Nacional de Cultura* 6, Panama.

1978 The Occurrence in Panama of Two Types of Paleo-Indian Projectile Points. In *Early Man in America from a Circum-Pacific Perspective*, edited by A. Bryan, pp. 263–72. Occasional Paper 1. University of Alberta, Edmonton.

Bocherens, H., G. Pacaud, P. A. Lazarev, and A. Mariotti

1996 Stable Isotope Abundances (^{13}C, ^{15}N) in Collagen and Soft Tissues from Pleis-tocene Mammals from Yakutia: Implications for the Palaeobiology of the Mam-moth Steppe. *Palaeogeography, Palaeoclimatology, Palaeoecology* 126: 31–44.

Bonadonna, F., G. Leone, and G. Zanchetta

1995 Composición isotópica de los fósiles de gasterópodos continentales de la Pro-vincia de Buenos Aires. In *Indicaciones paleoclimáticas: Evolución biológica y climática de la región oampeana durante los ultimos cinco millones de años. Un ensayo de correlación con el Mediterráneo Occidental*, edited by M. T. Alberdi, G. Leone, and E. Tonni, pp. 77–104. Monografías del Museo Nacional de Cien-cias Naturales, Consejo Superior de Investigaciones Científicas, Madrid.

Bonnichsen, R.

1991 Clovis Origins. In *Clovis: Origins and Adaptations*, edited by R. Bonnichsen and K. L. Turnmire, pp. 309–29. Center for the Study of the First Americans, Oregon State University, Corvallis.

Bonnichsen, R., D. Stanford, and J. L. Fasthook

1987   Environmental Change and Developmental History of Human Adaptive Patterns: The Paleoindian Case. In *North America and Adjacent Oceans during the Last Deglaciation,* vol. *K-3,* edited by W. F. Ruddiman and H. E. Wright, pp. 403–24. Geological Society of America, Boulder, Colo.

Bonnichsen, R., and R. T. Will

1999   Radiocarbon Chronology of Northeastern Paleo-American Sites: Discriminating Natural and Human Burn Features. In *Ice Age People of North America: Environments, Origins, and Adaptations,* edited by R. Bonnichsen and K. L. Turnmire, pp. 395–415. Oregon State University Press, Corvallis.

Bonomo, M.

2005   *Costeando las llanuras. Arqueología del litoral marítimo pampeano.* Sociedad Argentina de Antropología. Buenos Aires.

Borrero, L. A.

1983   Distribuciones discontinuas de puntas de proyectil en Sudamérica. Paper presented at the 11th International Congress of Anthropological and Ethnological Sciences, Vancouver.

1984   Pleistocene Extinctions in South America. In *Quaternary of South America and Antarctic Peninsula,* edited by J. Rabassa, 2: 115–25. Balkema, Rotterdam.

1988   Problemas para la definición de sistemas adaptativos. In *Arqueología de las Américas,* edited by M. Rodríguez, pp. 247–62. Banco Popular, Bogotá.

1990   Fuego-Patagonian Bone Assemblages and the Problem of Guanaco Communal Hunting. In *Hunters of the Recent Past,* edited by L. B. Davis and B. K. Reeves, pp. 373–99. Unwin Hyman, London.

1997   La extinción de la megafauna en la Patagonia. *Anales del Instituto de la Patagonia* 25: 89–102.

1999   The Prehistoric Exploration and Colonization of Fuego-Patagonia. *Journal of World Prehistory* 13 (3): 321–55.

2001   Wild Horses. Paper presented at the 66th Annual Meeting of the Society for American Archaeology, New Orleans.

n.d.   Unpublished notes on bones from Junius Bird's collections from Fell's Cave. Manuscript on file at the American Museum of Natural History, New York.

Borrero, L. A., and N. V. Franco

1997   Early Patagonian Hunter-Gatherers: Subsistence and Technology. *Journal of Anthropological Research* 53: 219–39.

Borrero, L. A., J. L. Lanata, and P. Cárdenas

1991   Reestudiando cuevas: Nuevas excavaciones en Última Esperanza. *Anales del Instituto de la Patagonia* 20: 101–10.

Borrero, L. A., and F. M. Martin

1996   Tafonomía de carnívoros: Un enfoque regional. In *Arqueología: Sólo Patagonia,* edited by J. Gómez, pp. 189–98. CENPAT-CONICET, Puerto Madryn, Argentina.

Bradley, B. A.

1982   Flaked Stone Technology and Typology. In *The Agate Basin Site,* edited by G. C. Frison and D. J. Stanford, pp. 181–208. Academic Press, New York.

1993   Paleo-Indian Flaked Stone Technology in the North American High Plains. In *From Kostenki to Clovis: Upper Paleolithic–Paleo-Indian Adaptations*, edited by O. Soffer and N. D. Praslov, pp. 251–61. Plenum Press, New York.

Bradley, B. A., and D. Stanford

2004   The North Atlantic Ice-Edge Corridor: A Possible Palaeolithic Route to the New World. *World Archaeology* 36 (4): 459–78.

Bray, W.

1980   Fluted Points in Mesoamerica and the Isthmus: A Reply to Rovner. *American Antiquity* 45: 168–70.

Briceño, J.

1997   La tradición de puntas de proyectil "cola de pescado" en Quebrada Santa María y el problema del poblamiento temprano en los Andes centrales. *Revista de Arqueología Sian* 4: 2–6

Broecker, W. S., M. Andree, W. Wolfli, H. Oeschger, G. Bonani, J. Kennett, and D. Peteet

1988   The Chronology of the Last Deglaciation: Implications to the Cause of the Younger Dryas Event. *Paleoceanography* 3: 1–19.

Brose, D. S.

1994   Archaeological Investigations at the Paleo Crossing Site, a Paleoindian Occupation in Medina County, Ohio. In *The First Discovery of America: Archaeological Evidence of the Early Inhabitants of the Ohio Area*, edited by W. S. Dancey, pp. 61–76. Ohio Archaeological Council, Columbus.

Broster, J. B., and M. R. Norton

1996   Recent Paleoindian Research in Tennessee. In *The Paleoindian and Early Archaic Southeast*, edited by D. G. Anderson and K. E. Sassaman, pp. 288–97. University of Alabama Press, Tuscaloosa.

Brown, K. L.

1980   A Brief Report on Paleoindian-Archaic Occupation in the Quiche Basin, Guatemala. *American Antiquity* 45 (2): 313–24.

Bryan, A. L.

1978   An Overview of Paleo-American Prehistory from a Circum-Pacific Perspective. In *Early Man in America from a Circum-Pacific Perspective*, edited by A. L. Bryan, pp. 396–27. Occasional Papers 1. Department of Anthropology, University of Alberta, Edmonton.

1986   Paleoamerican Prehistory as Seen from South America. In *New Evidence for the Pleistocene Peopling of the Americas*, edited by A. L. Bryan, pp. 1–14. Center for the Study of Early Man, University of Maine, Orono.

1991   The Fluted Point Tradition in the Americas—One of Several Adaptations to Late Pleistocene American Environments. In *Clovis: Origins and Adaptations*, edited by R. Bonnichsen and K. L. Turnmire, pp. 15–33. Center for the Study of the First Americans, Corvallis, Ore.

Bryan, A., R. Casamiquela, J. M. Cruxent, R. Gruhn, and C. Ochsenius

1978   An El Jobo Mastodon Kill at Taima-Taima, Venezuela. *Science* 200: 1275–277.

Bryan, A. L., and R. Gruhn
2003 Some Difficulties in Modeling the Original Peopling of the Americas. *Quaternary International* 109–10: 175–79.

Bryant, V. M., and R. G. Holloway
1985 A Late-Quaternary Paleoenvironmental Record of Texas: An Overview of the Pollen Evidence. In *Pollen Records of Late-Quaternary North American Sediments*, edited by V. M. Bryant Jr. and R. G. Holloway, pp. 39–70. American Association of Stratigraphic Palynologists Foundation, Dallas.

Bullen, R. P.
1958 The Bolen Bluff Site on Paynes Prairie, Florida. *Contributions of the Florida State Museum Social Sciences* 4: 1–51.

1975 *A Guide to the Identification of Florida Projectile Points.* Kendall Books, Gainesville.

Burr, G. S., W. J. Beck, F. W. Taylor, J. Récy, R. L. Edwards, G. Cabioch, T. Corrège, D. J. Donahue, and J. M. O'Malley
1998 A High Resolution Radiocarbon Calibration between 11.7 and 12.4 k BP Derived from 230Th Ages of Corals from Espiritu Santo Island, Vanuatu. *Radiocarbon* 40: 1093–1105.

Bush, M., and P. Colinvaux
1990 A Pollen Record of a Complete Glacial Cycle from Lowland Panama. *Journal of Vegetation Science* 1: 105–18.

Butzer, K.
1991 An Old World Perspective on Potential Mid-Wisconsinan Settlement of the Americas. In *The First Americans: Search and Research*, edited by T. D. Dillehay and D. J. Meltzer, pp. 137–56. CRC Press, Boca Raton, Fla.

Byers, D. A., and A. Ugan
2005 Should We Expect Large Game Specialization in the Late Pleistocene? An Optimal Foraging Perspective on Early Paleoindian Prey Choice. *Journal of Archaeological Science* 32 (11): 1624–640.

Cambron, J. W., and D. C. Hulse
1964 *Handbook of Alabama Archaeology.* Part 1, *Point Types.* Archaeological Research Association of Alabama, Tuscaloosa.

Cardich, A.
1978 Recent Excavations at Lauricocha (Central Andes) and Los Toldos (Patagonia). In *Early Man in America from a Circum-Pacific Perspective*, edited by A. L. Bryan, pp. 296–300. Occasional Papers of the Department of Anthropology, University of Alberta, Edmonton.

Cartagena, I., L. Nuñez, and M. Grosjean
2002 Primeras evidencias de fauna extinta y ocupaciones humanas en la vertiente occidental de la Puna de Atacama. Paper presented at the Primer Congreso Latinoamericano de Paleontología de Vertebrados, Santiago.

Casamiquela, R.
1979 An Interpretation of the Fossil Vertebrates of the Taima-Taima Site. In *Taima-Taima: A Late Pleistocene Paleo-Indian Kill Site in Northernmost South Amer-*

ica—Final Reports of 1976 Excavations, edited by C. Ochsenius and R. Gruhn, pp. 59–76. CIPICS/South American Quaternary Documentation Program, Bonn, Germany.

Castillo C., D., E. Castillo O., M. Rojas G., and C. Valldeperas
1987 Análisis de la lítica lasqueada del sitio 9-FG-T en Turrialba. Unpublished B.A. thesis, Escuela de Antropología y Sociología, Universidad de Costa Rica.

Ceballos, R.
1982 El sitio Cuyín Manzano. *Series y Documentos* 9: 1–66.

Chason, H. L.
1987 *Treasures of the Chippola River Valley*. Father and Son Publishers, Tallahassee.

Chauchat, C.
1975 The Paiján Complex, Pampa de Cupisnique, Perú. *Nawpa Pacha* 13: 85–96.
1982 Le Paijanien du désert de Cupisnique: Recherches sur l'occupation préhistorique de la cote nor du Perou au début de l'Holocene. Ph.D. dissertation, Université de Bordeaux.
1988 Early Hunter-Gatherers on the Peruvian Coast. In *Peruvian Prehistory*, edited by R. W. Keating, pp. 41–66. Cambridge University Press, Cambridge.

Chilton, E. S.
2004 Beyond "Big": Gender, Age, and Subsistence Diversity in Paleoindian Societies. In *The Settlement of the American Continents: A Multidisciplinary Approach to Human Biogeography*, edited by C. M. Barton, G. A. Clark, D. R. Yesner, and G. A. Pearson, pp. 162–72. University of Arizona Press, Tucson.

Cinq-Mars, J., and R. E. Morlan
1999 Bluefish Caves and Old Crow Basin: A New Rapport. In *Ice Age People of North America: Environments, Origins, and Adaptations*, edited by R. Bonnichsen and K. L. Turnmire, pp. 200–12. Oregon State University Press, Corvallis.

Clague, J. J., R. W. Mathewes, and T. A. Ager
2004 Environments of Northwest North America, Northeast Asia, and Beringia before the Last Glacial Maximum. In *Entering America before the Last Glacial Maximum*, edited by D. B. Madsen, pp. 63–94. University of Utah Press, Salt Lake City.

Clark, D. W.
1984 Some Practical Applications of Obsidian Hydration Dating in the Subarctic. *Arctic* 37: 91–109.
1991 The Northern (Alaska-Yukon) Fluted Points. In *Clovis: Origins and Adaptations*, edited by R. Bonnichsen and K. L. Turnmire, pp. 35–48. Center for the Study of the First Americans, Corvallis, Ore.

Clausen, C. J., H. K. Brooks, and A. B. Wesolowsky
1975 The Early Man Site at Warm Mineral Springs, Florida. *Journal of Field Archaeology* 2 (3): 191–213.

Clausen, C. J., A. D. Cohen, C. Emiliani, J. A. Holman, and J. J. Stipp
1979 Little Salt Spring, Florida: A Unique Underwater Site. *Science* 203 (4381): 609–14.

Clements, F. E., and V. E. Shelford
1939 *Bioecology*. Wiley, London.

Clutton-Brock, J.

1988   The Carnivore Remains Excavated at Fell's Cave in 1970. In *Travels and Archaeology in South Chile*, by J. B. Bird, edited by J. Hyslop, pp. 188–95. University of Iowa Press, Iowa City.

Cockrell, W. A., and L. Murphy

1978   Pleistocene Man in Florida. *Archaeology of Eastern North America* 6: 1–13.

Coe, J. L.

1964   *The Formative Cultures of the Carolina Piedmont.* Transactions of the American Philosophical Society, vol. 54, part 5. Philadelphia.

Coe, M. D.

1960   A Fluted Point from Highland Guatemala. *American Antiquity* 25 (3): 412–13.

Collins, M. B.

1997   The Lithics from Monte Verde: a Descriptive-Morphological Analysis. In *Monte Verde: A Late Pleistocene Settlement in Chile*, vol. 2, *The Archaeological Context*, edited by T. D. Dillehay, pp. 383–506. Smithsonian Institution Press, Washington, D.C.

1999   *Clovis Blade Technology.* University of Texas Press, Austin.

2001   Archeology of the Lampasas Cut Plain from Paleoindians to Pioneers. *Texas Archeology* 45 (1): 3–6.

2002   The Gault Site, Texas, and Clovis Research. *Athena Review* 3 (2). http://www.athenapub.com/10gault.htm.

2003   Gault Site Dates and Findings. *Newsletter of the Friends of the Texas Archeological Research Laboratory*, May.

Coltrain, J. B., J. M. Harris, T. E. Cerling, J. R. Ehleringer, M. Dearing, J. Ward, and J. Allen

2004   Rancho la Brea Stable Isotope Biogeochemistry and Its Implications for the Palaeoecology of Late Pleistocene, Coastal Southern California. *Palaeogeography, Palaeoclimatology, Palaeoecology* 205: 199–219.

Cooke, R. G., and A. J. Ranere

1992a   The Origin of Wealth and Hierarchy in the Central Region of Panama (12,000–2,000 B.P.), with Observations on Its Relevance to the History and Phylogeny of Chibchan-Speaking Polities in Panama and Elsewhere. In *Wealth and Hierarchy in the Intermediate Area*, edited by F. W. Lange, pp. 243–316. Dumbarton Oaks, Washington, D.C.

1992b   Prehistoric Human Adaptations to the Seasonally Dry Forests of Panama. *World Archaeology* 24 (1): 114–33.

Cooke, R. G., and L. A. Sánchez

2004a   Panamá prehispánico. In *Historia General de Panama*, vol. 1, part 1, edited by A. Castillero C., pp. 3–46. Comité Nacional de Centenario de la República, Presidencia de la República, Panamá.

2004b   Panamá indígena (1501–1550). In *Historia General de Panama*, vol. 1, part 1, edited by A. Castillero C., pp. 47–78. Comité Nacional de Centenario de la República, Presidencia de la República, Panamá.

Correal, G.
1977   Exploraciones arqueológicas en la costa Atlántica y el valle del Magdalena. *Caldasia* 55: 33–129.
1981   *Evidencias culturales y megafauna pleistocénica en Colombia*. FIAN, Bogotá.
1983   Evidencia de cazadores especializados en el sitio de La Gloria, golfo de Uraba. *Revista de la Academia Colombiana de Ciencias Exactas, Físicas y Naturales* 58: 77–82.
1986   Apuntes sobre el medio ambiente pleistocénico Andino y el hombre prehistórico en Colombia. In *New Evidence from the Pleistocene Peopling of the Americas*, edited by A. L. Bryan, pp. 115–31. Center for the Study of Early Man, University of Maine, Orono.

Correal, G., and T. Van der Hammen
1977   *Investigaciones arqueológicas en los Abrigos Rocosos del Tequendama*. Banco Popular, Bogotá.

Cotter, J. L.
1937   The Occurrence of Flints and Extinct Animals in Pluvial Deposits near Clovis, New Mexico, part 4, Report on the Excavations at the Gravel Pit in 1936. *Proceedings of the Philadelphia Academy of Natural Sciences* 89: 1–16.

Coupland, R. T.
1992a Overview of the Grasslands of North America. In *Natural Grasslands: Introduction and Western Hemisphere*, edited by R. T. Coupland, pp. 147–49. Elsevier, Amsterdam.
1992b Mixed Prairie. In *Natural Grasslands: Introduction and Western Hemisphere*, edited by R. T. Coupland, pp. 151–82. Elsevier, Amsterdam.
1992c Overview of South American Grasslands. In *Natural Grasslands: Introduction and Western Hemisphere*, edited by R. T. Coupland, pp. 363–66. Elsevier, Amsterdam.

Cox, S. L.
1986   A Re-Analysis of the Shoop Site. *Archaeology of Eastern North America* 14: 101–70.

Crivelli, E. A., D. Curzio, and M. Silveira
1993   La estratigrafía de la cueva Traful 1. *Praehistoria* 1: 9–159.

Crivelli, E. A., E. Eugenio, U. Pardiñas, and M. Silveira
1997   Archaeological Investigation in the Plains of the Province of Buenos Aires, Llanura Interserrana Bonaerense. *Quaternary of South America and Antarctic Penninsula* 10 (1994): 167–207.

Crivelli, E. A., U. Pardiñas, M. M. Fernández, M. Bogazzi, A. Chauvin, V. Fernández, and M. Lezcano
1996   Cueva Epullán Grande (Pcia. Del Neuquén): Informe de avance. *Praehistoria* 2: 185–265.

Crownover, S.
1994   *Archaeological Assessment of the North Landfill Project, Biscuit Flat, Maricopa County, Arizona*. Archaeological Consulting Services, Tempe.

Crusoe, D. L., and J. H. Felton
1974   La Alvina de Parita: A Paleo-Indian Camp in Panama. *Florida Anthropologist* 27: 145–48.
Cruxent, J. M.
1970   Projectile Points with Pleistocene Mammals in Venezuela. *American Antiquity* 44: 223–25.
1979   Stone and Bone Artifacts from Taima-Taima. In *Taima-Taima: A Late Pleistocene Paleo-Indian Kill Site in Northernmost South America*, edited by C. Ochsenius and R. Gruhn, pp. 77–88. CIPICS/South American Quaternary Documentation Program, Germany.
Daniel, I. R., and M. Wisenbaker
1987   *Harney Flats: A Florida Paleo-Indian Site*. Baywood Publishing, New York.
Davis, L. B.
2001   Folsom Complex Antecedents in Montana: The MacHaffie and Indian Creek Paleoindian Occupational Sequences. Paper presented at the meeting of Canadian Archaeological Association, Banff, May 10.
Davis, L. B., and M. Baumler
2000   Clovis and Folsom Occupations at Indian Creek. *Current Research in the Pleistocene* 17: 17–18.
de Lumley, H., M. A. de Lumley, M. Beltrao, Y. Yokoyama, J. Labeyrie, J. Danon, G. Delibrias, C. Falgueres, and J. Bischoff
1988   Decouverte d'outils tailles associes a des faunes du Pleistocene moyen dans la Toca da Esperança, Etat de Bahia, Bresil. *Comptes Rendus de l'Academie des Sciences* 306: 241–47.
Dennell, R. W., and W. Roebroeks
1996   The Earliest Colonization of Europe: The Short Chronology Revisited. *Antiquity* 70: 535–42.
Dent, R. J.
1999   Shawnee Minisink: New Dates on the Paleoindian Component. Poster presented at the 64th Annual Meeting of the Society for American Archaeology, Chicago.
Derbyshire, E.
1992   Loess and the Argentine Pampa. *Leicester University Geography Department Occasional Paper* 23: 1–71.
Dewar, E.
2002   *Bones: Discovering the First Americans*. Carroll and Graf, New York.
Dibble, D. S., and D. Lorrain
1968   Bonfire Shelter: A Stratified Bison Kill Site, Val Verde County, Texas. *Texas Memorial Museum Miscellaneous Papers* 1: 1–138.
Dillehay, T. D. (Editor)
1989   *Monte Verde: A Late Pleistocene Settlement in Chile*. Vol. 1, *Palaeoenvironment and Site Context*. Smithsonian Institution Press, Washington, D.C.
1997a   *Monte Verde: A Late Pleistocene Settlement in Chile*. Vol. 2, *The Archaeological Context and Interpretation*. Smithsonian Institution Press, Washington, D.C.

Dillehay, T. D.
1997b Zooarchaeological remains. In *Monte Verde: A Late Pleistocene Settlement in Chile*, vol. 2, *The Archaeological Context*, edited by T. D. Dillehay, pp. 661–750. Smithsonian Institution Press, Washington, D.C.
2000 *The Settlement of the Americas*. Basic Books, New York.
2002 *Errata*. In *Monte Verde: A Late Pleistocene Settlement in Chile*, vol. 2, *The Archaeological Context and Interpretation*. Smithsonian Institution Press, Washington, D.C.

Dillehay, T. D., G. Ardila, G. Politis, and M. Beltrao
1992 Earliest Hunters and Gatherers of South America. *Journal of World Prehistory* 6: 145–204.

Dillehay, T. D., and M. Pino
1997 Radiocarbon Chronology. In *Monte Verde: A Late Pleistocene Settlement in Chile*, vol. 2, *The Archaeological Context and Interpretation*, edited by T. D. Dillehay, pp. 41–52. Smithsonian Institution Press, Washington, D.C.

Dillehay, T. D., and J. Rossen
1997 Integrity and Distribution of Archaeobotanical Collection. In *Monte Verde: A Late Pleistocene Settlement in Chile*, vol. 2, *The Archaeological Context and Interpretation*, edited by T. D. Dillehay, pp. 351–81. Smithsonian Institution Press, Washington, D.C.
2002 Plant Foods and Its Implications for the Peopling of the New World: A View from South America. In *The First Americans: The Pleistocene Colonization of the New World*, edited by N. G. Jablonski, pp 237–53. Memoirs of the California Academy of Sciences 27. San Francisco.

Dillehay, T. D., J. Rossen, G. Maggard, K. Stackelbeck, and P. Netherly
2003 Localization and Possible Social Aggregation in the Late Pleistocene and Early Holocene on the North Coast of Peru. *Quaternary International* 109–10: 3–11.

Dillehay, T. D., J. Rossen, P. Netherly, G. Maggard, and K. Stackelbeck
2003 New Evidence of the Paiján Culture on the North Coast of Peru and Its Importance in Early Andean Prehistory. *Where the South Winds Blow: Ancient Evidence of Paleo South Americans*, edited by L. Miotti, M. Salemme, and N. Flegenheimer, pp. 13–15. Center for the Study of the First Americans, Texas A&M University, College Station.

Dincauze, D. F.
1993a Fluted Points in the Eastern Forests. In *From Kostenki to Clovis*, edited by O. Soffer and N. D. Praslov, pp. 279–92. Plenum Press, New York.
1993b Pioneering in the Pleistocene: Large Paleoindian Sites in the Northeast. In *Archaeology of Eastern North America: Papers in Honor of Stephen Williams*, edited by J. B. Stoltman, pp. 43–60. Archaeological Report 25. Mississippi Department of Archives and History, Jackson.

Di Peso, C. C.
1953 Clovis Fluted Points from Southeastern Arizona. *American Antiquity* 19: 82–85.

Dixon, E. J.

1993 *Quest for the Origins of the First Americans.* University of New Mexico Press. Albuquerque, New Mexico.

1999 *Bones, Boats, and Bison: Archaeology and the First Colonization of Western North America.* University of New Mexico Press, Albuquerque.

2001 Human Colonization of the Americas: Timing, Technology, and Process. *Quaternary Science Reviews* 20: 277–29.

Dolan, E. M., and G. T. Allen

1961 *An Investigation of the Darby and Hornsby Springs Sites, Alachua County, Florida.* Florida Geological Survey Special Publication 7. Tallahassee.

Dorn, R. I.

1996 Uncertainties in the Radiocarbon Dating of Organics Associated with Rock Varnish: A Plea for Caution. *Physical Geography* 17 (6): 585–91.

Downum, C. E.

1993 Evidence of a Clovis Presence at Wupatki National Monument. *Kiva* 58: 487–94.

Driskell, B. N.

1996 Stratified Late Pleistocene and Early Holocene Deposits at Dust Cave, Northwestern Alabama. In *Paleoindian and Early Archaic Southeast,* edited by D. G. Anderson and K. E. Sassaman, pp. 315–30. University of Alabama Press, Tuscaloosa.

Drucker, D. G., and D. Henry-Gambier

2005 Determination of the dietary habits of a Magdalenian Woman from Saint-Germain-la-Rivière in Southwestern France Using stable isotopes. *Journal of Human Evolution* 49 (1): 19–35.

Dunbar, J.

1991 Resource Orientation of Clovis and Suwannee Age Paleoindian Sites in Florida. In *Clovis: Origins and Adaptations,* edited by R. Bonnichsen and K. L. Turnmire, pp. 185–213. Center for the Study of the First Americans, Oregon State University, Corvallis.

2002 Chronostratigraphy and Paleoclimate of Late Pleistocene Florida and the Implications of Changing Paleoindian Land Use. Masters thesis, Department of Anthropology, Florida State University, Tallahassee.

Dunbar, J. S., and B. I. Waller

1983 A Distribution Analysis of the Clovis/Suwannee Paleo-Indian Sites of Florida— A Geographic Approach. *Florida Anthropologist* 36: 18–30.

Dunbar, J. S., and D. S. Webb

1996 Bone and Ivory Tools from Submerged Paleoindian Sites in Florida. In *The Paleoindian and Early Archaic Southeast,* edited by D. G. Anderson and K. E. Sassaman, pp. 331–53. University of Alabama Press, Tuscaloosa.

Dunbar, J. S., S. D. Webb, and D. Cring

1989 Culturally and Naturally Modified Bones from a Paleoindian Site in the Aucilla River, North Florida. In *Bone Modification,* edited by R. Bonnichsen and M. H. Sorg, pp. 473–97. Center for the Study of Early Man, Orono, Maine.

Dunbar, J. S., S. D. Webb, and M. K. Faught
1988   Page/Ladson (8 Je 591): An Underwater Paleo-Indian Site in Northwestern Florida. *Florida Anthropologist* 41 (4): 442–52.

Dunnell, R. C.
1986   Methodological Issues in Artifact Classification. In *Advances in Archaeological Method and Theory*, vol. 9, edited by M. B. Schiffer, pp. 267–87. Academic Press, New York.

Dyke, A. S., J. T. Andrews, P. U. Clark, J. H. England, G. H. Miller, J. Shaw, and J. J. Veillette
2002   The Laurentide and Innuitian Ice Sheets during the Last Glacial Maximum. *Quaternary Science Reviews* 21 (1–3): 9–31.

Dyke, A. S., A. Moore, and L. Robertson
2002   Revised North American Deglaciation Maps. Geological Survey of Canada. Poster presented at the 114th Annual Meeting of the Geological Society of America, Denver.

Edmund, A. G.
1985   The Armor of Fossil Giant Armadillos (Pampatheriidae, Xenarthra, Mammalia). *Texas Memorial Museum, Pierce-Sellards Series* 40: 1–20.

Elkin, D.
1996a El uso del recurso fauna por los primeros habitantes de Antofagasta de la Sierra (Puna de Catamarca). In *Actas del Primer Congreso de Investigación Social, Región y Sociedad en Latino-América*, pp. 202–9. Universidad Nacional de Tucuman, Tucumán.

1996b Arqueozoología de Quebrada Seca 3: Indicadores de subsistencia humana temprana en la puna meridional argentina. Ph.D. dissertation, Universidad de Buenos Aires, Buenos Aires.

Ellis, C. J., and D. B. Deller
1988   Some Distinctive Early Paleo-Indian Tool Types from the Lower Great Lakes Region. *Midcontinental Journal of Archaeology* 13: 111–58.

Ellis, C., A. C. Goodyear, D. F. Morse, and K. B. Tankersley
1998   Archaeology of the Pleistocene-Holocene Transition in Eastern North America. *Quaternary International* 50: 151–66.

Emperaire, J., A. L. Emperaire, and H. Reichlen
1963   Grotte de Fell et autres sites de la region volcanique de la Patagonie Chilienne. *Journal de la Societé de Americanistes* 52: 167–255.

Erlandson, J. M.
2001   The Archaeology of Aquatic Adaptation: Paradigms for a New Millennium. *Journal of Archaeological Research* 9: 287–350.

Erlandson, J. M., and M. L. Moss
1996   The Pleistocene-Holocene Transition along the Pacific Coast of North America. In *Humans at the End of the Ice Age: The Archaeology of the Pleistocene-Holocene Transition*, edited by L. G. Straus, B. V. Eriksen, J. M. Erlandson, and D. R. Yesner, pp. 277–301. Plenum Press, New York.

Fabian, J.

1983   *Time and the Other.* Columbia University Press, New York.

Fairbanks, R. G., R. A. Mortlock, T. C. Chiu, L. Cao, A. Kaplan, T. P. Guilderson, T. W. Fairbanks, A. L. Bloom, P. M. Grootes, and M. J. Nadeau

2005   Radiocarbon Calibration Curve Spanning 0 to 50,000 Years BP Based on Paired ^{230}Th/^{234}U/^{238}U and ^{14}C Dates on Pristine Corals. *Quaternary Science Reviews* 24 (16–17): 1781–796.

Faught, M. K.

1988   Inundated Sites in the Apalachee Bay Area of the Eastern Gulf of Mexico. *Florida Anthropologist* 41 (1): 185–90.

1996   Clovis Origins and Underwater Prehistoric Archaeology in Northwestern Florida. Ph.D. dissertation, University of Arizona, Tucson.

2004   The Underwater Archaeology of Paleolandscapes, Apalachee Bay, Florida. *American Antiquity* 69 (2): 235–49.

n.d.a   Roots of Human Diversity in the New World: Three Different Regions with Earliest Radiocarbon Ages. Manuscript in possession of the author.

n.d.b   Evidence for Fluted Point Paleoindian and Early Archaic Settlement Continuity in Peninsular Florida. Manuscript in possession of the author.

Faught, M. K., and D. G. Anderson

1996   Across the Straits, Down the Corridor, Around the Bend, and Off the Shelf: An Evaluation of Paleoindian Colonization Models. Paper presented at the 61st Annual Meeting of the Society for American Archaeology, New Orleans.

Faught, M. K., and B. Carter

1998   Early Human Occupation and Environmental Change in Northwestern Florida. *Quaternary International* 50: 167–76.

Faught, M. K., M. Hornum, B. Carter, R. Christopher Goodwin, and S. D. Webb

2003   Earliest Holocene Tool Assemblages from Northern Florida with Stratigraphically Controlled Radiocarbon Estimates (Sites 8LE2105 and 8JE591). *Current Research in the Pleistocene* 20: 16–18.

FAUNMAP Working Group

1994   *FAUNMAP: A Database Documenting Late Quaternary Distributions of Mammal Species in the United States.* Illinois State Museum Scientific Papers 25. Springfield.

Favier Dubois, C.

2006   Dinámica fluvial, paleoambientes y ocupaciones humanas en la localidad Paso Otero, río Quequén Grande, Provincia de Buenos Aires. *Intersecciones en Antropología* 7 (in press).

Feathers, J. K.

1997   The Application of Luminescence Dating in American Archaeology. *Journal of Archaeological Method and Theory* 4 (1): 1–66.

Feng, Z. D., W. C. Johnson, D. R. Sprowl, and Y. L. Lu

1994   Loess Accumulation and Soil Formation in Central Kansas, United States, during the Past 400,000 Years. *Earth Surface Processes and Landforms* 19: 55–67.

Fenneman, N. M.

1931   *Physiography of Western United States.* McGraw-Hill, New York.

Feranec, R. S.

2004   Isotopic Evidence of Saber-Tooth Development, Growth Rate, and Diet from the Adult Canine of *Smilodon fatalis* from Rancho la Brea. *Palaeogeography, Palaeoclimatology, Palaeoecology* 206: 303–10.

Fernández, J., V. Markgraf, H. O. Panarello, M. Albero, F. E. Angiolini, S. Valencia, and M. Arriaga

1991   Late Pleistocene/Early Holocene Environments and Climates, Fauna and Human Occupation in the Argentine Altiplano. *Geoarchaeology* 6: 251–72.

Ferrari, M. A., C. C. Olrog, G. Montes, and E. Saibene

1984   El Ñandú. In *Fauna Argentina: Aves,* vol. 1, edited by G. Montes and M. A. Palermo, pp. 1–32. Centro Editor de América Latina, Buenos Aires.

Ferring, C. R.

1995   The Late Quaternary Geology and Archaeology of the Aubrey Clovis Site, Texas: A Preliminary Report. In *Ancient Peoples and Landscapes,* edited by E. Johnson, pp. 273–81. Museum of Texas Tech University, Lubbock.

2001   *The Archaeology and Paleoecology of the Aubrey Clovis Site (41DN479), Denton County, Texas.* Center for Environmental Archaeology, Department of Geography, University of North Texas, Denton.

Fidalgo, F., U. Colado, and O. de Franceso

1973   Sobre ingresiones marinas cuaternarias en los Partidos de Castelli, Chascomús y Magdalena, Prov. de Buenos Aires. *Congreso Geológico Argentino Actas* 3: 227–40.

Fidalgo, F., L.M.M. Guzmán, G. G. Politis, M. C. Salemme, and E. P. Tonni

1986   Investigaciones arqueológicas en el sitio 2 de Arroyo Seco (Pdo. de Tres Arroyos-Pcia. de Buenos Aires–República Argentina). In *New Evidence for the Pleistocene Peopling of the Americas,* edited by A. L. Bryan, pp. 221–70. Center for the Study of Early Man, University of Maine, Orono.

Fidalgo, F., and E. Tonni

1981   Sedimentos eólicos del pleistoceno tardío y reciente en el Área Interserrana Bonaerense. *Actas del Congreso Geológico Argentino* 3: 33–39.

Fiedel, S. J.

1996   Paleoindians in the Brazilian Amazon. *Science* 274: 1823–824.

1999a Older than We Thought: Implications of Corrected Dates for Paleoindians. *American Antiquity* 64 (1): 95–116.

1999b Artifact Provenience at Monte Verde: Confusion and Contradictions. *Scientific American Discovering Archaeology* Special Report 1 (6): 1–12.

2000   The Peopling of the New World: Present Evidence, New Theories, and Future Directions. *Journal of Archaeological Research* 8 (1): 39–103.

2002   Initial Human Colonization of the Americas: An Overview of the Issues and the Evidence. *Radiocarbon* 44 (2): 407–36.

2005   Man's Best Friend, Mammoth's Worst Enemy? A Speculative Essay on the Role of Dogs in Paleoindian Colonization and Megafaunal Extinction. *World Archaeology* 37 (1): 11–25.

Fladmark, K. R.

1979   Routes: Alternate Migration Corridors for Early Man in North America. *American Antiquity* 44 (1): 55–69.

Flannery, T. F.

1999   Debating Extinction. *Science* 283: 182–83.

Flegenheimer, N.

1980   Hallazgos de Puntas "cola de pescado" en la Provincia de Buenos Aires. *Relaciones de la Sociedad Argentina de Antropología* 14 (1): 169–76.

1986   Excavaciones en el sitio 3 de la localidad Cerro la China. *Relaciones de la Sociedad Argentina de Antropología* 17: 7–28.

1987   Recent Research at Localities Cerro la China and Cerro el Sombrero, Argentina. *Current Research in the Pleistocene* 4: 148–49.

Flegenheimer, N, C. Bayón, M. Valente, J. Baeza, and J. Femenías

2003   Long distance tool stone transport in the Argentine Pampas. *Quaternary International* 109–10: 49–64.

Flegenheimer, N., and M. Zarate

1997   Considerations on Radiocarbon and Calibrated Dates from Cerro la China and Cerro el Sombrero, Argentina. *Current Research in the Pleistocene* 14: 27–28.

Foit, F. F., P. J. Mehringer, and J. C. Sheppard

1993   Age, Distribution, and Stratigraphy of Glacier Peak Tephra in Eastern Washington and Western Montana, United States. *Canadian Journal of Earth Sciences* 30: 535–52.

Fredlund, G. G., and L. L. Tieszen

1997   Phytolith and Carbon Isotope Evidence for Late Quaternary Vegetation and Climate Change in the Southern Black Hills, South Dakota. *Quaternary Research* 47: 206–17.

Freeman, A. K. L., E. E. Smith Jr., and K. B. Tankersley

1996   A Stone's Throw from Kimmswick: Clovis Period Research in Kentucky. In *The Paleoindian and Early Archaic Southeast*, edited by D. G. Anderson and K. E. Sassaman, pp. 385–403. University of Alabama Press, Tuscaloosa.

Frenguelli, J.

1946   Las grandes unidades físicas del territorio argentino: Geografía de la República Argentina. *Anales de la Sociedad Argentina para el Estudio de la Geografía* 3: 1–114.

Friedrich, M., B. Kromer, K. F. Kaiser, M. Spurk, K. A. Hughen, and S. J. Johnsen

2001   High-Resolution Climate Signals in the Bølling-Allerød Interstadial (Greenland Interstadial 1) as Reflected in European Tree-Ring Chronologies Compared to Marine Varves and Ice-Core Records. *Quaternary Science Reviews* 20: 1223–232.

Friedrich, M., B. Kromer, M. Spurk, J. Hofmann, and K. F. Kaiser

1999   Paleo-Environment and Radiocarbon Calibration as Derived from Lateglacial/Early Holocene Tree-Ring Chronologies. *Quaternary International* 61: 27–39.

Friedrich, M., S. Remmele, B. Kromer, J. Hofmann, M. Spurk, K. F. Kaiser, C. Orcel, and M. Küppers

2004   The 12,460-Year Hohenheim Oak and Pine Tree-Ring Chronology from Central Europe—a Unique Annual Record for Radiocarbon Calibration and Paleoenvironment Reconstructions. *Radiocarbon* 46 (3): 1111–122.

Frison, G. C.

1982   Bison Dentition Studies. In *The Agate Basin Site: A Record of Paleoindian Occupation of the Northwestern Plains*, edited by G. C. Frison and D. J. Stanford, pp. 240–60. Academic Press, New York.

1987   Prehistoric, Plains-Mountain, Large-Mammal, Communal Hunting Strategies. In *The Evolution of Human Hunting*, edited by M. H. Nitecki and D. V. Nitecki, pp. 177–223. Plenum Press, New York.

1991a *Prehistoric Hunters of the High Plains*. 2nd ed. Academic Press, San Diego.

1991b The Clovis Cultural Complex: New Data from Caches of Flaked Stone and Worked Bone Artifacts. In *Raw Material Economies among Hunter Gatherers*, edited by A. Montet-White and S. Holen, pp. 321–33. Publications in Anthropology 19. University of Kansas Press, Lawrence.

1991c The Goshen Paleoindian Complex: New Data for Paleoindian Research. In *Clovis: Origins and Adaptations*, edited by R. Bonnichsen and K. L. Turmine, pp. 133–51. Center for the Study of the First Americans, Oregon State University, Corvallis.

Frison, G. C. (Editor)

1996   *The Mill Iron Site*. University of New Mexico Press, Albuquerque.

Frison, G. C., and R. Bonnichsen

1996   The Pleistocene-Holocene Transition on the Plains and Rocky Mountains of North America. In *Humans at the End of the Ice Age: The Archaeology of the Pleistocene-Holocene Transition*, edited by L. G. Straus, B. V. Eriksen, J. M. Erlandson, and D. R. Yesner, pp. 303–18. Plenum Press, New York.

Frison, G. C., C. V. Haynes, and M. L. Larson

1996   Discussion and Conclusions. In *The Mill Iron Site 24CT30 and the Goshen-Plainview Cultural Complex on the Northern High Plains*, edited by G. C. Frison, pp. 205–16. University of New Mexico Press, Albuquerque.

Frison, G. C., and D. Stanford

1982   *The Agate Basin Site: A Record of Paleoindian Occupation of the Northwestern Plains*. Academic Press, New York.

Frison, G. C., and L. C. Todd

1986   *The Colby Mammoth Site: Taphonomy and Archaeology of a Clovis Kill in Northern Wyoming*. University of New Mexico Press, Albuquerque.

Frison, G. C., and G. N. Zeimens

1980   Bone Projectile Points: An Addition to the Folsom Cultural Complex. *American Antiquity* 45: 231–37.

Fullagar, R. L., D. M. Price, and L. M. Head

1996   Early Human Occupation of Northern Australia: Archaeology and Thermoluminescence Dating of Jinmium Rock Shelter, Northern Territory. *Antiquity* 70: 751–73.

Futato, E. M.
1996   A Synopsis of Paleoindian and Early Archaic Research in Alabama. In *The Paleoindian and Early Archaic Southeast*, edited by D. G. Anderson and K. E. Sassaman, pp. 298–314. University of Alabama Press, Tuscaloosa.

Gálvez, C. A.
1992   Investigaciones sobre el Paleolítico de la costa de los Andes Centrales (1948–1992). In *Il Curso de Prehistoria de América Hispana*, pp. 15–38. Universidad de Murcia, Murcia, Spain.

Gamble, C.
1993   The Center at the Edge. In *From Kostienki to Clovis: Upper Paleolithic-Paleo-Indian Adaptations*, edited by O. Soffer and N. D. Praslov, pp. 313–21. Plenum Press, New York.
1999   *The Palaeolithic Societies of Europe*. Cambridge University Press, Cambridge.

García, A.
1995   Agua de la Cueva Rockshelter and Its Relationships to the Early Peopling of Central West Argentina. *Current Research in the Pleistocene* 12: 13–14.
1997a   La ocupación humana del centro-oeste Argentino hacia el límite pleistoceno-holoceno: El complejo Paleoindio del sitio Agua de la Cueva, sector sur. Ph.D. dissertation, Universidad Nacional de Cuyo, Mendoza, Argentina.
1997b   Connotaciones y uso del término "Paleoindio" en el centro oeste Argentino. *Revista de Estudios Regionales* 15: 7–18
2003   *Los primeros pobladores de los Andes centrales argentinos*. Zeta Editores, Mendoza.

Garcia-Barcena, J.
1979   *Una punta acanalada de la cueva Los Grifos, Ocozocoautla, Chiapas*. Cuaderno de Trabajo 17. Departamento de Prehistoria, INAH, México.
1982   *El preceramico de Aguacatenango, Chiapas, México*. Colección Cientifica 111. INAH, México.

Gardner, W. M.
1974   *The Flint Run PaleoIndian Complex: A Preliminary Report, 1971 through 1973 Seasons*. Occasional Paper 1. Catholic University of America, Archaeology Laboratory, Washington, D.C.
1983   Stop Me If You've Heard This One Before: The Flint Run PaleoIndian Complex Revisited. *Archaeology of Eastern North America* 11: 49–59.

Geib, P. R.
1995   Two Fluted Points from the Kaibito Plateau, Northeastern Arizona. *Kiva* 61: 89–97.

Geist, V.
1999   Periglacial Ecology, Large Mammals, and Their Significance to Human Ecology. In *Ice Age People of North America, Environments, Origins, and Adaptations*, edited by R. Bonnichsen and K. L. Turnmire, pp. 78–94. Oregon State University Press, Corvallis.

Gerrell, P. R., J. F. Scarry, and J. S. Dunbar
1991   Analysis of Early Archaic Unifacial Adzes from North Florida. *Florida Anthropologist* 44 (1): 3–16.

Gil, A., G. Neme, and A. García
1997 Preliminary zooarchaeological results at Agua de la Cueva-Sector Sur Shelter. *Current Research in the Pleistoene* 14: 139–40.

Gillespie, R.
2002 Dating the First Australians. *Radiocarbon* 44 (2): 455–72.

Gnecco, C.
2000 *Ocupación temprana de bosques tropicales de montaña.* Editorial Universidad del Cauca, Popayán, Colombia.

Gnecco, C., and S. Mora
1997 Late Pleistocene/Early Holocene Tropical Forest Occupations at San Isidro and Peña Roja, Colombia. *Antiquity* 71: 683–90.

Gnecco, C., and H. Salgado
1989 Adaptaciones precerámicas en el suroccidente de Colombia. *Boletín del Museo del Oro* 24: 34–53.

Goebel, T.
1998 The Siberian Upper Paleolithic: Hard Environments, Limiting Factors, and Human Range Expansion into Northern Asia. Paper presented at the 63rd Annual Meeting of the Society for American Archaeology, Seattle.
2004 In Search for a Clovis Progenitor in SubAntarctic Siberia. In *Entering America: Northeast Asia and Beringia before the Last Glacial Maximum*, edited by D. B. Madsen, pp. 311–56. University of Utah Press, Salt Lake City.

Goebel, T., and M. Aksenov
1995 Accelerator Radiocarbon Dating of the Initial Upper Palaeolithic in Southeastern Siberia. *Antiquity* 69: 349–57.

Goebel, T., R. Powers, and N. Bigelow
1991 The Nenana Complex of Alaska and Clovis Origins. In *Clovis: Origins and Adaptations*, edited by R. Bonnichsen and K. L. Turnmire, pp. 49–80. Center for the Study of the First Americans, Corvallis, Ore.

Gonzalez, S., J. C. Jimenez-Lopez, R. Hedges, D. Huddart, J. C. Ohman, A. Turner, and J. A. Pompa
2003 Earliest Humans in the Americas: New Evidence from Mexico. *Journal of Human Evolution* 44 (3): 379–87.

Goode, G. T., and R. J. Mallouf
1991 The Evant Cores: Polyhedral Blade Cores from North-Central Texas. *Current Research in the Pleistocene* 8: 67–70.

Goodyear, A. C., S. B. Upchurch, M. J. Brooks, and N. N. Goodyear
1983 Paleo-Indian Manifestations in the Tampa Bay Region, Florida. *Florida Anthropologist* 36 (1): 40–66.

Goslar, T., M. Arnold, L. N. Tisnerat, J. Czernik, and K. Wieckowski
2000 Variations of Younger Dryas Atmospheric Radiocarbon Explicable without Ocean Circulation Changes. *Nature* 403: 877–80.

Goslar, T., B. Wohlfarth, S. Bjorck, G. Possnert, and J. Bjorck
1999 Variations of Atmospheric ^{14}C Concentrations over the Allerød–Younger Dryas Transition. *Climate Dynamics* 15: 29–42.

Graham, R. W.

1990   Evolution of New Ecosystems at the End of the Pleistocene. In *Megafauna and Man: Discovery of America's Heartland*, edited by L. D. Agenbroad, J. I. Mead, and L. W. Nelson, pp. 54–60. The Mammoth Site of Hot Springs Scientific Papers 1. Hot Springs.

1998   Mammals' Eye View of Environmental Change in the United States at the End of the Pleistocene. Paper presented at 63rd Annual Meeting of the Society for American Archaeology, Seattle.

Graham, R. W., and E. L. Lundelius

1984   Coevolutionary Disequilibrium and Pleistocene Extinctions. In *Quaternary Extinctions: A Prehistoric Revolution*, edited by P. S. Martin and R. G. Klein, pp. 223–49. University of Arizona Press, Tucson.

1994   FAUNMAP: A Database Documenting Late Quaternary Distributions of Mammal Species in the United States. *Scientific Papers* 25 (1): 1–287.

Graham, R. W., and J. I. Mead

1987   Environmental Fluctuations and Evolution of Mammalian Faunas during the Last Deglaciation in North America. In *North America and Adjacent Oceans during the Last Deglaciation*, edited by W. F. Ruddiman and H. E. Wright, pp. 371–402. Geological Society of America, Boulder, Colo.

Graham, R., T. Stafford, E. Lundelius, H. Semken, and J. Southon

2002   C-14 Chronostratigraphy and Litho-Stratigraphy of Late Pleistocene Megafauna Extinctions in the New World. Paper presented at the 67th Annual Meeting of the Society for American Archaeology, Denver.

Gramly, R. M.

1993   *The Richey Clovis Cache: Earliest Americans along the Columbia River*. Persimmon Press, Buffalo, New York.

Gray, R. S.

1967   Petrology of the Upper Cenozoic Non-Marine Sediments in the San Pedro Valley, Arizona. *Journal of Sedimentary Petrology* 37: 774–89.

Grayson, D. K.

1991   Late Pleistocene Extinctions in North America: Taxonomy, Chronology, and Explanations. *Journal of World Prehistory* 5: 193–232.

Grayson, Donald K., and D. J. Meltzer

2003   A requiem for North American overkill. *Journal of Archaeological Science* 30: 585–93.

Green, F. E.

1963   The Clovis Blades: An Important Addition to the Llano Complex. *American Antiquity* 29: 145–65.

Green, T. J., B. Cochran, T. W. Fenton, J. C. Woods, G. L. Titmus, L. Tieszen, M. A. Davis, and S. J. Miller

1998   The Buhl Burial: A Paleoindian Woman from Southern Idaho. *American Antiquity* 63 (3): 437–56.

Greenberg, J. H.

1987   *Language in the Americas*. Stanford University Press, Stanford, Calif.

Grey, D. C.
1963 Fossil Mammoth Bone from Kaufmann Cave. *Plains Anthropologist* 8: 53–54

Grill, S., A. M. Borromei, G. Martínez, M. A. Gutierrez, M.E. Cornou, and D. Olivera
2005 Palynofacial analysis in alkaline soils—Paso Otero 5 archaeological site—Necochea district, Buenos Aires province, Argentina). *Journal of South American Earth Sciences* (in press).

Grimm, E. C., G. L. Jacobson, W. A. Watts, B. C. Hansen, and K. A. Maasch
1993 A 50,000-Year Record of Climate Oscillations from Florida and Its Temporal Correlation with the Heinrich Events. *Science* 261: 198–200.

Gruhn, R., A. L. Bryan, and J. D. Nance
1977 Los Tapiales: A Paleo-Indian Campsite in the Guatemalan Highlands. *Proceedings of the American Philosophical Society* 121 (3): 235–73.

Guidon, N., and G. Delibrias
1986 Carbon-14 Dates Point to Man in the Americas 32,000 Years Ago. *Nature* 321 (6072): 769–71.

Guthrie, R. D.
2003 Rapid Body Size Decline in Alaskan Pleistocene Horses before Extinction. *Science* 426: 169–71.
2004 Radiocarbon Evidence of Mid-Holocene Mammoths Stranded on an Alaskan Bering Sea Island. *Nature* 429: 746–49.

Gutierrez, M. A.
1998 Taphonomic Effects and State of Preservation of the Guanaco (*Lama guanicoe*) Bone Bed from Paso Otero 1 (Buenos Aires Province, Argentina). Master's thesis, Texas Tech University, Lubbock.
2004 Análisis Tafonómicos en el Area Interserrana (Pcia. de Buenos Aires). Ph.D. dissertation, Facultad de Ciencias Naturales y Museo, Universidad Nacional de La Plata, La Plata, Argentina.

Gutierrez, M. A., and C. A. Kaufmann
2006 Paso Otero 1. In *INCUAPA 10 años. Perspectivas actuales de la arqueología en las regiones pampeana y norpatagónica*, edited by G. Politis. Serie Monográfica del INCUAPA 5. FACSO-UNCPBA, Olavarría (in press).

Gutierrez, M. A., G. Martínez, E. Johnson, G. G. Politis, and W. Hartwell
1994 Nuevos análisis oseos en el sitio Paso Otero 1. Actas y Memorias del XI Congreso Nacional de Arqueología. *Revista del Museo de Historia Natural de San Rafael (Mendoza)* 16 (1/4): 222–24.

Gutierrez, M. A., G. G. Politis, and E. Johnson
2000 La ocupación más temprana en Arroyo Seco 2. Paper presented at the 2nd Congreso de Arqueología de la Región Pampeana, Argentina, Mar del Plata.

Guzmán, L.
1984 Informe de las excavaciones arqueológicas en el sitio La Olla. Manuscript on file at the Museo de La Plata, Universidad Nacional de La Plata, La Plata.

Haas, M. R.
1958 A New Lingusitic Relationship in North America: Algonkian and the Gulf Languages. *Southwestern Journal of Anthropology* 14 (3): 231–64.

Haberle, S. G., and M. P. Ledru

2001   Correlations among Charcoal Records of Fires from the Past 16,000 Years in Indonesia, Papua New Guinea, and Central and South America. *Quaternary Research* 55 (1): 97–104.

Hageman, B. P.

1972   Reports of the International Quaternary Association Subcommission on the Study of the Holocene. *Bulletin* 6: 1–6.

Hajdas, I., G. Bonani, P. Boden, D. M. Peteet, and D. H. Mann

1998   Cold Reversal on Kodiak Island, Alaska, Correlated with the European Younger Dryas by Using Variations of Atmospheric ^{14}C Content. *Geology* 26 (11): 1047–1050.

Hajdas, I., G. Bonani, P. I. Moreno, and D. Ariztegui

2003   Precise Radiocarbon Dating of Late-Glacial Cooling in Mid-Latitude South America. *Quaternary Research* 59: 70–78.

Hajdas, I., S. D. Ivy-Ochs, and G. Bonani

1995a Problems in the Extension of the Radiocarbon Calibration Curve (10–13 KYr B.P.). *Radiocarbon* 37: 75–79.

Hajdas, I., S. D. Ivy-Ochs, G. Bonani, A. F. Lotter, B. Zollitschka, and C. Schluchter

1995b Radiocarbon Age of the Laacher See Tephra: 11,230±40 B.P. *Radiocarbon* 37 (2): 149–54.

Hajduk, A., A. Albornoz, and M. Lezcano

2004   El "Mylodon" en el patio de atrás: Informe preliminar sobre los trabajos en el sitio El Trébol, ejido urbano de Bariloche, Provincia de Río Negro. In *Contra Viento y Marea: Arqueología de Patagonia*, edited by M. T. Civalero, P. M. Fernández, and A. G. Guráieb, pp. 715–31. INAPL-SAA, Buenos Aires.

Hall, D. A.

1996   Good Luck and Careful Science Provide New Insights about Clovis. *Mammoth Trumpet* 11: 5–9.

Hamilton, T. D., and T. Goebel

1999   Late Pleistocene Peopling of Alaska. In *Ice Age People of North America: Environments, Origins, and Adaptations*, edited by R. Bonnichsen and K. L. Turnmire, pp. 156–99. Oregon State University Press, Corvallis.

Hannus, L. A.

1990   Mammoth Hunting in the New World. In *Hunters of the Recent Past*, edited by L. B. Davis and B. O. Reeves, pp. 47–67. Unwin Hyman, London.

Hartley, W.

1950   The Global Distribution of Tribes of the Gramineae in Relation to Historical and Environmental Factors. *Australian Journal of Agricultural Research* 1: 355–73.

Hartwell, W. T.

1995   The Ryan's Site Cache: Comparisons to Plainview. *Plains Anthropologist* 40 (152): 165–84.

Haury, E. W., E. Antevs, and J. F. Lance

1953   Artifacts with Mammoth Remains, Naco, Arizona. *American Antiquity* 19: 1–24.

Haury, E. W., E. B. Sayles, and W. W. Wasley

1959 The Lehner Mammoth Site. *American Antiquity* 25: 2–30.

Hawkes, K., K. Hill, and J. O'Connell

1982 Why Hunters Gather: Optimal Foraging in the Ache of Eastern Paraguay. *American Ethnologist* 9: 379–98.

Hayden, B.

1981 Research and Development in the Stone Age: Technological Transitions among Hunter-Gatherers. *Current Anthropology* 22: 519–48.

Haynes, C. V.

1964 Fluted Projectile Points: Their Age and Dispersion. *Science* 145: 1408–413.

1966 Elephant-Hunting in North America. *Scientific American* 214 (6): 104–12.

1976 Archaeological Investigations at the Mummy Springs Site, Arizona, 1968. *National Geographic Society Research Reports*, 1968 Projects, pp. 165–71.

1979 Archaeological Investigations at the Murray Springs Site, Arizona, 1970. *National Geographic Society Research Reports*, 1970 Projects, pp. 261–67.

1980 The Clovis Culture. *Canadian Journal of Anthropology* 1: 115–21.

1982 Archaeological Investigations at the Lehner Site, Arizona, 1974–75. *National Geographic Society Research Reports* 14: 325–34.

1984 Stratigraphy and Late Pleistocene Extinction in the United States. In *Quaternary Extinctions*, edited by P. S. Martin and R. G. Klein, pp. 345–53. University of Arizona Press, Tucson.

1987 Curry Draw, Cochise County, Arizona: A Late Quaternary Stratigraphic Record of Pleistocene Extinction and Paleo-Indian Activities. *Geological Society of America Centennial Field Guide*, Cordilleran Section, pp. 23–28.

1991 Geoarchaeological and Paleohyrological Evidence for a Clovis Age Drought in North America and Its Bearing on Extinction. *Quaternary Research* 35 (3): 438–50.

1992 Contributions of Radiocarbon Dating to the Geochronology of the Peopling of the New World. In *Radiocarbon after Four Decades*, edited by R. E. Taylor, A. Long, and R. S. Kra, pp. 355–74. Springer-Verlag, New York.

1993 Clovis-Folsom Geochronology and Climate Change. In *From Kostenki to Clovis: Upper Paleolithic-Paleo-Indian Adaptations*, edited by O. Soffer and N. D. Praslov, pp. 219–36. Plenum Press, New York.

1995 Geochronology of Paleoenvironmental Change, Clovis Type Site, Blackwater Draw, New Mexico. *Geoarchaeology* 10: 317–88

1997 Dating a Paleoindian Site in the Amazon in Comparison with Clovis Culture. *Science* 275: 1048–1949

1998 Geochronology of the Stratigraphic Manifestation of Paleoclimatic Events at Paleoindian Sites. Paper presented at the 63rd Annual Meeting of the Society for American Archaeology, Seattle.

n.d. Clovis, Pre-Clovis, Climate Change, and Extinction. Unpublished manuscript in possession of the author.

Haynes, C. V., R. P. Beukens, A. J. Jull, and D. Davis

1992 New Radiocarbon Dates for Some Old Folsom Sites: Accelerator Technology. In

Ice Age Hunters of the Rockies, edited by D. J. Stanford and J. S. Day, pp. 83–100. University Press of Colorado, Niwot.

Haynes, C. V., and E. T. Hemmings

1968   Mammoth-Bone Shaft Wrench from Murray Springs, Arizona. *Science* 159: 186–87.

Haynes, G.

1991   *Mammoths, Mastodons, and Elephants: Biology, Behavior, and the Fossil Record.* Cambridge University Press, New York.

1995   Pre-Clovis and Clovis Megamammals: A Comparison of Carcass Disturbance, Age Profiles and Other Characteristics in Light of Recent Actualistic Studies. In *Ancient Peoples and Landscapes,* edited by E. Johnson, pp. 9–27. Museum of Texas Tech University, Lubbock.

2002   *The Early Settlement of North America: The Clovis Era.* Cambridge University Press, Cambridge.

Hemmings, C. A.

1998   Probable Association of Paleoindian Artifacts and Mastodon Remains from Sloth Hole, Aucilla River, North Florida. *Current Research in the Pleistocene* 15: 16–18.

2004   The Organic Clovis: A Single Continent-Wide Cultural Adaptation. Ph.D. dissertation, University of Florida, Gainesville.

Hemmings, E. T.

1970   Early Man in the San Pedro Valley, Arizona. Ph.D. dissertation, University of Arizona, Tuscon.

1975   The Silver Springs Site: Prehistory in the Silver Springs Valley, Florida. *Florida Anthropologist* 28 (4): 141–58.

2006   Buried Animal Kills and Processing Localities. In *Murray Springs: A Clovis Site with Multiple Activity Areas in the San Pedro Valley, Arizona,* edited by C. V. Haynes and B. B. Huckell. Anthropological Papers of the University of Arizona. University of Arizona Press, Tucson.

Hemmings, E. T., and C. V. Haynes

1969   The Escapule Mammoth and Associated Projectile Points, San Pedro Valley, Arizona. *Journal of Arizona Academy of Science* 5: 184–88.

Hester, J. J.

1972   *Blackwater Locality No. 1: A Stratified Early Man Site in Eastern New Mexico.* Southern Methodist University, Dallas.

Hester, T. R., T. C. Kelly, and G. Ligabue

1981   *A Fluted Paleo-Indian Projectile Point from Belize, Central America.* Working Papers 1. Center for Archaeological Research, University of Texas, San Antonio.

Hicks, B. A. (Editor)

2004   *Marmes Rockshelter: A Final Report on 11,000 Years of Cultural Use.* Washington State University Press, Pullman.

Higham, T. F.
2004 AMS Dating of Archaeological Bone from Mexico: Problems and Future Directions. Paper presented at the 2nd International Symposium, Early Man in America, Mexico City.

Hilgers, A., A. S. Murray, N. Schlaak, and U. Radtke
2001 Comparison of Quartz OSL Protocols Using Lateglacial and Holocene Dune Sands from Brandenburg, Germany. *Quaternary Science Reviews* 20 (5–9): 731–36.

Hoffecker, J. F., W. R. Powers, and T. Goebel
1993 The Colonization of Beringia and the Peopling of the New World. *Science* 259: 46–53

Hofman, J. L.
1992 Recognition and Interpretation of Folsom Technological Variability on the Southern Plains. In *Ice Age Hunters of the Rockies*, edited by D. J. Stanford and J. S. Day, pp. 193–224. University of Colorado Press, Niwot.
1994 Paleoindian Aggregations on the Great Plains. *Journal of Anthropological Archaeology* 13: 341–70.

Hofman, J. L., L. C. Todd, C. B. Schultz, and W. Hendy
1991 The Lipscomb Bison Quarry: Continuing Investigation at a Folsom Site on the Southern Plains. *Bulletin of the Texas Archeological Society* 60: 149–89.

Holliday, V. T.
1989 Middle Holocene Drought on the Southern High Plains. *Quaternary Research* 31 (1): 74–82.
1995a Late Quaternary Stratigraphy of the Southern High Plains. In *Ancient Peoples and Landscapes*, edited by E. Johnson, pp. 289–313. Museum of Texas Tech University, Lubbock.
1995b Stratigraphy and Paleoenvironments of Late Quaternary Valley Fills on the Southern High Plains. *Geological Society of America Memoir* 186: 1–136.
1997 *Paleoindian Geoarchaeology of the Southern High Plains*. University of Texas Press, Austin.
2000 The Evolution of Paleoindian Geochronology and Typology on the Great Plains. *Geoarchaeology* 15 (3): 227–290.

Holliday, V. T., C. V. Haynes, J. L. Hofman, and D. J. Meltzer
1994 Geoarchaeology and Geochronology of the Miami (Clovis) Site, Southern High Plains of Texas. *Quaternary Research* 41 (2): 234–44.

Holliday, V. T., J. C. Knox, G. L. Running IV, R. D. Mandel, and C. R. Ferring
2002 The Central Lowlands and Great Plains. In *The Physical Geography of North America*, edited by A. R. Orme, pp. 335–62. Oxford University Press, New York.

Holliday, V. T., G. Martínez, E. Johnson, and B. Buchanan
2003 Geoarchaeology of Paso Otero 5 (Pampas of Argentina). In *Where the South Winds Blow: Ancient Evidence of Paleo South Americans*, edited by L. Miotti, M. Salemme, and N. Flegenheimer, pp. 37–43. Center for the Study of the First Americans, Texas A&M University, College Station.

Holmes, C.

1996   Broken Mammoth. In *American Beginnings: The Prehistory and Paleoecology of Beringia*, edited by F. H. West, pp. 312–18. University of Chicago Press, Chicago.

Holmes, C. E., and D. R. Yesner

1992   Investigating the Earliest Alaskans: The Broken Mammoth Archaeological Project. *Arctic Research* 6: 6–9.

Hoppe, K. A.

2004   Late Pleistocene Mammoth Herd Structure, Migration Patterns, and Clovis Hunting Strategies Inferred from Isotopic Analyses of Multiple Death Assemblages. *Paleobiology* 30 (1): 129–45.

Howard, C. D.

1990   The Clovis Point: Characteristics and Type Description. *Plains Anthropologist* 35 (129): 255–62.

Huckell, B. B.

1974   The Navarrete Site: A Third Clovis Locality on Greenbush Draw. Manuscript on file, Arizona State Museum Archives, University of Arizona, Tucson.

1982   *The Distribution of Fluted Points in Arizona: A Review and Update.* Arizona State Museum Archaeological Series 145. University of Arizona, Tucson.

2006   Clovis Lithic Technology: A View from the Upper San Pedro Valley. In *Murray Springs: A Clovis Site with Multiple Activity Areas in the San Pedro Valley, Arizona*, edited by C. V. Haynes and B. B. Huckell. Anthropological Papers of the University of Arizona. University of Arizona Press, Tucson.

Hughen, K. A., T. I. Eglinton, L. Xu, and M. Makou

2004   Abrupt Tropical Vegetation Response to Rapid Climate Changes. *Science* 304: 1955–1959.

Hughen, K. A., J. T. Overpeck, S. J. Lehman, M. Kashgarian, J. R. Southon, L. C. Peterson, R. Alley, and D. M. Sigman

1998   Deglacial Changes in Ocean Circulation from an Extended Radiocarbon Calibration. *Nature* 391: 65–68.

Hughen, K. A., J. R. Southon, S. J. Lehman, and J. T. Overpeck

2000   Synchronous Radiocarbon and Climate Shifts during the Last Deglaciation. *Science* 290: 1951–1954.

Humphrey, P. S., J. E. Pafaur, and P. C. Rasmussen

1993   Avifauna of Three Holocene Cave Deposits in Southern Chile. *Occasional Papers of the Museum of Natural History* 154: 1–37. University of Kansas, Lawrence.

Hunt, C. B.

1967   *Physiography of the United States.* W. H. Freeman, San Francisco.

Hurt W., T. Van der Hammen, and G. Correal

1972   Preceramic Sequences in the El Abra Rock-Shelters, Colombia. *Science* 175: 1106.

Ibarra, D. E.

1971   *Argentina indígena y prehistoria Sudamericana.* TEA, Buenos Aires.

Iriondo, M. H., and N. O. Garcia
1993 Climatic Variations in the Argentine Plains during the Last 18,000 Years. *Palaeogeography, Palaeoclimatology, Palaeoecology* 101: 209–20.

Isla, F.
1989 Holocene Sea-Level Fluctuation in the Southern Hemisphere. *Quaternary Science Reviews* 8: 359–68.

Isla. F., J. Fasano, L. Ferrero, M. Espinosa, and E. Schnack
1990 Late Quaternary marine-estuarine sequences of the south-eastern coast of Buenos Aires Province, Argentina. *Quaternary of South America and Antarctic Peninsula* 6 (1988): 137–55.

Jackson, D.
1993 Datación radiocarbónica para una adaptación costera del Arcaico temprano en el Norte Chico, Comuna de Los Vilos. *Boletín de la Sociedad Chilena de Arqueología* 16: 28–31.
1997 Coexistencia e interacción de comunidades cazadores-recolectores del Arcaico temprano en el semiárido de Chile. *Valles* 3: 13–36.
2002 *Los instrumentos líticos de los primeros cazadores de Tierra del Fuego.* Dirección de Bibliotecas, Archivos y Museos, Santiago.

Jackson, D., and M. Massone
n.d. Punta de proyectil acanalada en la provincial de Arauco, VIII Region, Chile. Unpublished manuscript on file with the authors.

Jackson, D., C. Méndez, and R. Seguel
2003 Late Pleistocene Human Occupations in the Semiarid Coast of Chile: A Comment. *Current Research in the Pleistocene* 20: 35–37.

Jackson, L. J.
1986 New Evidence for Early Woodland Seasonal Adaptation from Southern Ontario, Canada. *American Antiquity* 51 (2): 389–401.
1989 Notes on 1989 Examination of Fell's Cave Collections at American Museum of Natural History, New York. Manuscript in possession of author.
1995 A Clovis Point from South Coastal Chile. *Current Research in the Pleistocene* 12: 21–23.
1999 El Jobo Points: Age, Context, and Definition. *Current Research in the Pleistocene* 16: 41–43.

Jahren, A. H., L. C. Todd, and R. G. Amundson
1998 Stable Isotope Dietary Analysis of Bison Bone Samples from the Hudson-Meng Bonebed: Effects of Paleotopography. *Journal of Archaeological Science* 25: 465–75.

Jaimes, A.
1997 Northwestern Venezuela: A Regional Intersection for Cultural Dynamics in the Late Pleistocene. Paper presented at the 62nd Annual Meeting of the Society for American Archaeology, Nashville.
1999 Nuevas evidencias de cazadores-recolectores y aproximación al entendimiento del uso del espacio geográfico en el noroccidente de Venezuela: Sus implicaciones en el contexto sudamericano. *Arqueología del Área Intermedia* 1: 83–120

Jelinek, A.

1992   Perspectives from the Old World on the Habitation of the New. *American Antiquity* 57: 345–48.

Johnson, E.

1982   Paleoindian Bone Expediency Tools—Lubbock Lake and Bonfire Shelter. *Canadian Journal of Anthropology* 2 (2): 145–57.

1985   Current Developments in Bone Technology. In *Advances in Archaeological Method and Theory*, edited by M. B. Schiffer, pp. 157–235. Academic Press, New York.

1986   Late Pleistocene and Early Holocene Paleoenvironments and Vertebrates on the Southern High Plains (USA). *Geographic Physique et Quaternaire* 40 (3): 249–61.

1987   *Lubbock Lake: Late Quaternary Studies on the Southern High Plains*. Texas A&M University Press, College Station.

1989   Human Modified Bone from Early Southern Plains Sites. In *Bone Modification*, edited by R. Bonnichsen and M. Sorg, pp. 431–71. Center for the Study of the First Americans, Orono, Maine.

1991a   Late Pleistocene Cultural Occupation of the Southern Plains. In *Clovis: Origins and Adaptations*, edited by R. Bonnichsen and K. L. Turnmire, pp. 215–36. Center for the Study of the First Americans, Corvallis, Ore.

1991b   Paleoindian Hunters on the Southern Plains: The Lubbock Lake Perspective. Paper presented at the 2nd Soviet-American Symposium on Upper Paleolithic-Paleoindian Adaptations, Denver.

1995a   Site Formation and Disturbance Processes at Lubbock Lake (Southern High Plains, USA) during the Terminal Pleistocene. In *Ancient Peoples and Landscapes*, edited by E. Johnson, pp. 315–40. Museum of Texas Tech University, Lubbock.

1995b   Southern High Plains Paleoindian Subsistence Patterns—Beyond Mammoth and Ancient Bison. Symposium paper presented at the 61st Annual Meeting of the Society for American Archaeology, Minneapolis.

1997   Late Quaternary Bison Utilization at Lubbock Lake on the Southern High Plains of Texas. *Plains Anthropologist Memoir* 29: 1–16.

2005   Late Wisconsinan Mammoth Procurement in the North American Grasslands. In *Paleoamerican Origins: Beyond Clovis*, edited by R. Bonnichsen, B. Lepper, D. Steele, D. Stanford, C. N. Warren, and R. Gruhn, pp. 115–35. Center for the Study of the First Americans, Texas A&M University Press, College Station.

Johnson, E., M. A. Gutierrez, G. Politis, G. Martínez, and W. T. Hartwell

1996   Holocene Taphonomy at Paso Otero 1 on the Eastern Pampas of Argentina. In *Proceedings of the 1993 Bone Modification Conference, Hot Springs, South Dakota*, edited by L. A. Hannus and R. P. Winham, pp. 50–64. Occasional Publication 1. Archaeology Laboratory, Augustana College, South Dakota.

Johnson, E., and V. T. Holliday

1986   The Archaic Record at Lubbock Lake. *Plains Anthropologist Memoir* 21: 7–54.

1989   Lubbock Lake: Late Quaternary Cultural and Environmental Change on the Southern High Plains, USA. *Journal of Quaternary Science* 4 (2): 145–65.

1995   Archeology and Late Quaternary Environments of the Southern High Plains. *Bulletin of the Texas Archeological Society* 66: 519–40.

1997   Analysis of Paleoindian Bone Beds at the Clovis Site: New Data from Old Excavations. *Plains Anthropologist* 42: 329–52.

Johnson, E., G. Politis, and M. Gutierrez

2000   Early Holocene Bone Technology at the La Olla 1 Site, Atlantic Coast of the Argentine Pampas. *Journal of Archaeological Science* 27 (6): 463–77.

Johnson, E., G. Politis, G. Martínez, W. T. Hartwell, M. A. Gutierrez, and H. Haas

1998   Radiocarbon Chronology of Paso Otero 1 in the Pampean Region of Argentina. *Quaternary of South America and Antarctic Peninsula* 16: 15–25.

Johnson, N. M., N. D. Opdyke, and E. H. Lindsay

1975   Magnetic Polarity Stratigraphy of Pliocene-Pleistocene Terrestrial Deposits and Vertebrate Faunas, San Pedro Valley, Arizona. *Geological Society of American Bulletin* 86: 5–12.

Jones, M. D., P. J. Sheppard, and D. G. Sutton

1997   Soil Temperature and Obsidian Hydration Dating: A Clarification of Variables Affecting Accuracy. *Journal of Archaeological Science* 24: 505–17.

Jones, S.

1996   The Anzick Site: An Analysis of a Clovis Burial Assemblage. M.A. thesis, Oregon State University, Corvallis.

Jones, S., and R. Bonnichsen

1994   The Anzick Clovis Burial. *Current Research in the Pleistocene* 11: 42–44.

Josenhans, H., D. Fedje, R. Pienitz, and J. Southon

1997   Early Humans and Rapidly Changing Holocene Sea Levels in the Queen Charlotte Islands–Hecate Strait, British Columbia, Canada. *Science* 277: 71–74.

Justice, N. D.

1987   *Stone Age Spear and Arrow Points of the Midcontinent and Eastern United States.* Indiana University Press, Bloomington.

Kaiser, K. F.

1989   Late Glacial Reforestation in the Swiss Mittelland, as Illustrated by the Dättnau Valley. In *Quaternary Type Sections: Imagination or Reality?* edited by J. Rose and C. Schluchter, pp. 161–78. Balkema, Rotterdam.

n.d.   [14]C and Dendro Years, Dättnau: Boelling/Alleroed Chronologies. Graph formerly posted at www.wsl.ch/forest/dendro/images/dendroy.jpg.

Karathanasis, A. D.

1997   X-ray Diffraction, X-ray Fluorescence, and Differential Scanning Calorimetry Analysis of Sediments from Selected Features and Bones. In *Monte Verde: A Late Pleistocene Settlement in Chile*, vol.2, *The Archaeological Context and Interpretation*, edited by T. D. Dillehay, pp. 817–24. Smithsonian Institution Press, Washington, D.C.

Kaufmann, C. A., and M. A. Gutierrez

2004   Dispersión potencial de huesos de guanaco en medios fluviales y lacustres. In *Aproximaciones Contemporáneas a la Arqueología Pampeana. Perspectivas teóricas, metodológicas, análiticas y casos de estudio*, edited by G. Martínez,

M. A. Gutierrez, R. Curtoni, M. Berón, and P. Madrid, pp. 129–46. Facultad de Ciencias Sociales, UNCPBA, Olavarría.

Keefer, D. K., S. D. deFrance, M. E. Moseley, J. B. Richardson III, D. R. Satterlee, and A. Day-Lewis

1998   Early Maritime Economy and El Niño Events at Quebrada Tacahuay. *Science* 281: 1833–835.

Keeley, L. H.

1980   *Experimental Determination of Stone Tool Uses: A Microwear Analysis.* University of Chicago Press, Chicago.

Kelly, R. L.

1995   *The Foraging Spectrum: Diversity in Hunter-Gatherer Lifeways.* Smithsonian Institution Press, Washington, D.C.

2003   Maybe We Do Know When People First Came to North America. *Quaternary International* 109–10: 133–45.

Kelly, R. L., and L. C. Todd

1988   Coming into the Country: Early Paleoindian Hunting and Mobility. *American Antiquity* 53: 231–44.

Kelly, T. C.

1993   Preceramic Projectile-Point Typology in Belize. *Ancient Mesoamerica* 4: 205–27.

Kennett, D. J., B. L. Ingram, J. R. Southon, and K. Wise

2002   Differences in ^{14}C Age between Stratigraphically Associated Charcoal and Marine Shell from the Archaic Period Site of Kilometer 4, Southern Peru: Old Wood or Old Water? *Radiocarbon* 44 (1): 53–58.

Kershaw, A.

1995   Environmental Change in Greater Australia. *Antiquity* 265 (69): 656–75.

Kitigawa, H., and J. van der Plicht

1998   Atmospheric Radiocarbon Calibration to 45,000 Yr B.P.: Late Glacial Fluctuations and Cosmogenic Isotope Production. *Science* 279: 1187–190.

2000   Atmospheric Radiocarbon Calibration beyond 11,900 cal B.P. from Lake Suigetsu Laminated Sediments. *Radiocarbon* 42 (3): 369–80.

Kreutzer, L. A.

1988   Megafaunal Butchering at Lubbock Lake, Texas: A Taphonomic Reanalysis. *Quaternary Research* 30: 221–31.

1996   The Taphonomy of the Mill Iron Site Bison Bonebed. In *The Mill Iron Site 24CT30 and the Goshen-Plainview Cultural Complex on the Northern High Plains,* edited by G. C. Frison, pp. 101–43. University of New Mexico Press, Albuquerque.

Krieger, A.

1964   Early Man in the New World. In *Prehistoric Man in the New World,* edited by J. Jennings and E. Norbeck, pp. 23–81. University of Chicago Press, Chicago.

Kromer, B., M. Friedrich, K. A. Hughen, F. Kaiser, S. Remmele, M. Schaub, and S. Talamo

2004   Late Glacial ^{14}C Ages from a Floating, 1382-Ring Pine Chronology. *Radiocarbon* 46 (3): 1203–209.

Kromer, B., S. W. Manning, P. I. Kuniholm, M. W. Newton, M. Spurk, and I. Levin
2001 Regional $^{14}CO_2$ Offsets in the Troposphere: Magnitude, Mechanisms, and Consequences. *Science* 294: 2529–532.

Kunz, M. L. and R. E. Reanier
1994 Paleoindians in Beringia: Evidence from Arctic Alaska. *Science* 263: 660–62.
1996 The Mesa Site, Iteriak Creek. In *American Beginnings: The Prehistory and Palaeoecology of Beringia*, edited by F. H. West, pp. 497–504. University of Chicago Press, Chicago.

Lahren, L. A.
2001 The On-Going Odyssey of the Anzick Clovis Burial in Park County, Montana (24PA506): Part 1. *Archaeology in Montana* 42: 55–59.

Lahren, L. A., and R. Bonnichsen
1974 Bone Foreshafts from a Clovis Burial in Southwestern Montana. *Science* 186: 147–50.

Largent, F.
2004 Pre-Clovis Traces at Swan Point, Alaska. *Mammoth Trumpet* 20 (1): 4–7.

Laub, R. S., and G. Haynes
1998 Fluted Points, Mastodons, and Evidence of Late-Pleistocene Drought at the Hiscock Site, Western New York State. *Current Research in the Pleistocene* 15: 32–34.

Laub, R. S., J. Tomenchuk, and P. L. Storck
1996 A Dated Mastodon Artifact from the Late Pleistocene of New York. *Archaeology of Eastern North America* 24: 1–17.

Lauenroth, W. K., and D. G. Milchunas
1992 Short-Grass Steppe. In *Natural Grasslands*, edited by R. Coupland, pp. 183–226. Elsevier, Amsterdam.

Leonard, J. A., R. K. Wayne, J. Wheeler, R. Valadez, S. Guillen, and C. Vila
2002 Ancient DNA evidence for Old World Origin of New World dogs. *Science* 298: 1613–616.

Leyden, B. W.
1984 Guatemalan Forest Synthesis after Pleistocene Aridity. *Proceedings of the National Academy of Sciences* 81: 4856–859.
1985 Late Quaternary Aridity and Holocene Moisture Fluctuations in the Lake Valencia Basin, Venezuela. *Ecology* 66 (4): 1279–295.

Lindsay, E. H., G. A. Smith, C. V. Haynes, and N. D. Opdyke
1990 Sediments, Geomorphology, Magnetostratigraphy, and Vertebrate Paleontology in the San Pedro Valley, Arizona. *Journal of Geology* 98: 605–19.

Litt, T., H. U. Schmincke, and B. Kromer
2003 Environmental Response to Climate and Volcanic Events in Central Europe during the Weichselian Lateglacial. *Quaternary Science Reviews* 22: 7–32.

Llagostera, A.
1979 9000 Years of Maritime Subsistence on the Pacific: An Analysis by Means of Bioindicators in the North of Chile. *American Antiquity* 44: 309–24.

López, C. E.

1991   *Investigaciones arqueológicas en el Magdalena Medio, Cuenca del Río Carare (Departamento de Santander).* FIAN, Bogotá.

1994   Aproximación al medio ambiente, recursos y ocupaciones tempranas del valle del río Magdalena. *Informes Antropológicos* 7: 5–15.

1999   *Ocupaciones tempranas en las Tierras Bajas Tropicales del Valle Medio del Río Magdalena, Sitio 05-YON-002, Yondó-Antioquia.* FIAN, Bogotá.

Lothrop, S. K.

1961   Early Migrations to Central and South America: An Anthropological Problem in the Light of Other Sciences. *Journal of the Royal Anthropological Institute* 91: 97–123.

Lotter, A. F.

1991   Absolute Dating of the Late Glacial in Switzerland Using Annually Laminated Sediments. *Quaternary Research* 35: 321–30.

Lovvorn, M. B., G. C. Frison, and L. L. Tieszen

2001   Paleoclimate and Amerindians: Evidence from Stable Isotopes and Atmospheric Circulation. *Proceedings of the National Academy of Science* 98 (5): 2485–490.

Lundelius, E. L., R. W. Graham, E. Anderson, J. Guilday, J. A. Holman, D. W. Steadman, and S. D. Webb

1983   Terrestrial Vertebrate Faunas. In *Late-Quaternary Environments of the United States*, vol. 1, edited by S. C. Porter, pp. 311–53. University of Minnesota Press, Minneapolis.

Lyman, R. L., and M. J. O'Brien

1999   Prehistoric Osseous Rods from North America: Arguments on Function. *North American Archaeologist* 20 (4): 347–64.

Lynch, T. F.

1974   The Antiquity of Man in South America. *Quaternary Research* 4: 356–77.

1983   The South American Paleo-Indians. In *Ancient Native Americans*, edited by J. D. Jennings, pp. 87–137. W. H. Freeman, San Francisco.

1990   Glacial Age Man in South America? A Critical Review. *American Antiquity* 55: 12–36.

Lynch, T. F. (Editor)

1980   *Guiterrero Cave: Early Man in the Andes.* Academic Press, New York.

Lynch, T. F., and S. Pollock

1981   La arqueología de la Cueva Negra de Chobshi. *Miscelánea Antropológica Ecuatoriana* 1: 92–119.

Maat, P. B., and W. C. Johnson

1996   Thermoluminescence and New 14C Age Estimates for Late Quaternary Loesses in Southwestern Nebraska. *Geomorphology* 17: 115–28.

MacDonald, G. F.

1968   *Debert, a Paleo-Indian Site in Central Nova Scotia.* Anthropology Papers 16. National Museums of Canada, Ottawa.

MacNeish, R. S.

1979   The Early Man Remains from Pikimachay Cave, Ayacucho Basin, Highland Peru.

In *Pre-Llano Cultures of the Americas: Paradoxes and Possibilities*, edited by R. L. Humphrey and D. Stanford, pp. 1–47. Anthropological Society of Washington, D.C.

MacNeish, R. S., E. Berger, and R. Protsch
1970   Megafauna and Man from Ayacucho, Highland Peru. *Science* 168: 975–78.

MacNeish, R. S., and A. Nelken-Terner
1983   *Final Annual Report of the Belize Archaic Archaeological Reconnaissance*. Center for Archaeological Studies, Boston University, Boston.

Madsen, D. B. (Editor)
2004   *Entering America: Northeast Asia and Beringia before the Last Glacial Maximum*. University of Utah Press, Salt Lake City.

Mandryk, C. A.
1998   Evaluating Paleoenvironmental Constraints on Interior and Coastal Entry Routes into North America. Paper presented at the 63rd Annual Meeting of the Society for American Archaeology, Seattle.

Marshall, L. G., S. D. Webb, J. J. Sepkoski, and D. M. Raup
1982   Mammalian Evolution and the Great American Interchange. *Science* 215: 1351–357.

Martens, R. A., B. Koldehoff, J. E. Morrow, and T. A. Morrow
2004   The Surface Collection from the Martens site. *Missouri Archaeologist* 65: 1–43.

Martin, C. W.
1993   Radiocarbon Ages on Late Pleistocene Loess Stratigraphy of Nebraska and Kansas, Central Great Plains, U.S.A. *Quaternary Science Reviews* 12: 179–88.

Martin, P. S.
1973   The Discovery of America. *Science* 179: 969–74.

Martin, P. S., and J. E. Guilday
1967   A Bestiary for Pleistocene Biologists. In *Pleistocene Extinctions: The Search for a Cause*, edited by P. S. Martin and H. E. Wright, pp. 1–62. Yale University Press, New Haven, Conn.

Martínez, G. A.
1999   Tecnología, subsistencia y asentamiento en el curso medio del río Quequén Grande: Un enfoque arqueológico. Ph.D. dissertation, Universidad Nacional de La Plata, La Plata.

2001   "Fish-Tail" Projectile Points and Megamammals: New Evidence from Paso Otero 5 (Argentina). *Antiquity* 75: 523–28.

2002–4   Superficies de estabilización del paisaje (horizontes "A" de suelos enterrados) y el registro arqueológico de la localidad Paso Otero (río Quequén Grande, Pdo. de Necochea). *Arqueología* 12: 179–99.

2006   Arqueología del curso inferior del río Colorado: estado actual del conocimiento. In *INCUAPA 10 años Perspectivas actuales de la arqueología en las regiones pampeana y norpatagónica*, edited by Gustavo Politis. Serie Monográfica del INCUAPA 5. FACSO-UNCPBA, Olavarría (in press).

Martínez, G. A., and M. A. Gutierrez
2004   Tendencias en la explotación humana de la fauna durante el Pleistoceno final-

Holoceno en la Región Pampeana (Argentina). In *Zooarchaeology of South America*, edited by G. L. Mengoni Goñalons, pp. 81–98. BAR International Series 1298, Oxford.

2006   Paso Otero 5: integración de los resultados interdisciplinarios y estado actual de las investigaciones. In *INCUAPA 10 años. Perspectivas actuales de la arqueología en las regiones pampeana y norpatagónica*, edited by Gustavo Politis. Serie Monográfica del INCUAPA 5. FACSO-UNCPBA, Olavarría, Argentina (in press).

Martínez, G., M. A. Gutierrez, and G. Armentano

2005   The archaeology of Paso Otero 5, a late Pleistocene Site from the Pampa region, Argentina. Paper presented at the 70th Annual Meeting de la Society for American Archaeology. Salt Lake City, Utah.

Martínez, G., M. A. Gutierrez, and J. L. Prado

2004   New archaeological evidences from the late Pleistocene/early Holocene Paso Otero 5 site (Pampean region, Argentina). *Current Research in the Pleistocene* 21: 16–18.

Martínez, G., P. Messineo, M. E. Piñeyro, C. Kaufmann, and P. Barros

2001   Análisis preliminar de la estructura faunística del sitio Paso Otero 3 (Pdo. de Necochea, Pcia. de Buenos Aires, Argentina). *Arqueología Uruguaya Hacia el Fin del Milenio* 1: 505–20.

Mason, R. J.

1962   The Paleo-Indian Tradition in Eastern North America. *Current Anthropology* 3: 227–83.

Massone, M.

1983   10,400 años de colonización humana en Tierra del Fuego. *Informese* 14: 24–32.

1987   Los cazadores paleoindios de Tres Arroyos (Prov. de Bs. Ac.). *Etnia* 15: 1–18.

2004   *Los cazadores después del hielo*. Ediciones de la Dirección de Bibliotecas, Archivos y Museos. Santiago.

2005   *Los Cazadores Después del Hielo*. Centro Diego Barros Arana, Santiago.

Massone, M., D. Jackson, and A. Prieto

1993   *Perspectiva arqueológica de los Selk'nam*. Centro Diego Barros Arana, Santiago.

Massone, M., and A. Prieto

2004   Evaluación de la Modalidad Cultural Fell 1 En Magallanes. *Chungara, Revista de Anthropologia Chilena* 3: 303–15.

Massone, M., A. Prieto, D. Jackson, G. Cárdenas, M. Arroyo, and P. Cárdenas

1998   "Los cazadores tempranos y sus fogatas: una nueva historia para la Cueva Tres Arroyos 1, Tierra del Fuego. *Boletín de la Sociedad Chilena de Arqueología*, vol. 26, pp. 11–18. Santiago.

Matheus, P. E.

1995   Diet and Co-Ecology of Pleistocene Short-Faced Bears and Brown Bears in Eastern Beringia. *Quaternary Research* 44: 447–53.

Matheus, P. E., R. D. Guthrie, and M. L. Kunz

2003   Isotope Ecology of Late Quaternary Eastern Beringia. Paper presented at the 3rd International Mammoth Conference, Dawson City, Yukon, Canada.

Matos, R.
1992 El precerámico de Junín: del lítico al formativo. In *Prehistoria de Sudamérica. Nuevas Perspectivas*, edited by B. Meggers, pp. 327–32. Taraxacum, Washington, D. C..

Mayer-Oakes, W. J.
1984 Fluted Projectile Points: A North American Shibboleth Viewed in South American Perspective. *Archaeology of Eastern North America* 12: 231–47.
1986a Early Man Projectile Points and Lithic Technology in the Ecuadorian Sierra. In *New Evidences for the Pleistocene Peopling of the Americas*, edited by A. L. Bryan, pp. 133–56. Center for the Study of Early Man, University of Maine, Orono.
1986b *El Inga: A Paleo-Indian Site in the Sierra of Northern Ecuador*. Transactions of the American Philosophical Society, vol. 76, part 4. Philadelphia.

Mayewski, P. A., L. D. Mecker, S. Whitlow, M. S. Twickler, M. C. Morrison, R. B. Alley, P. Broomfield, and K. Taylor
1993 The Atmosphere during the Younger Dryas. *Science* 261: 195–97.

Mayle, F., A. E. Levesque, and L. C. Cwynar
1993 Accelerator-Mass-Spectrometer Ages for the Younger Dryas Event in Atlantic Canada. *Quaternary Research* 39: 355–60.

Mazzanti, D.
2003 Human settlements in caves and rockshelters during the pleistocene-holocene transition in the Eastern Tandilia Range, Pampean Region, Argentina. In *Ancient evidences for paleo south americans: from where the south winds blow*, edited by L. Miotti, M. Salemme, and N. Flegenheimer, pp. 57–61. Center for the Studies of the First Americans (CSFA) and Texas A&M University Press, College Station.

Mazzanti, D., and C. Quintana
1997 Asociación cultural de fauna extinguida en el sitio arqueológico Cueva Tixi, Provincia de Buenos Aires, Argentina. *Revista Española de Antropología Americana* 27: 11–21.
2001 *Cueva Tixi: cazadores y recolectores de las sierras de Tandilia oriental. Geología, Paleontología y Zooarqueología*. Publicación Especial 1. Laboratorio de Arqueología, Facultad de Humanidades (UNMP), Mar del Plata.

McAvoy, J. M., J. C. Baker, J. K. Feathers, R. L. Hodges, L. J. McWeeney, and T. R. Whyte
2002 Summary of Research at the Cactus Hill Archaeological Site, 44SX202, Sussex County, Virginia: Report to the National Geographic Society in Compliance with Stipulations of Grant #6345-98.

McAvoy, J. M., and L. D. McAvoy
1997 *Archaeological Investigations of Site 44SX202, Cactus Hill, Sussex County, Virginia*. Research Report Series 8. Virginia Department of Historic Resources, Richmond.

McCormac, F. G., P. J. Reimer, A. G. Hogg, T. F. Higham, M. G. Baillie, J. Palmer, and M. Stuiver
2004 Calibration of the Radiocarbon Time Scale for the Southern Hemisphere: AD 1850–950. *Radiocarbon* 46 (3): 641–51.

Mehringer, P. J., and F. F. Foit
1990   Volcanic Ash Dating of the Clovis Cache at East Wenatchee, Washington. *National Geographic Research* 6 (4): 495–503.

Mehringer, P. J., J. C. Sheppard, and F. F. Foit
1984   The Age of Glacier Peak Tephra in West-Central Montana. *Quaternary Research* 21: 36–41.

Meltzer, D. J.
1988   Late Pleistocene Human Adaptations in Eastern North America. *Journal of World Prehistory* 2: 1–53.
1989   Why Don't We Know When the First People Came to America? *American Antiquity* 54: 471–90.
1993   Is There a Clovis Adaptation? In *From Kostenki to Clovis*, edited by O. Soffer and N. D. Praslov, pp. 293–309. Plenum Press, New York.
1995   Clocking the First Americans. *Annual Review of Anthropology* 24: 21–45.
2001   Late Pleistocene Cultural and Technological Diversity of Beringia: A View from Down Under. *Arctic Anthropology* 38 (2): 206–13.
2002   What Do You Do When No One's Been There Before? Thoughts on the Exploration and Colonization of New Lands. In *The First Americans: The Pleistocene Colonization of the New World*, edited by N. G. Jablonski, pp. 27–58. Memoirs of the California Academy of Sciences 27. San Francisco.

Meltzer, D. J., J. M. Adovasio, and T. D. Dillehay
1994   On a Pleistocene Human Occupation at Pedra Furada, Brazil. *Antiquity* 68 (261): 695–714.

Meltzer, D. J., and B. Smith
1986   Paleoindians and Early Archaic Subsistence Strategies in Eastern North America. In *Foraging, Collecting, and Harvesting: Archaic Period Subsistence and Settlement in the Eastern Woodlands*, edited by S. W. Neusius, pp. 3–31, Center for Archeological Investigations Occasional Paper 6. Carbondale, Ill.

Menghin, O.
1952   Fundamentos cronológicos de la prehistoria de Patagonia. *Runa* 1: 23–43.

Mercier, N., H. Valladas, G. Valladas, J. L. Reyss, A. Jelinek, L. Meignen, and J. L. Joron
1995   TL Dates of Burnt Flints from Jelinek's Excavations at Tabun and Their Implications. *Journal of Archaeological Science* 22 (4): 495–509.

Messineo, P., and G. Politis
2006   Estado actual de las investigaciones en los sitios de La Moderna y Campo Laborde. In INCUAPA 10 años. *Perspectivas actuales de la arqueología en las regiones pampeana y norpatagónica*, edited by Gustavo Politis. Serie Monográfica del INCUAPA 5. FACSO-UNCPBA, Olavarría, Argentina (in press).

Mihlbachler, M. C., D. A. Hemmings, and S. D. Webb
2000   Reevaluation of the Alexon Bison Kill Site, Wacissa River. *Current Research in the Pleistocene* 17: 55–57.

Milanich, J. T.
1994   *Archaeology of Precolumbian Florida*. University Press of Florida, Gainesville

Miller, G. H., J. W. Magee, B. J. Johnson, M. L. Fogel, N. A. Spooner, M. T. McCulloch, and L. K. Ayliffe
1999 Pleistocene Extinction of *Genyornis newtoni*: Human Impact on Australian Megafauna. *Science* 283: 205–8.

Miotti, L.
1995 Piedra Museo Locality: A Special Place in the New World. *Current Research in the Pleistocene* 12: 36–38.
1996 Piedra Museo (Santa Cruz), nuevos datos para la ocupación pleistocénica en Patagonia. In *Arqueología: Sólo Patagonia*, edited by J. Gómez, pp. 27–38. CENPAT-CONICET, Puerto Madryn, Argentina.
2003a Radiocarbon Chronology at Piedra Museo Locality. In *Where the South Winds Blow: Ancient Evidence of Paleo South Americans*, edited by L. Miotti, M. Salemme, and N. Flegenheimer, pp. 99–104. Center for the Studies of the First Americans, Texas A&M University, College Station.
2003b Patagonia: A Paradox for Building Images of the First Americans during the Pleistocene/Holocene Transition. *Quaternary International* 109–10: 147–73.

Miotti, L. L., and R. Cattáneo
1997 Bifacial Technology at 13,000 Years Ago in Southern Patagonia. *Current Research in the Pleistocene* 14: 65–68.

Miotti, L. L., and M. C. Salemme
1999 Biodiversity, Taxonomic Richness and Specialists-Generalists during Late Pleistocene/Early Holocene Times in Pampa and Patagonia (Argentina, Southern South America). *Quaternary International* 53/54: 53–68.
2003 When Patagonia Was Colonized: People Mobility at High Latitudes during Pleistocene/Holocene Transition. *Quaternary International* 109–110: 95–111.
2004 Problamiento, movilidad y territories entre las sociedades cazadores-recolectoras de Patagonia. *Complutum* 15: 177–206.

Montané, J.
1968 Paleo-Indian Remains from Laguna de Tagua-Tagua, Central Chile. *Science* 161: 1137–138.

Montgomery, J., and J. Dickenson
1992 Additional Blades from Blackwater Draw Locality No. 1, Portales, New Mexico. *Current Research in the Pleistocene* 9: 32–33.

Mora, S.
2003 *Early Inhabitants of the Amazonian Tropical Rain Forest.* University of Pittsburgh Latin American Archaeology Reports 3. Pittsburgh.

Mora, S., and C. Gnecco
2003 Archaeological Hunter-Gatherers in Tropical Forests: A View from Colombia. In *Under the Canopy: The Archaeology of Tropical Rain Forests*, edited by J. Mercader, pp. 271–90. Rutgers University Press, New Brunswick, N.J.

Morrow, J. E.
1995 Clovis Projectile Point Manufacture: A Perspective from the Ready/Lincoln Hills Site, 11JY46, Jersey County, Illinois. *Midcontinental Journal of Archaeology* 20: 167–91.

1996   The Organization of Early Paleoindian Lithic Technology in the Confluence Region of the Mississippi, Illinois, and Missouri Rivers. Ph.D. dissertation, Washington University, St. Louis.

1998   Excavations at the Martens Site, 23SL222. *Missouri Archaeological Society Quarterly* 15 (1): 4–7.

2001a Metric and Morphologic Attributes Recorded on the Anzick Clovis Assemblage. Manuscript on file, Arkansas Archaeological Survey, Arkansas State University, Jonesboro.

2001b Notes on Ice Age Blades and Blade Technology. *Arkansas Archeological Society Field Notes* 303: 3–5.

Morrow, J., and S. Fiedel

2002   New Radiocarbon Dates for the Clovis Component of the Anzick Site (24PA506), Park County, Montana. Paper presented at the 60th Plains Anthropological Conference, Oklahoma City.

Morrow, J., and T. Morrow

1999   Geographic Variation in Fluted Projectile Points: A Hemispheric Perspective. *American Antiquity* 64 (2): 215–30.

2002   Exploring the Clovis-Gainey-Folsom Continuum: Technological and Morphological Variation in Midwestern Fluted Points. In *Folsom Technology and Lifeways*, edited by J. Clark and M. Collins. Special Publication 4, Lithic Technology. University of Tulsa, Tulsa, Oklahoma.

Morrow, T. A.

1992   The Fear of Fluting: A Modern Flintknapper's Perspective on the Ready Site Fluted Point Manufacturing Sequence. Paper presented at the Midwestern Archaeological Conference, Grand Rapids, Michigan.

Morse, D. F., D. G. Anderson, and A. C. Goodyear

1996   The Pleistocene-Holocene Transition in the Eastern United States. In *Humans at the End of the Ice Age: The Archaeology of the Pleistocene-Holocene Transition*, edited by L. G. Straus, B. V. Eriksen, J. M. Erlandson, and D. R. Yesner, pp. 319–38. Plenum Press, New York.

Morse, D. F., and A. C. Goodyear

1973   The Significance of the Dalton Adze in Northeast Arkansas. *Plains Anthropologist* 18 (62): 316–22.

Mortensen, A. K., M. Bigler, K. Grönvold, J. P. Steffensen, and S. J. Johnsen

2005   Volcanic Ash Layers from the Last Glacial Termination in the NGRIP Ice core. *Journal of Quaternary Science* 20 (3): 209–19.

Morwood, M. J., F. Aziz, P. O'Sullivan, D. Nasruddin, R. Hobbs, and A. Raza

1999   Archaeological and Palaeontological Research in Central Flores, East Indonesia: Results of Fieldwork 1997–98. *Antiquity* 73: 273–86.

Mosimann, J. E., and P. S. Martin

1975   Simulating Overkill by Paleoindians. *American Scientist* 63: 304–13.

Nami, H. G.

1987   Cueva del Medio: Perspectivas arqueológicas para la Patagonia austral. *Anales del Instituto de la Patagonia* 17: 73–106.

1993 Observaciones sobre desechos de talla procedentes de las ocupaciones tempranas de Tres Arroyos (Tierra del Fuego, Chile). *Anales del Instituto de la Patagonia* 22: 175–80.

1994 Reseña sobre los avances de la arqueología Finipleistocénica del extremo sur de Sudamérica. *Revista Chungara* 26 (2): 145–63.

1996a New Assessments on Early Human Occupations in the Southern Cone. In *Prehistoric Mongoloid Dispersals*, edited by T. Akazawa and E. J. Szathmry, pp. 254–69. Oxford University Press, Oxford.

1996b Investigaciones actualísticas para discutir aspectos técnicos de los cazadores-recolectores del tardiglacial: el problema Clovis-cueva Fell. *Anales del Instituto de la Patagonia* 25: 151–86.

1997 Experiments to Understand North and South American Late Pleistocene Lithic Reduction Sequence. Paper presented at the 62nd Annual Meeting of the Society for American Archaeology, Nashville.

Nami, H. G., and A. Menegaz

1991 Cueva del Medio: Aportes para el conocimiento de la diversidad faunística hacia el pleistoceno-holoceno en Patagonia austral. *Anales del Instituto de la Patagonia* 20: 117–32.

Nami, H. G., and T. Nakamura

1995 Cronologia radiocarbónica con AMS sobre muestras de hueso procedentes del sitio Cueva del Medio (Ultima Esperanza, Chile). *Anales del Instituto de la Patagonia* 23: 125–33.

Narosky, T., and D. Yzurieta

1993 *Birds of Argentina and Uruguay: A Field Guide*. Vazquez Mazzini Editores, Buenos Aires.

Neill, W. T.

1958 A Stratified Early Site at Silver Springs, Florida. *Florida Anthropologist* 11 (2): 33–52.

1964 The Association of Suwannee Points and Extinct Animals in Florida. *Florida Anthropologist* 17: 17–32.

Nichols, J.

1998 The First Four Discoveries of America. Paper presented at the 164th Annual Meeting of the American Association for the Advancement of Science, Philadelphia.

Niemeyer, F., and C. Villagrán

1994 Cuenca de Taguatagua en Chile: El ambiente del Pleistoceno y ocupaciones humanas. *Revista Chilena de Historia Natural* 67: 503–19.

Normile, D.

2001 Japanese Fraud Highlights Media-Driven Research Ethic. *Science* 291: 34–35.

Nuñez, L., J. Varela, R. Casamiquela, V. Schiappacasse, H. F. Niemeyer, and C. Villagrán

1994 Cuenca de Taguatagua en Chile: el embiente de Pleistocene y Ocupaciones humanas. *Revista Chilena de Historia Natural* 67: 503–19.

O'Brien, M. J., J. Darwent, and R. L. Lyman
2001   Cladistics Is Useful for Reconstructing Archaeological Phylogenies: Paleoindian Points from the Southeastern United States. *Journal of Archaeological Science* 28: 1115–136.

Ochsenius, C., and R. Gruhn (Editors)
1979   *Taima-Taima: A Late Pleistocene Paleo-Indian Kill Site in Northernmost South America—Final Reports of 1976 Excavations.* CIPICS/South American Quaternary Documentation Program, Bonn, Germany.

O'Connell, J. F., and K. Hawkes
1981   Alyawara Plant Use and Optimal Foraging Theory. In *Hunter-Gatherer Strategies: Ethnographies and Archaeological Analyses*, edited by B. Winterhalder and E. A. Smith, pp. 99–125. University of Chicago Press, Chicago.

Oliva, F., J. Moirano, and M. Saghesi
1991   Estado de las investigaciones arqueológicas en el sitio Laguna de Puán 1. *Boletín del Centro* 2: 127–38.

Oliver, S. C.
1935   Noticia sobre el hallazgo de restos de mastodontes en la región del Lago Budi. *Revue Universitaria* 4: 5.

Ossa, P. P., and E. Moseley
1972   La Cumbre: A Preliminary Report on Research into the Lithic Occupation of the Moche Valley, Peru. *Nawpa Pacha* 9: 1–16.

Owen-Smith, N.
1987   Pleistocene Extinctions: The Pivotal Role of Megaherbivores. *Paleobiology* 13: 351–62.

Owsley, D. W., and D. R. Hunt
2001   Clovis and Early Archaic Period Crania from the Anzick Site (24PA506), Park County, Montana. *Plains Anthropologist* 46: 115–24.

Parenti, F.
1996   Problemática da Pre-Historia do Pleistoceno superior no Nordeste do Brasil: O abrigo da Pedra Furada em seu contexto regional. *Fundhamentos* 1 (1): 15–53.

Paunero, R. S.
2003   The Cerro Tres Tetas (C3T) Locality in the Central Plateau of Santa Cruz, Argentina. In *Where the South Winds Blow: Ancient Evidence of Paleo South Americans*, edited by L. Miotti, M. Salemme, and N. Flegenheimer, pp. 133–40. Center for the Study of the First Americans, Oregon State University, Corvallis.

Pearson, G.
1998   Reduction Strategy for Secondary Source Lithic Raw Materials at Guardiria (Turrialba, FG-T-9), Costa Rica. *Current Research in the Pleistocene* 15: 84–85.
1999   North American Paleoindian Bi-Beveled Bone and Ivory Rods: A New Interpretation. *North American Archaeologist* 20: 81–103.
2002   Pan-Continental Paleoindian Expansions and Interactions as Viewed from the Earliest Lithic Industries of Lower Central America. Ph.D. dissertation, University of Kansas, Lawrence.

2003 First Report of a New Paleoindian Quarry Site on the Isthmus of Panama. *Latin American Antiquity* 14 (3): 311–42.

2004 Pan-American Paleoindian Dispersal and the Origins of Fishtail Projectile Points as Seen through the Lithic Raw-Material Reduction Strategies and Tool-Manufacturing Techniques at the Guardiría Site, Turrialba Valley, Costa Rica. In *The Settlement of the American Continents: A Multidisciplinary Approach to Human Biogeography*, edited by C. M. Barton, G. A. Clark, D. R. Yesner, and G. A. Pearson, pp. 85–102. University of Arizona Press, Tucson.

Pearson, G. A., and R. G. Cooke

2003 The Role of the Panamanian Land Bridge during the Initial Colonization of the Americas. *Antiquity* 76 (294): 931–32.

Pérez, E.

1956 *Plantas útiles de Colombia*. Rivadeneyra, Madrid.

Perrins, C. M.

1996 *The Illustrated Encyclopedia of Birds*. Barnes and Noble Books, New York.

Phillips, D. A., M. C. Slaughter, and S. B. Bierer

1993 Archaeological Studies at Kartchner Caverns State Park, Cochise County, Arizona. *SWCA Archaeological Report 93-26*, pp. 7.18 and 7.20. SWCA, Inc., Environmental Consultants, Flagstaff and Tucson, Arizona.

Pielou, E. C.

1991 *After the Ice Age: The Return of Life to Glaciated North America*. University of Chicago Press, Chicago.

Piperno, D.

1985 Phytolithic Analysis of Geological Sediments from Panama. *Antiquity* 59: 13–19.

1989 Paleoethnobotany in the Neotropics from Microfossils: New Insights into Ancient Plant Use and Agricultural Origins in the Tropical Forest. *Journal of World Prehistory* 12 (4): 393–449.

Piperno, D. R., M. B. Bush, and P. A. Colinvaux

1991 Paleoecological Perspectives on Human Adaptation in Panama, 1: The Pleistocene. *Geoarchaeology* 6 (3): 201–26.

Piperno, D. R., and J. G. Jones

2003 Paleoecological and Archaeological Implications of a Late Pleistocene/Early Holocene Record of Vegetation and Climate Change from the Pacific Coastal Plain of Panama. *Quaternary Research* 59: 79–86.

Piperno, D. R., and D. Pearsall

1998 *The Origins of Agriculture in the Lowland Neotropics*. Academic Press, San Diego.

Piperno, D., A. Ranere, I. Holst, and P. Hansell

2000 Starch Grains Reveal Early Root Crop Horticulture in the Panamanian Tropical Forest. *Nature* 407: 894–97.

Pitulko, V. V., P. A. Nikolsky, E. Y. Girya, A. E. Basilyan, V. E. Tumskoy, S. A. Koulakov, S. N. Astakhov, E. Y. Pavlova, and M. A. Anisimov

2004 The Yana RHS Site: Humans in the Arctic before the Last Glacial Maximum. *Science* 303: 52–56.

Politis, G.

1984   Arqueología del Área Interserrana Bonaerense. Ph.D. dissertation, Universidad Nacional de La Plata, La Plata.

1989   ¿Quien mató al megaterio? *Ciencia Hoy* 1 (2): 26–35.

1991   Fishtail Projectile Points in the Southern Cone of South America: An Overview. In *Clovis: Origins and Adaptations*, edited by R. Bonnichsen and K. L. Turnmire, pp. 287–301. Center for the Study of the First Americans, Oregon State University, Corvallis.

1996a A Review of the Late Pleistocene Sites of Argentina. *Fundhamentos* 1 (1): 153–70.

1996b Moving to Produce: Nukak Mobility and Settlement Patterns in Amazonia. *World Archaeology* 27: 492–511.

Politis, G. G., and R. Beukens

1991   Nuevos datos sobre la extinción del megaterio. *Ciencia Hoy* 20 (11): 6–7.

Politis, G., and M. A. Gutierrez

1998   Gliptodontes y cazadores recolectores en la región pampeana de Argentina. *Latin American Antiquity* 9 (2): 111–34.

Politis, G. G., M. A. Gutierrez, and G. Martínez

1991   Informe preliminar de las investigaciones en el sitio Paso Otero 1 (Pd. de Necochea, Pcia. de Buenos Aires). *Boletín del Centro de Registro Arqueológico y Paleontológica* 3: 80–90.

Politis, G., E. Johnson, M. A. Gutierrez, and W. T. Hartwell

2003   Survival of Pleistocene Fauna: New Radiocarbon Dates on Organic Sediments from La Moderna (Pampean Region, Argentina). In *Where the South Winds Blow: Ancient Evidence of Paleo South Americans*, edited by L. Miotti, M. A. Salemme, and N. Flegenheimer, pp. 45–50. Center for the Study of the First Americans, Texas A&M University, College Station.

Politis, G. G., and P. Lozano

1988   Informe preliminar del sitio costero La Olla (Pdo. Coronel de Marina Leonardo Rosales, Pcia. de Buenos Aires). *Resúmenes de las Ponencias Científicas Presentadas al IX Congreso Nacional de Arqueología Argentina*, p. 108. Buenos Aires.

Politis, G. G., P. Madrid, and G. Barrientos

1992   Informe de la Campaña 1992 al Sitio Arroyo Seco 2 (Pdo. de Tres Arroyos, Pcia. de Buenos Aires, Argentina). *Palimpsesto* 1: 80–85.

Politis, G. G., P. Messineo, and C. Kaufmann

2004   El problamiento temperano de las llanuras pampeanas de Argentina y Uruguay. *Complutum* 15: 207–24.

Politis, G. G., and D. M. Olmo

1986   Preliminary Analysis of the Lithic Collection of the La Moderna Site, Argentina. *Current Research in the Pleistocene* 3: 36–38.

Politis, G., J. L. Prado, and R. P. Beukens

1995   The Human Impact in Pleistocene-Holocene Extinctions in South America. In *Ancient Peoples and Landscapes*, edited by E. Johnson, pp. 187–205. Museum of Texas Tech University, Lubbock.

Politis, G. G., and E. P. Tonni
1997 El Guanaco en la Pcia. de Buenos Aires: Contrastación del modelo. *Resúmenes del XII Congreso Nacional de Arqueología Argentina*, p. 29. Universidad Nacional de La Plata, La Plata.

Posey, D. A.
1984 A Preliminary Report on Diversified Management of Tropical Forests by the Kayapó Indians of the Brazilian Amazon. *Advances in Economic Botany* 1: 112–26.

Price, T. D.
1991 The View from Europe: Concepts and Questions about Terminal Pleistocene Societies. In *The First Americans: Search and Research*, edited by T. D. Dillehay and D. J. Meltzer, pp. 267–74. CRC Press, Boca Raton, Fla.

Prieto, Aldo
1996 Late Quaternary Vegetational and Climatic Changes in the Pampa Grassland of Argentina. *Quaternary Research* 45 (1): 73–88.

Prieto, Alfredo R.
1991 Cazadores tempranos y tardíos en Cueva Lago Sofía 1. *Anales del Instituto de la Patagonia* 20: 75–100.

Prous, A.
1991 Fouilles de l'Abri du Boquete, Minas Gerais, Brasil. *Journal de la Societé des Americanistes* 78: 77–109.

Purdy, B. A.
1991 *The Art and Archaeology of Florida's Wetlands*. CRC Press, Boca Raton, Fla.

Quade, J., R. M. Forester, W. L. Pratt, and C. Carter
1998 Black Mats, Spring-Fed Streams, and Late Glacial Age Recharge in the Southern Great Basin. *Quaternary Research* 49: 129–48.

Quattrocchio, M. E., A. M. Borromei, and S. Grill
1995 Cambios vegetacionales y fluctuaciones paleoclimáticas durante el Pleistoceno tardío-Holoceno en el sudeste de la provincia de Buenos Aires (Argentina). *Actas del VI Congreso Argentino de Paleontología y Bioestratigrafía*, pp. 221–29. Trelew.

Quattrocchio, M. E., C. Deschamps, C. Zabala, A. M. Borromei, S. Grill, and G. R. Guerstein
1993 Cuaternario del sur de la Provincia del Buenos Aires. Estratigrafía e inferencias paleoambientales. In *El Holoceno de la Argentina*, edited by M. H. Iriondo, pp. 22–34. CADINQUA, Buenos Aires.

Ranere, A. J.
1980 Human Movement into Tropical America at the End of the Pleistocene. In *Anthropological Papers in Honor of Earl H. Swanson*, edited by L. Harten, C. Warren, and D. Tuohy, pp. 41–47. Idaho State University Press, Pocatello.
2000 Paleoindian Expansion into Central America: The view from Panama. In *Archaeological Passages: A Volume in Honor of Claude N. Warren*, edited by J. Schneider, R. Yohe III, and J. Gardner, pp. 110–22. Western Center for Archaeology and Paleontology, Publications in Archaeology 1. Hemet, Calif.

Ranere, A., and R. Cooke

1991   Paleoindian Occupation in the Central American Tropics. In *Clovis: Origins and Adaptations*, edited by R. Bonnichsen and K. L. Turnmire, pp. 237–53. Center for the Study of the First Americans, Oregon State University, Corvallis.

1995   Evidencias de ocupación humana en Panamá a postrimerías del pleistoceno y a comienzos del holoceno. In *Ámbito y ocupaciones tempranas de la América tropical*, edited by I. Cavelier and S. Mora, pp. 5–26. Fundación Erigiae–Instituto Colombiano de Antropología, Bogotá.

1996   Stone Tools and Cultural Boundaries in Prehistoric Panamá: An Initial Assessment. In *Paths to Central American Prehistory*, edited by F. W. Lange, pp. 49–78. University Press of Colorado, Niwot.

2003   Late Glacial and Early Holocene Occupation of Central American Tropical Forests. In *Under the Canopy: The Archaeology of Tropical Rain Forests*, edited by J. Mercader, pp. 219–48. Rutgers University Press, New Brunswick, N.J.

Redford, K. H., and J. F. Eisenberg

1992   *Mammals of the Neotropics*. Vol. 2, *The Southern Cone*. University of Chicago Press, Chicago.

Redmond, B. G., and K. B. Tankersley

2005   Evidence of Early Paleoindian Bone Modification and Use at the Sheriden Cave Site (33WY252), Wyandot County, Ohio. *American Antiquity* 70: 503–26

Reimer, P. J., M. Baillie, E. Bard, A. Bayliss, J. W. Beck, C. J. H. Bertrand, P. G. Blackwell, C. E. Buck, G. S. Burr, K. B. Cutler, P. E. Damon, R. L. Edwards, R. G. Fairbanks, M. Friedrich, T. P. Guilderson, A. G. Hogg, K. A. Hughen, B. Kromer, G. McCormac, S. Manning, C. B. Ramsey, R. W. Reimer, S. Remmele, J. R. Southon, M. Stuiver, S. Talamo, F. W. Taylor, J. van der Plicht, and C. E. Weyhenmeyer

2004   IntCal04 Terrestrial Radiocarbon Age Calibration, 0–26 Cal Kyr BP. *Radiocarbon* 46 (3): 1029–1058.

Rich, J., and S. Stokes

2001   Optical Dating of Geoarchaeologically Significant Sites from the Southern High Plains and South Texas, USA. *Quaternary Science Reviews* 20 (5–9): 949–59.

Richards, M. P., S. Mays, and B. T. Fuller

2002   Stable Carbon and Nitrogen Isotope Values of Bone and Teeth Reflect Weaning Age at the Medieval Wharram Percy Site, Yorkshire, UK. *American Journal of Physical Anthropology* 119: 205–10.

Rick, J. W.

1980   *Prehistoric Hunters of the High Andes*. Academic Press, New York.

1988   The Character and Context of Highland Preceramic Society. In *Peruvian Prehistory*, edited by R. W. Keating, pp. 3–40. Cambridge University Press, Cambridge.

Rick, J. W., and K. M. Moore

2001   Specialized Meat-Eating in the Holocene: An Archaeological Case from the Frigid Tropics of High-Altitude Peru. In *Meat-Eating and Human Evolution*, edited by C. B. Stanford and H. T. Bunn, pp. 237–60. Oxford University Press, Oxford.

Ridings, R.
1996 Where in the World Does Obsidian Hydration Dating Work? *American Antiquity* 61 (1): 136–48.

Rindos, D.
1984 *The Origins of Agriculture: An Evolutionary Perspective.* Academic Press, San Diego.

Roberts, F. H.
1940 Developments in the Problem of the North American Paleo-Indian. *Smithsonian Miscellaneous Collections* 100: 51–116.

Roberts, R., M. Bird, J. Olley, R. Galbraith, E. Lawson, G. Laslett, H. Yoshida, R. Jones, R. Fullagar, G. Jacobsen, and Q. Hua.
1998 Optical and Radiocarbon Dating at Jinmium Rockshelter in Northern Australia. *Nature* 393: 358–60.

Roberts, R. G., T. F. Flannery, L. K. Ayliffe, H. Yoshida, J. M. Olley, G. J. Prideaux, G. M. Laslett, A. Baynes, M. A. Smith, R. Jones, and B. L. Smith
2001 New Ages for the Last Australian Megafauna: Continent-Wide Extinction about 46,000 years ago. *Science* 292: 1888.

Roebroeks, W., and T. Van Kolfschoten
1994 The Earliest Occupation of Europe: A Short Chronology. *Antiquity* 68: 489–503.

Roebroeks, W., and T. Van Kolfschoten (Editors)
1995 *The Earliest Occupation of Europe.* Analecta Praehistorica Leidensia 27. University of Leiden, Leiden.

Rogers, R. N.
2006 Chemical Evaluation of the Black Mat Deposit at Murray Springs. Appendix B in *Murray Springs: A Clovis Site with Multiple Activity Areas in the San Pedro Valley, Arizona*, edited by C. V. Haynes and B. B. Huckell. Anthropological Papers of the University of Arizona. University of Arizona Press, Tucson.

Roosa, W. B.
1965 Some Great Lakes Fluted Point Types. *Michigan Archaeologist* 11: 89–102.

Roosevelt, A. C., L. Brown, J. Douglas, M. O'Connell, E. Quinn, and J. Kemp
1997 Dating a Paleoindian Site in the Amazon in Comparison with Clovis Culture: Technical Comments. *Science* 275: 1950–1952.

Roosevelt, A. C., J. Douglas, and L. Brown
2002 The Migrations and Adaptations of the First Americans: Clovis and Pre-Clovis Viewed from South America. In *The First Americans: The Pleistocene Colonization of the New World*, edited by N. G. Jablonski, pp. 159–236. California Academy of Sciences Memoir 27. San Francisco.

Roosevelt, A. C., M. Lima da Costa, C. Lopes Machado, M. Michab, N. Mercier, H. Vallada, J. Feathers, W. Barnet, M. Imazio da Silveira, A. Henderson, J. Sliva, B. Chernoff, D. S. Reese, J. A. Holman, N. Toth, and K. Schick
1996 Paleoindian Cave Dwellers in the Amazon: The Peopling of the Americas. *Science* 272: 373–84.

Roseveare, G. M.

1948   The Grasslands of Latin America. [Imperial Bureau Pastures and Field Crops, Aberystwyth] *Bulletin* 36: 1–291.

Roth, B. J.

1993   A Clovis Point from East-Central Arizona. *Kiva* 58: 495–98.

Rovner, I.

1980   Comment on Bray's "An Eighteenth Century Reference to a Fluted Point from Guatemala." *American Antiquity* 45: 165–67.

Rutherford, A. A., and J. Wittenberg

1979   Evidence in Support of Soluble Collagen Extraction for Radiocarbon Bone Dating. *Saskatchewan Research Council Report* C79-22: 1–8.

Sabin, T., and V. T. Holliday

1995   Morphological and Spatial Relationships of Playas and Lunettes on the Southern High Plains. *Annals of the Association of American Geographers* 25: 286–305.

Salemme, M. C.

1987   Paleoetnozoología del Sector Bonaerense de la Región Pampeana con especial atención a los Mamíferos. Ph.D. dissertation, Universidad Nacional de La Plata, La Plata.

Salemme, M. C., and L. L. Miotti

1987   Zooarchaeology and Palaeoenvironments: Some Examples from the Patagonian and Pampean Regions (Argentina). *Quaternary of South America and Antarctic Peninsula* 5: 33–57.

Sandweiss, D. H.

2003   Terminal Pleistocene through Mid-Holocene Archaeological Sites as Paleoclimatic Archives for the Peruvian Coast. *Palaeogeography, Palaeoclimatology, Palaeoecology* 194: 23–40.

Sandweiss, D. H., H. McInnis, R. L. Burger, A. Cano, B. Ojeda, R. Paredes, M. C. Sandweiss, and M. Glascock

1998   Quebrada Jaguay: Early South American Maritime Adaptations. *Science* 281 (5384): 1830–832.

Sanguinetti, A. C.

1976   Excavaciones prehistóricas en la cueva Las Buitreras. *Relaciones de la Sociedad Argentina de Antropología* 10: 271–92.

Sanguinetti, A. C., and L. A. Borrero

1977   Los niveles con fauna extinta de la cueva Las Buitreras. *Relaciones de la Sociedad Argentina de Antropología* 11: 167–81.

Santoro, C.

1989   Antiguos cazadores de la Puna (9.000 a 6.000 a.C.). In *Culturas de Chile: Prehistoria, desde sus orígenes hasta los albores de la conquista*, edited by J. Hidalgo, pp. 33–55. Editorial Andrés Bello, Santiago.

Sassaman, K. E.

1996   Early Archaic Settlement in the South Carolina Coastal Plain. In *The Paleoindian and Early Archaic Southeast*, edited by D. G. Anderson and K. E. Sassaman, pp. 58–84. University of Alabama Press, Tuscaloosa.

Sauer, C. O.
1944 A Geographic Sketch of Early Man in America. *Geographical Review* 34: 529–73.

Saunders, J. J.
1983 Late Pleistocene Vertebrates of the San Pedro Valley. Manuscript on file, Arizona State Museum Archives, University of Arizona, Tucson.

Savolainen, P., Y. Zhang, J. Luo, J. Lunberg, and T. Leitner
2002 Genetic Evidence for an East Asian Origin for Domestic Dogs. *Science* 298: 1610–613.

Saxon, E. C.
1979 Natural Prehistory: The Archaeology of Fuego-Patagonian Ecology. *Quaternaria* 21: 339–56.

Scabuzzo, C., and G. Politis
2006 Early Holocene Secondary Burials in the Pampas of Argentina. Archaeology Department, Facultad de Ciencias Naturales y Museo, Universidad Nacional de La Plata. MS.

Schaub, M., K. F. Kaiser, B. Kromer, S. Talamo, M. Friedrich, G. Bonani, and I. Hajdas
2003 Records of Lateglacial Pioneer Forests on the Swiss Plateau Provide a High Resolution Archive. Poster presented at the 16th INQUA Congress, Reno, Nevada, July 23–30.

Scheinsohn, V., and J. L. Ferretti
1995 Mechanical Properties of Bone Materials as Related to Design and Function of Prehistoric Tools from Tierra del Fuego (Argentina). *Journal of Archeological Science* 22: 711–17.

Schmitz, P. I.
1986 Cazadores antiguos en el sudoeste de Goias, Brasil. In *New Evidences for the Pleistocene Peopling of the Americas*, edited by A. L. Bryan, pp. 183–94. Center for the Study of Early Man, University of Maine, Orono.
1987 Prehistoric Hunters and Gatherers of Brazil. *Journal of World Prehistory* 1: 53–126.

Schmutz, E. M., E. L. Smith, P. R. Ogden, M. L. Cox, J. O. Klemmedson, J. J. Norris, and L. C. Fierro
1992 Desert Grassland. In *Natural Grasslands: Introduction and Western Hemisphere*, edited by R. T. Coupland, pp. 337–62. Elsevier, Amsterdam.

Schobinger, J.
1969 *Prehistoria de Suramérica*. Labor, Barcelona.
1973 Nuevos hallazgos de puntas "cola de pescado," y consideraciones en torno al origen y dispersión de la cultura de cazadores superiores toldense (Fell I) en Sudamérica. In *Atti del XL Congresso Internazionale degli Americanisti*, Vol. 1: 33–50. Tilgher, Génova, Italy.
1988 200.000 años del hombre en América: ¿qué pensar? *Prehistoria* 1: 375–95.

Schubert, B. W., R. W. Graham, H. Gregory McDonald, E. C. Grimm, and T. W. Stafford
2004 Latest Pleistocene Paleoecology of Jefferson's Ground Sloth (*Megalonyx jefferso-*

nii) and Elk-Moose (*Cervalces scotti*) in Northern Illinois. *Quaternary Research* 61 (2): 231–40.

Schwander, J., U. Eicher, and B. Ammann

2000   Oxygen Isotopes of Lake Marl at Gerzensee and Leysin (Switzerland) Covering the Younger Dryas and Two Minor Oscillations and Their Correlation to the GRIP Ice Core. *Palaeogeography, Palaeoclimatology, Palaeoecology* 159: 203–14.

Seguel, Z., and O. Campana

1975   Presencia de megafauna en la Provincia de Osorno (Chile) y sus posibles relaciones con cazadores superiores. In *Actas y trabajo del 1 Congreso de Arqueologia Argentina*, pp. 237–42. Museo Historico Provincial Dr. Julio Marc, Osorno, Chile.

Sellards, E. H.

1952   *Early Man in America*. University of Texas Press, Austin.

Shackley, M. S.

2006   Sources of Obsidian at the Murray Springs Clovis Site: A Semi-Quantitative X-Ray Fluorescence (XRF) Analysis. Appendix C in *Murray Springs: A Clovis Site with Multiple Activity Areas in the San Pedro Valley, Arizona*, edited by C. V. Haynes and B. B. Huckell. Anthropological Papers of the University of Arizona. University of Arizona Press, Tucson.

Sheets, P. D.

1994   Chipped Stone Artifacts from the Cordillera de Tilaran. In *Archaeology, Volcanism, and Remote Sensing in the Arenal Region, Costa Rica*, edited by P. D. Sheets and B. R. McKee, pp. 211–54. University of Texas Press, Austin.

Sheldrick, C., J. J. Lowe, and M. J. Reynier

1997   Palaeolithic Barbed Point from Gransmoor, East Yorkshire, England. *Proceedings of the Prehistoric Society* 63: 359–70.

Shetrone, H. C.

1936   The Folsom Phenomena as Seen from Ohio. *Ohio State Archaeological and Historical Quarterly* 45: 240–56.

Shipman, P.

1997   Cut Marks and Other Features on Selected Bone Specimens. In *Monte Verde: A Late Pleistocene Settlement in Chile*, vol. 2, *The Archaeological Context and Interpretation*, edited by T. D. Dillehay, pp. 759–66. Smithsonian Institution Press, Washington, D.C.

Shott, M. J.

1986   Technological organization and settlment mobility: an ethnographic examination. *Journal of Anthropoligical Research* 42: 15–51.

1992   Radiocarbon Dating as a Probabilistic Technique: The Childers Site and Late Woodland Occupation in the Ohio Valley. *American Antiquity* 57 (2): 202–30.

1996   An Exegesis of the Curation Concept. *Journal of Anthropological Research* 52: 259–80.

Silveira, M.

1979   Análisis e interpretación de los restos faunísticos de la Cueva Grande del Arroyo Feo. *Relaciones de la Sociedad Argentina de Antropología* 13: 229–53.

Smith, C.
1966 Archaeological Evidence for Selection in Avocado. *Economic Botany* 20: 169–75.
1969 Additional Notes on Pre-Conquest Avocados in Mexico. *Economic Botany* 23: 135–40.

Snarskis, M. J.
1979 Turrialba: A Paleo-Indian Quarry and Workshop Site in Eastern Costa Rica. *American Antiquity* 44 (1): 125–38.

Soriano, A.
1979 Distribution of Grasses and Grasslands in South America. In *Ecology of Grasslands and Bamboolands in the World*, edited by M. Numata, pp. 84–91. VEB Gustav Fischer, Jena, Germany.

Soriano, A., R. J. León, O. E. Sala, R. S. Lavado, V. A. Deregibus, M. A. Cauhépé, O. A. Scaglia, C. A. Velázquez, and J. H. Lemcoff
1992 Río de la Plata Grasslands. In *Natural Grasslands: Introduction and Western Hemisphere*, edited by R. T. Coupland, pp. 367–413. Elsevier, Amsterdam.

Soriano, A., W. Volkheimer, H. Walter, E. O. Box, A. A. Marcolin, J. A. Vallerini, C. P. Movia, R. J. León, J. M. Gallardo, M. Rumboll, M. Canevari, P. Canevari, and W. G. Vasina
1983 Deserts and Semi-Deserts of Patagonia. In *Temperate Deserts and Semi-Deserts*, edited by N. E. West, pp. 423–60. Elsevier, Amsterdam.

Southon, J.
2002 A First Step to Reconciling the GRIP and GISP2 Ice-Core Chronologies, 0–14,500 Yr B.P. *Quaternary Research* 57: 32–37.

Stafford, T. W.
1994 Accelerator C-14 Dating of Human Fossil Skeletons: Assessing Accuracy and Results on New World Specimens. In *Method and Theory for Investigating the Peopling of the Americas*, edited by R. Bonnichsen and D. G. Steele, pp. 45–56. Center for the Study of the First Americans, Corvallis, Ore.

Stanford, D.
1991 Clovis Origins and Adaptations: An Introductory Perspective. In *Clovis: Origins and Adaptations*, edited by R. Bonnichsen and K. L. Turmine, pp. 1–13. Center for the Study of the First Americans, Oregon State University, Corvallis.

Stanford, D., and B. Bradley
2002 Ocean Trails and Prairie Paths? Thoughts about Clovis Origins. In *The First Americans: The Pleistocene Colonization of the New World*, edited by N. G. Jablonski, pp. 255–71. California Academy of Sciences Memoirs no. 27. San Francisco.

Stanford, D., and M. A. Jodry
1988 The Drake Clovis Cache. *Current Research in the Pleistocene* 5: 21–22.

Steele, J., J. Adams, and T. Sluckin
1998 Modelling Paleoindian Dispersals. *Antiquity* 30 (2): 286–305.

Steele, J., G. G. Politis, and P. Pettitt
2001 AMS Radiocarbon Dating of the Earliest Paleoindian Occupation of the South-

ern Cone of South America. Paper presented at the 66th Annual Meeting of the Society for American Archaeology, New Orleans.

Steen-McIntyre, V., R. Fryxell, and H. E. Malde

1981   Geologic Evidence for Age of Deposits at Hueyatlaco Archeological Site, Valsequillo, Mexico. *Quaternary Research* 16: 1–17.

Storck, P. L.

1991   Imperialists without a State: The Cultural Dynamics of Early Paleoindian Colonization as Seen from the Great Lakes Region. In *Clovis: Origins and Adaptations*, edited by R. Bonnichsen and K. L. Turnmire, pp. 153–62. Center for the Study of the First Americans, Oregon State University, Corvallis.

Storck, P. L., and A. E. Spiess

1994   The Significance of New Faunal Identifications Attributed to an Early Paleoindian (Gainey Complex) Occupation at the Udora Site, Ontario. *American Antiquity* 59: 121–42.

Stothert, K. E.

1985   The Preceramic Las Vegas Culture of Coastal Ecuador. *American Antiquity* 50: 613–37.

1988   *La prehistoria temprana de la península de Santa Elena, Ecuador: Cultura Las Vegas*. Miscelánea Antropológica Ecuatoriana, Serie Monográfica 10. Guayaquil.

Stothert, K., D. Piperno, and T. Andres

2003   Terminal Pleistocene/Early Holocene Human Adaptation in Coastal Ecuador: The Las Vegas Evidence. *Quaternary International* 109–10: 23–43.

Straus, L. G., B. V. Eriksen, J. M. Erlandson, and D. R. Yesner (Editors)

1996   *Humans at the End of the Ice Age: The Archaeology of the Pleistocene-Holocene Transition*. Plenum Press, New York.

Stuart, A. J., P. A. Kosintsev, T. F. Higham, and A. M. Lister

2004   Pleistocene to Holocene Extinction Dynamics in Giant Deer and Woolly Mammoth. *Nature* 431: 684–89.

Stuiver, M. P., M. Grootes, and T. F. Braziunas

1995   The GISP2 $\delta^{18}O$ Climate Record of the Past 16,500 Years and the Role of the Sun, Ocean, and Volcanoes. *Quaternary Research* 44: 341–54.

Stuiver, M., and P. J. Reimer

1993   Extended ^{14}C Data Base and Revised Calib 3.0 ^{14}C Age Calibration Program. *Radiocarbon* 35: 215–30.

Stuiver, M., P. J. Reimer, E. Bard, W. J. Beck, G. S. Burr, K. A. Hughen, B. Kromer, F. G. McCormac, J. van der Plicht, M. Spurk

1998   INTCAL98 Radiocarbon Age Calibration 24,000–0 Cal B.P. *Radiocarbon* 40: 1041–1083.

Surovell, T. A.

2000   Early Paleoindian Women, Children, Mobility, and Fertility. *American Antiquity* 65 (3): 493–509.

Swauger, J. L., and W. J. Mayer-Oakes

1952   A Fluted Point from Costa Rica. *American Antiquity* 17: 264–65.

Szabo, B. J., H. E. Malde, and C. Irwin-Williams
1969 Dilemma Posed by Uranium-Series Dates on Archaeologically Significant Bones from Valsequillo, Puebla, Mexico. *Earth and Planetary Science Letters* 6: 237–44.

Tankersley, K. B.
1990 Late Pleistocene Lithic Exploitation in the Midwest and Midsouth: Indiana, Ohio and Kentucky. In *Early Paleoindian Economies of Eastern North America*, edited by K. B. Tankersley and B. L. Isaac, pp. 259–99. Jai Press, Greenwich, Conn.
1994 The Effects of Stone and Technology on Fluted-Point Morphometry. *American Antiquity* 59: 498–510.
1997 Sheriden: A Clovis Cave in Eastern North America. *Geoarchaeology* 12: 713–24.

Taylor, D. C.
1969 The Wilsall Excavations: An Exercise in Frustration. *Proceedings of the Montana Academy of Sciences* 29: 147–50.

Taylor, R. E.
1992 Radiocarbon Dating of Bone: To Collagen and Beyond. In *Radiocarbon after Four Decades: An Interdisciplinary Perspective*, edited by R. E. Taylor, A. Long, and R. S. Kra, pp. 375–402. Springer-Verlag, New York.

Taylor, R. E., C. V. Haynes, and M. Stuiver
1996 Clovis and Folsom Age Estimates: Stratigraphic Context and Radiocarbon Calibration. *Antiquity* 70 (269): 515–25.

Taylor, R. E., D. L. Kirner, J. R. Southon, and J. C. Chatters
1998 Radiocarbon Dates of Kennewick Man. *Science* 280: 1171–172.

Tecchi, R. A.
1983 Contenido de silicofitolitos en suelos del sector sudoriental de la pampa ondulada. *Ciencia del Suelo* 1: 75–82.

Temme, M.
1982 Cubilán: Un sitio precerámico al sur del Ecuador. *Miscelánea Antropológica Ecuatoriana* 2: 135–64.

Tonni, E. P.
1985 Mamiferos del Holoceno del Partido de Lobería, Provincia de Buenos Aires: Aspectos paleoambientales y bioestratigraficos del Holoceno del sector oriental de Tandilia y Area Interserrana. *Ameghiniana* 22 (3–4): 283–88.
1992 Mamíferos y clima del Holoceno en la Provincia de Buenos Aires. In *Holoceno en la Argentina*, edited by M. Iriondo, pp. 64–78. CADINQUA, Buenos Aires.

Tonni, E. P., M. S. Bargo, and J. L. Prado
1988 Los cambios ambientales en el Pleistoceno Tardio y Holoceno del sudeste de la Provincia de Buenos Aires a través de una secuencia de mamíferos. *Ameghiniana* 25 (2): 99–110.

Tonni, E. P., and A. Cione
1995 Los mamíferos como indicadores de cambios climáticos en el Cuaternario de la región pampeana de la Argentina. In *Climas Cuaternarios en América del Sur*, edited by J. Argollo and P. Mouguiart, pp. 319–26. Orstom, La Paz.

1997   Did the Argentine Pampean Ecosystem Exist in the Pleistocene? *Current Research in the Pleistocene* 14: 131–33.

Tonni, E. P., A. Cione, and A. Figini

1999   Predominance of arid climates indicated by mammals in the Pampas of Argentina during the Late Pleistocene and Holocene. *Palaeogeography, Palaeoclimatology, Palaeoecology* 147: 257–81.

Tonni, E. P., R. A. Huarte, J. E. Carbonari, and A. Figini

2003   New radiocarbon chronology for the Guerrero Member of the Luján Formation (Buenos Aires, Argentina): paleoclimatic significance. *Quaternary International* 109–10: 45–48.

Torrence, R.

1983   Time Budgeting and Hunter-Gatherer Technology. In *Pleistocene Hunters and Gatherers in Europe*, edited by G. Bailey, pp 11–22. Cambridge University Press, Cambridge.

Turner, A.

1992   Large Carnivores and Earliest European Hominids: Changing Determinants of Resource Availability during the Lower and Middle Pleistocene. *Journal of Human Evolution* 22: 109–26.

Turner, C. G., II

2002   Teeth, Needles, Dogs, and Siberia: Bioarchaeological Evidence for the Colonization of the New World. In *The First Americans: The Pleistocene Colonization of the New World*, edited by N. G. Jablonski, pp. 123–58. California Academy of Sciences, Memoirs no. 27. San Francisco.

Turney, C. S., M. I. Bird, L. K. Fifield, R. G. Roberts, M. Smith, C. E. Dortch, R. Gruhn, E. Lawson, L. K. Ayliffe, G. H. Miller, J. Dortch, and R. G. Cresswell

2001   Early Human Occupation at Devil's Lair, Southwestern Australia, 50,000 Years Ago. *Quaternary Research* 55 (1): 3–13.

Turney, C. S., G. R. Coope, D. D. Harkness, J. J. Lowe, and M. J. Walker

2000   Implications for the Dating of Wisconsinan (Weichselian) Late-Glacial Events of Systematic Radiocarbon Age Differences between Terrestrial Plant Macrofossils from a Site in SW Ireland. *Quaternary Research* 53 (1): 114–21.

Turney, C. S., M. S. McGlone, and J. M. Wilmshurst

2003   Asynchronous Climate Change between New Zealand and the North Atlantic during the Last Deglaciation. *Geology* 31 (3): 223–26.

Turpin, S. A., L. C. Bement, and H. H. Eling

1992   Big Lake: A Playa Bison Kill Site in West Texas. *Current Research in the Pleistocene* 9: 45–46.

1997   Stuck in the Mud: The Big Lake Bison Kill Site (41RG13), West Texas. In *Southern Plains Bison Procurement and Utilization from Paleoindian to Historic*, edited by L. C. Bement and K. J Buehler, pp. 119–33. *Plains Anthropologist Memoir* 29.

Ugent, D.

1997   The Tuberous Plant Remains of Monte Verde. In *Monte Verde: A Late Pleistocene Settlement in Chile*, vol. 2, *The Archaeological Context and Interpretation*, edited by T. D. Dillehay, pp. 903–10. Smithsonian Institution Press, Washington, D.C.

Van der Hammen, T.

1974 The Pleistocene Changes of Vegetation and Climate in Tropical South America. *Journal of Biogeography* 1: 3–26.

Vasil'ev, S. A., Y. V. Kuzmin, L. A. Orlova, and V. N. Dementiev

2002 Radiocarbon-Based Chronology of the Paleolithic in Siberia and Its Relevance to the Peopling of the New World. *Radiocarbon* 44 (2): 503–30.

Voigt, E.

2002 Archaeological Data Recovery at the Brook Run Jasper Quarry (Site 44CU122) Associated with the Proposed Route 3 Improvements, Culpeper County, Virginia. Draft report to Virginia Department of Transportation from Louis Berger Group.

Waguespak, N. M., and T. A. Surovell

2003 Clovis Hunting Strategies, or How to Make Out on Plentiful Resources. *American Antiquity* 68 (2): 333–52.

Walker, D. N.

1982 Early Holocene Vertebrate Fauna. In *The Agate Basin Site: A Record of Paleoindian Occupation of the Northwestern Plains*, edited by G. C. Frison and D. J. Stanford, pp. 274–308. Academic Press, New York.

Walker, R. B., K. R. Detwiler, S. C. Meeks, and B. N. Driskell

2001 Berries, Bones and Blades: Reconstructing Late Pleistocene Subsistence Economies at Dust Cave, Alabama. *Midcontinental Journal of Archaeology* 26: 169–97.

Walter, H.

1967 Das Pampa problem in Vergleichend Ökolo-gischer Betrachtung und seine Lösung. *Erdkunde* 21: 181–203.

Walthall, J. A.

1998 Rockshelters and Hunter-Gatherer Adaptation to the Pleistocene/Holocene Transition. *American Antiquity* 63: 223–38.

Warren, S. H.

1914 The Experimental Investigation of Flint Fracture and Its Application to Problems of Human Implements. *Journal of the Royal Anthropological Institute* 44: 412–50.

Watanabe, S., W. E. Ayta, H. Hamaguchi, N. Guidon, E. S. La Salvia, S. Maranca, and O. Baffa Filho

2003 Some Evidence of a Date of First Humans to Arrive in Brazil. *Journal of Archaeological Science* 30 (3): 351–54.

Waters, M. R., S. L. Forman, and J. M. Pierson

1997 Diring Yuriakh: A Lower Paleolithic Site in Central Siberia. *Science* 275: 1281–284.

Watts, W. A., and B. C. S. Hansen

1988 Environments of Florida in the Late Wisconsin and Holocene. In *Wet Sites Archaeology*, edited by B. A. Purdy, pp. 307–23. Telford Press, Caldwell, N.J.

Watts, W. A., B. C. Hansen, and E. C. Grimm
1992   Camel Lake: A 40,000 Yr Record of Vegetational and Forest History from Northwest Florida. *Ecology* 73 (3): 1056–1066.

Webb, S. D.
1974   *Pleistocene Mammals of Florida*. University of Florida Presses, Gainesville.
1985   Late Cenozoic Mammal Dispersals between the Americas. In *The Great American Biotic Interchange*, edited by F. G. Stehli and D. S. Webb, pp. 357–86. Plenum Press, New York.
2006   *First Floridians and Last Mastodons*. University Press of Florida, Gainesville.

Webb, S. D., J. T. Milanich, R. Alexon, and J. S. Dunbar
1984   A Bison Antiquus Kill Site, Wacissa River, Jefferson County, Florida. *American Antiquity* 49 (2): 384–92.

Wheat, J. B.
1972   The Olsen-Chubbuck Site: A Paleo-Indian Bison Kill. *Society for American Archaeology Memoirs* 26: 1–179.
1979   The Jurgens Site. *Plains Anthropologist Memoir* 15: 1–153.

Whitley, D. S., and R. I. Dorn
1993   New Perspectives on the Clovis vs. Pre-Clovis Controversy. *American Antiquity* 58 (4): 626–47.

Wijmstra, T. A., and T. Van der Hammen
1966   Palynological Data on the History of Tropical Savannas in Northern South America. *Leidse Geologische Mededelingen* 38: 71–90.

Wilke, P. J., J. J. Flenniken, and T. L. Ozbun
1991   Clovis Technology at the Anzick Site, Montana. *Journal of California and Great Basin Anthropology* 13: 242–72.

Willey, G. R.
1958   Archaeological Perspective on Algonkian-Gulf Linguistic Relationships. *Southwestern Journal of Anthropology* 14: 265–72.
1966   *An Introduction to American Archaeology*. Vol. 1, *North and Middle America*. Prentice Hall, Englewood Cliffs, N.J.
1971   *An Introduction to American Archaeology*. Vol. 2, *South America*. Prentice Hall, Englewood Cliffs, N.J.

Williams, J. W., D. M. Post, L. C. Cwynar, A. F. Lotter, and A. J. Levesque
2002   Rapid and Widespread Vegetation Responses to Past Climate Change in the North Atlantic Region. *Geology* 30 (11): 971–74.

Wilmsen, E. N., and F. H. Roberts
1984   *Lindenmeier, 1934–1974: Concluding Report on Investigations*. Smithsonian Contributions to Anthropology 24. Smithsonian Institution Press, Washington, D.C.

Witthoft, J.
1952   A Paleo-Indian Site in Eastern Pennsylvania: An Early Hunting Culture. *Proceedings of the American Philosophical Society* 96: 464–95.

Wohlfarth, B.
1996   The Chronology of the Last Termination: A Review of Radiocarbon-Dated,

High-Resolution Terrestrial Stratigraphies. *Quaternary Science Reviews* 15: 267–84.

Wohlfarth, B., S. Bjorck, G. Possnert, and B. Holmquist

1998 An 800-Year-Long, Radiocarbon-Dated Varve Chronology from South-Eastern Sweden. *Boreas* 27: 243–57.

Woods, J. C., and G. L. Titmus

1985 A Review of the Simon Clovis Collection. *Idaho Archaeologist* 8: 3–8.

Yacobaccio, H. D.

1995 Biomasa animal y consumo en el Pleistoceno-Holoceno sur andino. *Arqueología* 4: 43–71.

1996 The evolution of South Andean Hunter-Gatherers. *Proceedings of the XIII Congress of the International Union of Prehistoric and Protohistoric Sciences*, pp. 389–94. Forlì, Italy.

Yacobaccio, H. D., and C. M. Madero

1992 Zooarqueología de Huachichocana III (Jujuy, Argentina). *Arqueologia* 2: 149–88.

Yesner, D. R.

1995 Paleoindian Dietary Diversity in Interior Alaska: Evidence from the Broken Mammoth Site. Paper presented at the 60th Annual Meeting of the Society for American Archaeology, Minneapolis.

1996a Human Adaptation at the Pleistocene-Holocene Boundary (circa 13,000 to 8,000 yr BP) in Eastern Beringia. In *Humans at the End of the Ice Age: The Archaeology of the Pleistocene-Holocene Transition*, edited by L. G. Straus, B. V. Eriksen, J. M. Erlandson, and D. R. Yesner, pp. 255–76. Plenum Press, New York.

1996b Environments and Peoples at the Pleistocene-Holocene Boundary in the Americas. In *Humans at the End of the Ice Age: The Archaeology of the Pleistocene-Holocene Transition*, edited by L. G. Straus, B. V. Eriksen, J. M. Erlandson, and D. R. Yesner, pp. 243–53. Plenum Press, New York.

Yu, Z.

2000 Ecosystem Response to Lateglacial and Early Holocene Climate Oscillations in the Great Lakes Region of North America. *Quaternary Science Reviews* 19: 1723–747.

Yu, Z., and H. E. Wright

2001 Response of Interior North America to Abrupt Climate Oscillations in the North Atlantic Region during the Last Deglaciation. *Earth-Science Reviews* 52: 333–69.

Zárate, M.

1989 Estratigrafía y geología del Cenozoico Tardíoaflorante en los acantilados marinos comprendidos entre Playa San Carlos y el Arroyo Chapadmalal, Partido de General Pueyrredón, Provincia de Buenos Aires. Ph.D. dissertation, Universidad Nacional de Mar del Plata, Mar del Plata.

Zárate, M., and A. Blasi

1993 Late Pleistocene-Holocene Eolian Deposits of the Southern Buenos Aires Province, Argentina: A Preliminary Model. *Quaternary International* 17: 15–20.

Zárate, M., and N. Flegenheimer

1990 *Loess Stratigraphy and Geomorpholgy of the Pampas: Field Guide.* Centro de Geología de Costas y Cuaternario y Universidad Nacional de Mar del Plata, Mar del Plata.

Zárate, M., R. A. Kemp, M. Espinosa, and L. Ferrero

2000 Pedosedimentary and palaeoenvironmental significance of a Holocene alluvial sequence in the Southern Pampas, Argentina. *The Holocene* 10(4):481-88.

Zdanowicz, C. M., G. A. Zielinski, and M. S. Germani

1999 Mount Mazama Eruption: Calendrical Age Verified and Atmospheric Impact Assessed. *Geology* 27 (7): 621–24.

Zielinski, G. A., P. A. Mayewski, L. D. Meeker, S. Whitlow, and M. S. Twickler

1996 A 110,000-Yr Record of Explosive Volcanism from the GISP2 (Greenland) Ice Core. *Quaternary Research* 45 (2): 109–18.

Contributors

Javier Aceituno is a professor in the Departamento de Antropología, Universidad de Antioquia, Medellín, Colombia.

Luis Alberto Borrero works for the Programa de Estudios Prehistóricos in Buenos Aires, Argentina.

Michael Faught is a principal investigator with Panamerican Consultants in Tallahassee, Florida.

Stuart J. Fiedel is a principal investigator for the Louis Berger Group in Washington, D.C.

Cristóbal Gnecco is a professor in the Departamento de Antropología, Universidad del Cauca, Popayán, Colombia.

María Gutierrez is a research archaeologist with CONICET, a professor at Universidad Nacional del Centro, INCUAPA, Olavarría, Argentina, and a research associate with the Museum of Texas Tech University.

C. Vance Haynes is an emeritus professor of anthropology and quaternary geology in the Department of Anthropology and Geosciences at the University of Arizona, Tucson.

Lawrence Jackson is an adjunct professor in the Department of Anthropology at Western Ontario University and manages his own archaeological consulting firm, Northeast Archaeological Associates.

Eileen Johnson is curator of anthropology at the Museum of Texas Tech University, a professor in the Museum Science Program at Texas Tech University, and director of the Lubbock Lake Landmark.

Gustavo Martínez is a research archaeologist with CONICET, a professor at Universidad Nacional del Centro, INCUAPA, Olavarría, Argentina, and a research associate with the Museum of Texas Tech University.

Laura Miotti is a research archaeologist with CONICET and a professor at Universidad Nacional de La Plata, La Plata, Argentina.

Juliet E. Morrow is station archeologist with the Arkansas Archeological Survey at Arkansas State University and an associate professor at the University of Arkansas–Fayetteville.

Gustavo Politis is a research archaeologist with CONICET, a professor with Universidad Nacional de La Plata, La Plata, Argentina, and a research associate with the Museum of Texas Tech University.

Anthony Ranere is a professor in the Department of Anthropology at Temple University in Philadelphia and research associate with the Smithsonian Tropical Research Institute in Panama.

Index

CPSIA information can be obtained
at www.ICGtesting.com
Printed in the USA
LVHW090927090421
683923LV00001B/6